BECOMING BATMAN

BECOMING BATMAN

The Possibility
of a Superhero

E. PAUL ZEHR

THE JOHNS HOPKINS
UNIVERSITY PRESS
Baltimore

To my daughters, Andi and Jordan

May you become whatever you wish to become

© 2008 The Johns Hopkins University Press
All rights reserved. Published 2008
Printed in the United States of America on acid-free paper
9 8 7 6 5 4 3 2 1

The Johns Hopkins University Press
2715 North Charles Street
Baltimore, Maryland 21218-4363
www.press.jhu.edu

Library of Congress Cataloging-in-Publication Data
Zehr, E. Paul.
Becoming Batman : the possibility of a superhero / by E. Paul Zehr.
    p. cm.
Includes bibliographical references and index.
ISBN-13: 978-0-8018-9063-5 (hbk. : alk. paper)
ISBN-10: 0-8018-9063-2 (hbk. : alk. paper)
1. Batman (Fictitious character)   2. Physical education and train-
ing.   3. Human physiology.   I. Title.
PN6728.B363Z45 2008
613.7—dc22   2008011325

A catalog record for this book is available from the British Library.

*Special discounts are available for bulk purchases of this book. For more
information, please contact Special Sales at 410-516-6936 or specialsales@
press.jhu.edu.*

Contents

PART I. BAT-BUILDING BLOCKS
Exploring what Batman became
by beginning where he started

PART II. BASIC BATBODY TRAINING
Laying the foundation for Batman's
physical prowess to be later exploited
by his skill

Foreword

From the very beginning, he was expected to be completely similar to, and totally different from, Superman.

In 1939 National Periodicals was looking to bottle lightning a second time. Having struck a nerve with American comic book buyers the year before with the publication of Action Comics #1, featuring the debut of the Kryptonian man of steel, the editors charged young cartoonist Bob Kane with creating a new character for Detective Comics that would be as popular as Superman. Kane was a far better businessman than a creator of superheroes. (He had signed his first contract with National while a minor, which they learned when trying to renegotiate that contract. They discovered that they either did it on his terms or risked losing the rights to Batman entirely as Kane's previous work was based on an invalid contract.)

Kane's initial design of a red-costumed, mechanical-winged crimefighter called "Bird-Man" was reworked by colleague Bill Finger into the gray-and-black clad, mysterious, dark knight detective Bat-Man. Combining the swashbuckling of Douglas Fairbanks, the detective skills of Sherlock Holmes, the dark costuming and socialite alter ego of the Shadow, and the technological utility belt of Doc Savage, Finger and Kane managed to satisfy their editor's edict, and their creation, now known as Batman, has joined Superman as perhaps the world's two finest superheroes.

As an aside, Batman's debt to the pulp novel hero the Shadow is quite strong. The Batcopter, the Batarang, and Batman's skill at disguises follow from the Shadow's auto-gyro, boomerang, and trademark renown as a master of disguise. Bruce Wayne's friendship with Police Commissioner Gordon is an echo of the Shadow's alter ego Lamont Cranston's association with Police Commissioner Weston. In addition, the plot of Bat-Man's first adventure, "The Case of the Chemical Syndicate," which appeared in Detective Comics #27 (July 1939), is a direct takeoff of "Partners of Peril," published in *The Shadow Magazine* (November 1936) and written by Theodore Tinsley under the house name of Maxwell Grant. An amusing coincidence: Batman, inspired in part by the Shadow, first appeared in Detective Comics. The character of the Shadow was introduced as the host of a radio program, *The Detective Story Hour,* that featured tales drawn from its sponsor, the pulp magazine *Detective Story Magazine.*

Batman might not have enjoyed enduring popularity had he not been radically different from Superman. Whereas Superman is a strange visitor from another planet with powers and abilities far beyond those of mortal men, Batman is, after all, a mortal man. Batman does not possess super strength; he cannot fly or stretch like a rubber band; he cannot even cloud men's minds like his forebear the Shadow. His complete lack of superpowers accounts in part for his appeal. No matter how tempted we might be to wallow in radioactive waste, some small part of our brain recognizes that this will not enable us to run faster than a speeding bullet or climb the sides of buildings like a spider. But Detective Comics #27 in 1939 held out the hope that with sufficient training and preparation—and a willingness to go out in public dressed like Dracula—we could become Batman.

At least, that is what we have always been told. Now E. Paul Zehr, armed with advanced degrees in kinesiology and neuroscience, addresses whether it is physically and biologically possible to become Batman. In so doing, he provides a first-rate introduction to human physiology, neurology, the biomechanics of martial arts, the influence of diet and hormones (natural and synthetic) on strength training, and the materials science of protective clothing, such as Kevlar. Along the way we learn the physical mechanisms by which our muscles provide force, what changes occur at the cellular level in our bones as a consequence of weight training, and how Bruce Wayne's daytime meal provides the energy for Batman's nighttime crime fighting. We also find out why the martial arts are called "the martial arts," whether Batman really knows 127 different martial arts, what the expression "muscle memory" really means, the physical and biological means by which we heal from injuries, and the physiological changes that occur in aging. Dr. Zehr explains all this and more, in a fun and accessible manner, through the related concepts of stress and homeostasis. In addition to having a PhD in neuroscience, Paul Zehr possesses a black belt in Shito-ryu karate. The doctor knows whereof he speaks!

Finally, you will learn not only whether it is possible to become Batman but, perhaps more important, whether you can *stay* Batman! Body building and strength training is all well and good, expert proficiency in the martial arts is important—but can you keep it up year after year, in a never-ending battle against the petty crooks and supervillain escapees from Arkham Asylum?

By using the Caped Crusader as the medium by which he explains his subject matter, Dr. Zehr also points out the most important way by which we can all become Batman, even those of us who do not lift a single weight or step one foot out of our secret cave headquarters. Batman has such a hold on our collective imagination because he is a mere human who nevertheless acts like a true superhero. As Superman explains to Wonder Woman in the graphic novel *Trinity,* by way of excusing Batman's brusque manners: "I've seen him throw himself in harm's way time and again, all to rescue the lives of innocents." Reminding Wonder Woman that, unlike themselves, Batman has no extraphysical prowess, Superman wonders: "If I were an ordinary man, would I show the same valor?" Indeed, it is Batman's courage, dedication, and commitment—bravery that even a Superman can admire—that we all would like to believe we are capable of, and can at least strive for, if only we have the will. Paul Zehr shows us the way. The rest is up to us.

—James Kakalios, author of *The Physics of Superheroes*
(Gotham, 2005)

Preface

The Batman has no super-powers, so I
have to make myself the best I can be . . .
Always.
—Bruce Wayne reflecting on his alter ego in
"You May See a Stranger" (Batman: Dark
Detective #2, 2005)

This book is an examination of a superhero. It seeks to answer a simple question: Is it possible for any human to attain the skills and abilities of Batman? Batman is the perfect superhero about whom to ask this question as there is nothing supernatural about his abilities. He is a man in disguise, with powers that seem within reach. But are they? The question may be simple, but as we shall see, the answers are not.

Because I am a scholar who studies the control of movement, my lifelong passions place me in an expert position to attempt to search out and answer questions relating to the feasibility of a real-life superhero like Batman. My day job is the study of the neural control of human movement using methods of neuroscience, exercise physiology, and biomechanics. My main "hobby" (but that word really fails to capture the extent of my devotion) is training in the martial arts of karate and Okinawan weapons (Ryukyu Kobujutsu), in which I hold advanced black belt ranks. In fact, my interest in martial arts not only came first (I started training in 1981 at the age of 13) but actually spurred my interest in science. I was interested in how people can move so fast with such precision in martial arts. That got me on the road to kinesiology, in which I hold a master of science degree, and neuroscience, in which I hold a PhD.

I only followed the scientific path related to martial arts for a while (but some of my earliest publications were on this topic) until diving full on into neural control of walking and rehabilitation. But every day I study and teach about movement control and then practice and teach about how to do real martial arts movements. You could say I practice what I preach, and you would be right.

Who hasn't wanted to become a superhero like Batman? As a kid I certainly remember donning my Batman mask at Halloween and zipping all over the neighborhood feeling pretty darn good about myself. However, when I imagined becoming a character like the Dark Knight, I am pretty sure I didn't have much of a concept about what it would take to actually become Batman. Instead, I devoted my energy to imagining ripping around in the Batmobile to arrive at the scene just in time to dispatch the Riddler, the Penguin, or the Joker—or maybe all of them at once—thus saving Gotham once again from mayhem and chaos. I could then secretly enjoy my successes as the multibillionaire Bruce Wayne attending some socialite ball sipping scotch on the rocks and then dumping my drink out while no one is looking!

We all admire Batman for his accomplishments and abilities, but if you think about it a little longer you might ask how difficult it would be to achieve those things. Batman and Bruce Wayne make it seem pretty easy. What would actually happen to your body, though? How hard would it be to train to become Batman?

In the introduction to *The Greatest Batman Stories Ever Told* the amazing artist and inker Dick Girodano—famous for his work on many comic book characters, including Batman—wrote, "I knew that I could aspire to be Batman but I couldn't aspire to be Superman . . . I could, if I started young enough, train myself the way young Bruce Wayne did and maybe some day be just like Batman. Well, I never started training and so remained ordinary, but I knew I could have, and that was a good portion of the character's appeal to the kids who read Batman."

This raises a point that is central to this book: Is it realistic to think you could train to become Batman? Does the human body possess the capability to respond and adapt to such extremes? Many costumed heroes such as Superman possess superhuman abilities and powers. But you don't really think in terms of a process for "becoming Superman" when you think of his powers. He has them because he was born on Krypton and now lives on Earth. The Batman, though, is a real flesh-and-blood human being from our planet. He has no superabilities. Only through his years of rigorous training has Batman pulled himself to near-superhuman status.

This part of the Batman mythology is what makes him so attractive and accessible to so many—it seems well-grounded in the reality of hard work and achievement. Is it, though? In *Tales of the Dark Knight: Batman's First Fifty Years: 1939–1989,* Mark Cotta Vaz quotes then president and editor-in-chief of DC Comics Jenette Kahn on Batman: "Batman is an ordinary mortal who made himself a superhero . . . Through discipline and determination and commitment, he made himself into the best. I always thought that meant that I could be anything I wanted to be." This sentiment was shared by the great silver age Batman artist Neal Adams: "You must remember, Batman is the only superhero who is not a superhero. He has no powers . . . He's a human being bent on a mission." And DC Comics Editor Dennis O'Neil wrote, "There isn't a great stretch between Batman's world and ours: he is the most 'realistic' of the great superheroes. To be blunt: the guy isn't very super. He didn't gain his powers by being lightning-struck, nor bathing in chemicals, nor by dint of being born on another planet, nor by the intervention of extraterrestrials or gods. To paraphrase an old commercial, he got them the old-fashioned way—he earned them . . . He wasn't bequeathed those abilities; he sweated for them."

It is clear that most of us have the perception that Batman's prowess and skill could be achieved by ordinary mortals if they had the resources, time, and motivation to pursue them. Perceptions aren't necessarily reality. And it's my goal in this book to use my extensive knowledge of science and martial arts to put perception to the test and explore the scientific possibility of becoming Batman.

Who is Batman? Batman first appeared in 1939 in Detective Comics #27. (By the way, in the bibliography you will find a chronological list of all the Batman comics that I talk about in the book.) This first story was called "The Case of the Chemical Syndicate," and Batman was known as "The Bat-Man." It was pretty vague about what Batman actually was or where he came from. More information was given in 1948 in Batman #47. Even there the training of Batman takes up only a few panels. The character of Batman was created by the artist Bob Kane, who in his autobiography said, "Inspired by Leonardo da Vinci's flying machine, I created my first experimental sketches of a bat-man when I was 13. I was fascinated by the idea of a man who could fly." Kane later revealed that further inspiration for the Batman character came from Zorro, The Bat, The Shadow, and Dick Tracy.

In the Batman's "prehistory," the parents of a young Bruce Wayne are tragically killed right before his eyes by a demented criminal. The teenage Bruce Wayne then flees Gotham on a worldwide pilgrimage to discover himself. Little is known about what happened to Bruce while he was away from Gotham City. An interesting story arc is presented by Frank Miller in *Batman: Year One*, where it is explained that Bruce Wayne, now in his mid-20s, returns to Gotham as a fully trained "almost Batman" 12 to 18 years after the murder of his parents.

Except for a few details, however, there is little information about the physical training that Batman would have undergone while he was away. In *Batman: The Ultimate Guide to the Dark Knight*, Scott Beatty summarizes Bruce's training by saying that he learned "jiu jutsu from the Kirgiz school and studied 127 styles of combat." Aside from this little bit of martial arts training evidence, there isn't much information about what Bruce Wayne did in those long years of training.

As is apparent, there are many gaps in Batman's history. These omissions create dramatic tension rather appropriate for the dark nature of the character. However, for someone trying to appreciate the effort and training necessary to become a real-life superhero, the lack of information is a bit frustrating. This book fills those gaps by outlining the kind of physical training that would have been needed to produce the consummate martial artist and superb athlete that you know of as Batman.

Batman is at the peak of physical human performance and ability. Neal Adams captured this well when he wrote that Batman "trained his body to a perfection reached by few. He became such a physical specimen as would make a Spartan wonder, and if he entered the Olympics, he would win, place or show in every event." The most notable aspects of Batman's ability that I focus on in this book are his martial arts and physical prowess while also exploring the reality of obtaining these capabilities. You will read about transforming a large but "normal" would-be Batman into "The Batman." What kind of training would be needed? What physical changes would occur to a human being who undertook a training program aimed at becoming Batman? What changes would happen in the body as a result of such training? How much would Batman need to eat to train this way? You will find the answers to these questions in the pages that follow.

In the end, Batman is the sum of his parts. He does not have his spectacular overall abilities because of ultimate performance in any one thing. Rather, he has elevated ability in all things which, taken together, give him his near-superhuman capacity for costumed crime fighting.

To evaluate the possibility of becoming Batman, we start with a description of the physical characteristics of our eventual superhero. By seeing what happens to Batman, you will explore the extreme limits of human performance. We will evaluate if there are real scientific underpinnings of these achievements. If Batman is considered the most realistic of superheroes, does that mean that becoming Batman could be a reality?

I have written this book in a way that I think Batman the detective would have appreciated. Batman is, above all, an information hound. As such, I provide much of the background of our explorations as we move along. Some of the history of key early discoveries and what those discoveries meant to science are things Batman would certainly be keen to learn.

The book is divided into five parts that relate to different aspects of Batman's physical development, skill training, and refinement. In Part I, we start with a fully fledged and "finished" Batman and cast backward in time to think about what his physical state was before he became Batman. That is, we take a long look at Bruce Wayne. What would he have been like physically had he not become Batman? How much could he really improve his physical prowess with training? It is important to think about his "trainability" in order to understand Bruce's turning into Batman. To help with this process I created an identical twin for Bruce Wayne—named Bob Wayne. I explain what Bruce Wayne achieved while becoming Batman by comparing what Bob achieves (or actually doesn't achieve).

Part II is all about understanding physical performance and acquiring prowess. How much can you improve factors like strength with physical training? What are reasonable expectations and what are the extreme outer limits for performance for Batman? Part III looks at acquiring the physical movement skills needed to become Batman. The main concentration is on the learning of motor skills in the nervous system through training in martial arts. What actually happens in the brain when we learn and perfect movement skills? What type of skill training would Batman need to become the Dark Knight?

Part IV examines the application of all the training and hard work. We learn what Batman could really achieve in action. How hard and fast can he kick and punch? How many bad guys could he fight at once? I'll explain how much energy is expended during this training and consider how much Batman would need to eat and drink every day to keep from wasting away.

Part V details pitfalls along the path to becoming Batman. What injuries would likely be sustained from his extreme training and from his crime-fighting encounters? What is it like to work night shifts all the time as does Batman? Would Batman take steroids? When should Batman retire? The answers to these questions will probably surprise you.

Together we will evaluate what it would take physically to actually become Batman. As you will see, it won't be easy to do. But it will be fun and easy to read about. Along the way you will learn about the extremes of human adaptability and the scientific basis for physical training and learning.

My interests in writing and in science were kindled and fed by numerous teachers. However, in particular I would credit my inspiration for reading (which led to the desire to write) to Doug Pratt who taught at Elderslie Central School in Ontario. My interest in science can be traced back to my biology teacher Larry Richardson and for writing to my English teacher Ross King at Chesley District High School.

I have been greatly inspired in all of my scientific activities by my two main mentors, Digby Sale at McMaster University and Richard Stein at the University of Alberta. I also thank my sister Pat Zehr for showing me that, no matter the hard work required, you must always pursue your goals.

I humbly thank my martial arts mentors Shane Higashi Sensei, Kisho Inoue Sensei, and Tsuyoshi Chitose Sensei. Also, I thank my first martial arts teacher, Police Constable Peter Zehr, for getting me started in karate and then serving as my martial arts role model.

I thank my mom, Marlene Mary Zehr, for supporting my interests in reading—including many, many comic books—throughout my childhood . . . and beyond.

I am grateful to Marc Klimstra for reading and providing helpful comments on an earlier draft of the manuscript. Roderick Haesevoets provided helpful assistance with the final preparation of the figures. I thank my colleagues in the Rehabilitation Neuroscience Laboratory at the University of Victoria for their support and understanding throughout the process of writing this book. At UVic, Ryan Rhodes deserves special commendation for helping kick start me into finally writing this book instead of just talking about it all the time! Related to the motivation for writing the book, I need to mention also Sean and Tracey Turriff. Without their help, particularly early on, my road forward would have been very difficult indeed.

I continue to remain impressed by the level of professionalism and competence at the Johns Hopkins University Press. In particular I thank Vince Burke for his help throughout the entire process and Michele T. Callaghan for her outstanding copyediting.

Last, I thank the three ladies in my life, Lori, Andi, and Jordan, for just being who they are.

PART I

BAT-BUILDING BLOCKS

**Exploring what Batman became
by beginning where he started**

CHAPTER 1

The "Before" Batman

HOW BUFF WAS BRUCE?

He will become the greatest crimefighter the
world has ever known . . . It won't be easy.
—*Batman: Year One* (1986) by Frank Miller

At some point in your life—maybe even just this year—you
probably tried an activity that combined physical ability and movement skill. It might have been baseball, gymnastics, hockey, or karate. You likely achieved some measure of success and saw various
physical changes in your body. After a time, it's also likely that you
no longer approached the activity with the same fervent, unrelenting
passion and may have even stopped participating altogether. Slowly,
those beneficial physical changes simply faded away.

This is pretty normal, really. It takes considerable devotion to
performance to achieve and maintain a high level of fitness. What
would happen, though, if you did make that commitment? What
would your life be like? What could you achieve and how much
could your body change?

You may be thinking that your level of success in improving
physical performance depends on the condition of your body when
you start. In other words, on the "raw material" that you start out
with. We have all seen images of Batman in action in comic books
and movies. Batman is depicted as a skilled and powerful athlete

with marvelous capabilities operating at the peak of human performance. But what are the limits of human performance, and how much did Batman's body improve through training? To explore these questions we will investigate Batman's training as he evolved from plain-old Bruce Wayne to someone who "strikes terror into the hearts of Gotham City's worst"—The Batman.

Everyone has a conception of what Batman is like: a powerful and well-built man. However, to understand the process of actually transforming an average guy (well, in this case an extremely wealthy average guy with unlimited financial resources and social contacts) into a man functioning at the peak of human performance, you need first to get a handle on what Batman was like before all his training. Basically, what we want to know is, "What sort of physical characteristics did Bruce Wayne have to start with?" Or, in other words, "How buff was Bruce Wayne?"

Well, in short, not that buff. Bruce Wayne was a pretty solid man with an athletic build, for sure. But we want to understand the transformation from a scientific perspective. Together we'll explore scientifically accepted measures to quantify physical changes in Bruce Wayne as he trained to become Batman. Along the way, we will ask, What's in our bodies? How can that potential for performance gains and responses to training be estimated or measured? After we have discussed how to determine changes in your body, we'll take another look at Wayne's original physical characteristics.

You Can't Judge a Bat by His Cover

One way to think about the "buffness" of Bruce or Batman is to talk about body composition. This means asking, What are the relative amounts of different tissues in our bodies? There are complex multiple-part models that can be used to examine the actual cell mass of the body (and that are useful for diagnostic medical evaluations). But for defining changes in body composition related to exercise activity, a basic two-part model works fine.

The two parts of the model are (1) adipose tissue—fat or fat mass, and (2) pretty much everything else. The "everything else" category includes mostly bone and muscle and is together called lean body mass. You might think you can easily tell the difference between fat mass and lean body mass just by looking at someone. You see a person and can tell whether they look fat, thin, or average. But the relative amounts of adipose and lean body mass change are determined by our exercise status and training as well as by our nutritional intake. You cannot really see this with the naked eye, so how can you measure it? One way might be to step on a scale and simply weigh yourself. But that will only tell you your actual mass, which includes everything in your body. To isolate the different components means taking some other measures.

For the longest time the "gold standard" measure for body composition was to do hydrodensitometry. This means finding out how much you weigh when you are immersed in water by using the Archimedes principle (say Eureka!). According to this principle, a body (in this case a real human body) submerged in water has a counterforce of buoyancy that is equal to the weight of the displaced water. Bone and muscle—the main components of the lean body mass—are denser than water and tend to sink. Lean body mass is about 70% water, while fat mass is about 10% water. As a result, fat mass tends to float and makes the body lighter in the water. Given that lean tissue sinks and fat floats in water, your underwater weight can be used as an estimate of the amount of fat mass you carry.

Conducting this measurement is rather difficult to do in your own bathtub with a standard bathroom scale. To understand why, let's talk for a minute about balloons. A balloon filled with air will float. Well, your lungs act just like balloons when they have air in them, and this makes it difficult to measure your actual weight in water. You'd need a way to measure the volume of air expelled when you breathe out as much air as possible. First, you'd have to take a deep breath, completely submerge yourself in water, and then be able to measure your weight. You'd take a second measurement after completely expelling air from your lungs. Perform a few calculations and you'd have a good idea about your body composition. But all this would require special equipment and special knowledge.

As it turns out, you cannot really do this at home. And the other ways to measure Batman's body composition aren't do-it-yourself projects either. One method would be to take a DEXA (dual x-ray absorptiometry) scan of Batman. This method relies on the differing absorption of low-level x-rays into body fat, bone, and muscle to calculate lean body mass. Similarly, CT (computerized tomography) or MRI (magnetic resonance imaging) scans of the body could give accurate data on body composition. All three types of scans are expensive and are not readily available to the average person.

There are a couple of additional measures that are cheaper and easier to do but that aren't nearly as accurate. One is using calipers to pinch the skin and fat layers at different parts of your body and measuring how thick the layers are. The other is bioelectrical impedance, which works by passing an electrical current through the body. Current travels at different speeds through fat mass and lean body mass because of differences in water content. If you used bioelectrical impedence on Batman when he was dehydrated from a night of crime fighting or had just eaten a meal after a midnight prowl, you'd get different answers. All these measures would be useful for finding the changes in body composition that would take place as Bruce becomes Batman; they aren't necessarily good at telling us what his body composition is at any given time.

Are All Bruces Created Equal?

Wouldn't it be easier if you could just measure Batman's height and weight and get some kind of indication of his body composition? Before we can answer this question, we have to look at another measure called the body mass index (or BMI for short), which gives a ballpark estimate of whether Batman has a "healthy" or not so healthy weight. Your family physician probably calculated your BMI at your last physical, and BMI is regularly used in many health surveys. The calculation involves looking at your body mass as a function of your height.

But where can we get an estimate of Batman's or Bruce Wayne's height and weight in the first place? What does "healthy" or "unhealthy" weight even mean? Is there an amount that an individual with certain characteristics should weigh? In one corner, an endless stream of diet experts tells everyone how much they should (or more often should not) weigh. In another corner, insurance companies use BMI and other indicators to determine whether to provide life insurance to someone. For these purposes, insurers use guides such as the Metropolitan Life Insurance Company tables.

According to the most recent of these tables (from 1983!), the "ideal weight" for a man ages 25–59, who is 1.9 meters (6'2") tall with a large frame is between 77 and 89 kilograms (172 and 197 pounds).

TABLE 1.1. Comparison of Bruce Wayne / Batman and other athletes

Athlete	Height	Weight (lb)	Body fat (%)	Body mass index
Bruce Wayne	6'2"	185	20	26
Batman	6'2"	210	10	27
Lance Armstrong	5'11"	172	10	24
Arnold Schwarzenegger	6'1"	245	5	32

I put Bruce right in the middle of this range and give him a weight of 83 kilograms (185 pounds). I also estimate that he would have been an average North American male with about 20% body fat. Batman, in contrast, would be in much better shape and have around 10% body fat.

For comparison purposes, let's look a little closer at the concept of body composition by considering a person in both extremes from Batman with respect to body fat, endurance cyclist like Lance Armstrong and former power builder like Arnold Schwarzenegger. Lance Armstrong would have averaged around 8–10% body fat over his cycling career. Competition bodybuilders such as Arnold would average about 3–5% body fat (only during competition because too little body fat is unhealthy).

You can find more about this in Table 1.1, which summarizes some basic physical characteristics for Batman and Bruce Wayne. This will help you understand what physical state Bruce was in when he began his training and how far he went as he became Batman.

We now have a baseline from which to judge the average Bruce Wayne. This will allow us to determine what type and degree of training would have been required to change Bruce Wayne into Batman. Now let's discuss different body types and how they respond to training.

Does Body Type Affect How Buff Can Bruce Get?

One of my favorite scenes from Batman comics on the topic of Batman's physical condition is in the story "Night of the Reaper" (Batman

#237, 1971). It contains probably one of the biggest understatements ever made in comics (in my biased view). Batman infiltrates a costume party and one of the other partygoers remarks on his excellent build. Batman responds with "Uh, thanks! I exercise a lot!" Does he ever!

We will talk a great deal in this book about the types of exercise Bruce did to become Batman and the effect of that exercise on his muscles and bones. But here I want to look at the concept of *body type*. To learn more about this concept, let's travel back to the 1940s when psychologist William Sheldon first characterized people according to body types using something called "somatotopy" (literally, body categories). According to this scheme, human bodies fall into three categories: ectomorphic, endomorphic, and mesomorphic. Although these categories can be useful in a general way, Sheldon also tried to relate them to criminality, personality, and other matters having to do with mental function. These concepts are now recognized as totally lacking scientific validity. Bear in mind that he came up with these ideas when things such as phrenology (measuring mental capacity by examining bumps on the skull!) were in vogue. Regardless of the poor conclusions of the original model, body typing can still be useful for physical characterization.

Let's take a closer look at the three body types. Ectomorphs have slim bodies and difficulty gaining weight, while endomorphs have thicker bodies and gain weight (particularly fat) easily. Mesomorphs are between ecto- and endomorphs, with a strong facility for gaining muscle mass. Although people cannot be categorized strictly according to these terms, they may be predisposed to one type. Mesomorphs constitute the largest grouping for athletes. Emaciated fashion models are an extreme example of an ectomorph.

Scientists now use a modified form of this typing to calculate somatotopy scores, recognizing that many people don't fit neatly into one category. Based upon his obvious response to training, Batman would be considered a blend of mesomorph and ectomorph. He began as a mesomorph but reached his full potential as he underwent training. In Chapter 2, I will return to a discussion of how much Batman could really achieve as a function of his training and how much as a function of his genetic makeup.

What does "response to training" mean? It doesn't just mean improving because a person does something more often. We all know that doing something more often—practicing—usually makes us better at that something. The rate at which people change or the

Figure 1.1. Changes in Batman's physique across the ages. Notice the increasing emphasis on Batman's musculature and physical prowess (indicated by arrows) from 1940 to 2000.

level of improvement they reach can vary. Is there a way to have an idea about how good somebody will be at something and how they will respond to training? And do body types have a role in how a person responds?

The modern version of Batman is closest to the mesomorph. But this wasn't always the case. And Batman's build has changed dramatically across the years. If we looked at Batman action figures from the 1940s, 1950s, 1970s, and 1990s, we would detect a dramatic shift, which is shown in Figure 1.1. Notice that the muscle definition and bulk are extremely different in the original Batman (top left) compared with the 1990s version (bottom left). Artists have increasingly (and somewhat unrealistically) emphasized mesomorphic characteristics since the 1940s. Certainly, Batman is an athletic figure, but he doesn't necessarily need huge muscles and six-pack abs to fight crime.

So now we have looked at Bruce's general body type. In the next chapter we turn our attention further to how much training can really do. We have observed that Bruce Wayne was a solid man, taller than average with a modest build. He wasn't starting from scratch, but he wasn't an all-star athlete either. How much potential would he have had for responding to his training? What are the limits based upon genetics? To determine which changes involved in becoming Batman are the result of training and which are the result of genetics, we will look at the same thing scientists would examine to make such a determination: studies of identical twins.

In the comics world, Bruce Wayne was an only child. But for our purposes, I have created a genetically identical twin brother for him: Robert (Bob) "Blocco" Wayne. After you meet Bruce's "twin" in the next chapter and observe him throughout the book, you will be better prepared to appreciate what Bruce's training accomplished. You will certainly see what would have happened—or, more correctly, would not have happened—to Bruce if he hadn't trained to become Batman.

CHAPTER 2

Guess Who's Coming for Dinner

BRUCE'S TWIN BROTHER, BOB, AND THE HUMAN GENOME

At a very early age, each and every one of us realized that we probably were not born on Krypton, we were unlikely to get bitten by a radioactive spider, and we were not the spawn of mud touched by the gods. We knew, however, that if given the proper motivations, we could become the Batman. More important, we knew that if we had to endure those motivations, becoming the Batman was probably the proper thing to do.
—*The Greatest Batman Stories Ever Told*, from the foreword by Mike Gold

In this part of our story, I turn to what you may consider to be a major factor underlying the potential to become someone like Batman: your genetic makeup. How much potential we have to improve or change our bodies with any kind of training depends a great deal on our genes. Before we meet Bruce's brother, Bob, and see how much of Batman's capabilities could be related to genetics and how much to his training and lifestyle, we need to review some basic concepts about how our cells function, what genes are, how DNA works, and why Gregor Mendel, James Watson, and Francis Crick are so important.

Under the Batscope

To understand genetics, let's take an imaginary microscopic view of the human body and look at the elementary functional unit of the human body: the cell. All living beings are made up of cells. We human beings are eukaryotes, or organisms composed of many cells. The essential features of the same cell type—for example, nerve or muscle cells—are virtually the same in different species, from Batman to actual bats. By the way, Batman has (as do you) approximately 100 trillion finely tuned cells in his body.

The first person to see what cells look like was the English scientist Robert Hooke (1635–1703). In 1663, using a light microscope, Hooke saw what he described as little "rooms," or "cells" (from the Latin *cellulae*), in a sample of cork. Not too long after this discovery in 1674, live cells were described in the algae *Spirogyra* by the Dutch anatomist Anton van Leeuwenhoek, who became known as the "father of microbiology." The work done by these two scientists and others eventually yielded the "cell theory," put forward in 1839 by Theodor Schwann and Matthias Schleiden, which stated that the cell is the basic unit of life.

In Figure 2.1 you can see some sketches of nerve cells (neurons) of different species done by Nobel Prize winner Santiago Ramon y Cajal (1852–1934) more than a hundred years ago. The neurons in panel A are from the periphery—such as nerve fibers coming from your spinal cord to your muscle; the neurons in the other panels are from the brain and spinal cord. If you look carefully at panel B, you will see some common elements of all cells. Let's briefly review those elements.

There are three main parts to consider in any cell: the cell membrane, the fluid in the cell (cytoplasm), and the nucleus. The cell membrane forms the walls of the cell, keeping what is supposed to stay in the cell inside and what is not supposed to be in the cell out. A key component of the cell membrane is cholesterol, which the cell must produce to maintain the strength and function of this barrier.

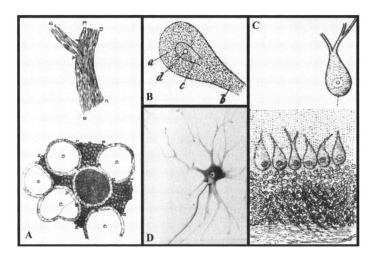

Figure 2.1. Sketches of nerve cells (neurons) drawn by Nobel Prize winner Santiago Ramon y Cajal (1852–1934) more than a hundred years ago. The neurons in panel A are from the periphery—such as nerve fibers from your spinal cord to your muscle—while the others are from the brain and spinal cord. Courtesy Lopez-Munoz (2006).

However, the cell is a very busy place and there is always a lot of movement across the cell wall.

Movement of ions—positively or negatively charged atoms—occurs largely through portholes or gates in the membrane known as ion channels. Sodium, potassium, and calcium are key ions. The body maintains specific concentrations of these ions on either side of the membrane. The cell membrane also detects chemical signals that may be used to modify the activity of the cell. It is also the literal point of contact of one cell to other cells. The cell membrane, then, has a complicated function serving as both a selective gateway and a barrier defining the boundaries of the cell and its surroundings.

Cytoplasm is the intracellular fluid in which the functional parts of the cell—called organelles—float around. There is also an extensive framework of tubes and tubules that make up a kind of scaffolding within the cell to give it strength and shape. Dissolved in the cytoplasm are all the ions, nutrients, and wastes that are needed and produced by the cellular organelles. Understanding the function and potential alterations of these organelles is crucial when

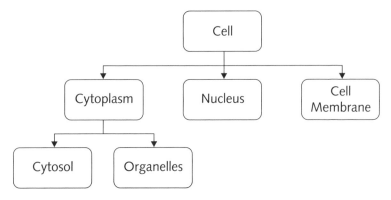

Figure 2.2. Outline of components of the cell.

discussing changes caused by training. Therefore we will revisit some organelles throughout the book, including the mitochondria (cellular power plants), Golgi apparatus, and ribosomes (producers of protein and fats).

The nucleus is the site of some of the most vital cell activity: cell division and replication. Inside the nucleus is the nucleolus, which contains the DNA, RNA, and other genetic material that determine all the cellular proteins and can ultimately define the function and type of the cell.

Cells are essentially of four different types: epithelial (skin, both inside and outside your body), connective (including tendons, ligaments, and bone), muscle, and nervous system. All of our bodies' tissues are created by assembling together many cells of each type. A key feature of connective tissue is the presence of collagen, which gives strength and durability and which needs vitamin C to be maintained. Muscle and nervous system tissues are both considered excitable tissues because they can generate electrical signals.

There is one other cell type that I should mention before we move on. You have probably heard of them before: stem cells. The important thing about stem cells is that they can become different types of cells—muscle, nervous system, and so on. This is why they are so crucial for function and have such enormous promise for use in degenerative diseases such as Parkinson's disease. We will talk about a kind of stem cell termed a satellite cell in Chapter 4 when we discuss muscles.

Do Genes Make the Bat?

Let's return to genetics in general. What does it mean when we hear about genetic coding and genetics? Genetics is a subbranch of the larger scientific discipline of biology. In genetics the main focus is on studying and explaining the physical traits or attributes that move from ancestors to their descendents. Physical traits that we can see are called phenotypes. For Batman, an observed phenotype would be his black hair. His black cape, however, is not a phenotype—that's a personal stylistic or environmental choice!

Although scientists have only relatively recently learned more specifically how genetics works, a basic awareness of the concept of inheritance of physical traits has been around since the earliest attempts to domesticate plants and animals. Ancient civilizations such as the Egyptians were known to domesticate dogs, sheep, goats, camels, and other animals as far back as 12,000 years ago. Once the process of domestication was under way, traits inherited from parents and expressed in the offspring were likely fairly easy to observe. Then, selective breeding of the offspring quickly led to distinct breeds of animals (for example, dogs) that met the needs of the human breeders. In fact, Charles Darwin (1809–1882) remarked that only 25 generations were needed in the mink to produce stock with widely varying fur colors.

Recently, Steve Britton and Lauren Koch at the University of Michigan implemented a breeding project in the rat. The point of the research was to see how much of a difference selective breeding could have on aspects of exercise capacity during running. They selectively bred the rats in two "directions": one direction was toward high capacity and one was toward low capacity. After only 11 generations of breeding, the difference between the two groups was almost 350%. This was a staggering result both for the extent of the difference and for the relative speed of the changes. This shows just what can happen in animal biology with an extreme selection process.

What really set the background for the modern concept of genetics and genetic manipulation was the work of the extraordinarily brilliant yet extremely shy eighteenth-century Augustinian monk by the name of Gregor Mendel (1822–1884). Mendel established the concept of heredity through his extensive study and documentation of pea and bean plants. He is the true father of modern genetics, a fact that was only recognized in the twentieth century when his work outlining the laws of genetic inheritance of physical traits from generation to generation was finally recognized. After an extended series of breeding experiments and detailed observations stretching over eight years and ten thousand plants, Mendel published his work in 1866. This detailed work on hybridization of pea plants was crucial in overturning the prevailing idea that heredity resulted from a "blending" of traits from the parents. That is, heredity had been understood as a literal averaging or mixing of the contributions from the parental plants or animals.

You see, when you were conceived, genetic information was transferred from your parents to you. You got about half your genetic material from your mother and about half from your father. This genetic material from both parents was of crucial importance to how you have grown and developed. However, the genetic material was not blended. Instead, there was a pairing of the genes from each parent that gave rise to the traits that were ultimately expressed. Mendel's experiments showed that heredity followed specific rules and laws, and they established that the "factors" (the forerunner of what we now call genes) from each parent are indeed combined in the children.

What Mendel's work did not show was how those traits or genes are actually stored in our cells. This would have to wait until the identification of DNA (which stands for deoxyribonucleic acid) in 1871 as well as evidence that genes were completely composed of DNA, which was provided by Oswald Avery in 1946. These discoveries led to the understanding that genetic information is stored in DNA, which is found in the nucleus of every cell. The actual functional units of genetics are formed from little molecules called nucleotides, which in turn are arranged so that they form a structure called a chromosome. You might be amazed to know that about three billion pairs of nucleotides yielding between 25,000 and 50,000 genes are all arranged on 23 pairs of chromosomes.

Before we continue on with chromosomes, we need to know a bit more about cells as well as where DNA is and how it works. Something else that Mendel introduced when he described his factors that determine traits—a.k.a. genes—was the concept of dominant and recessive expression. When you hear the word "expression" in genetics, remember that genes communicate a variety of things about you—the visible (such as hair color) and the invisible (such as the likelihood of getting a certain genetic disease): Genes can take on different forms, or "alleles" (from the Greek word that means "each other"). The set of alleles that a person—such as Bruce Wayne—has for a certain gene is what is called the genotype. Within a person's genotype, alleles may be dominant or recessive. Often the situation involves more than two alleles and more than just a dominant and recessive segregation, but this simple illustration will work for our purposes. If you have at least one dominant allele for a certain trait, that will be expressed, or shown. The recessive trait will be expressed only if you have recessive alleles in both pairs.

An important distinction is that the genes that you possess (your genotype) and the actual physical manifestation of those genes (your phenotype) are not always the same thing. Let's use blood type as an example of this because everybody has an identifiable blood type. The commonly used classification system for blood types was established by the Austrian scientist Karl Landsteiner (1868–1943) and is known as the A-B-O system. The A, B, O distinction represents the three alleles that exist for blood type, which when examined in all combinations give rise to six different pairings: AA, BB, OO, AB, AO, and BO. You (and every other person) have the possibility of four of these types, from the two alleles inherited from each of your parents. Figure 2.3 shows all the possible combinations of blood types.

Using this example of blood types illustrates fairly simply the ideas of what genotype and phenotype really mean. Your blood typing genotype refers to the actual genes that you possess, for example, AA or AO. But only one of these genotypes will actually be manifested (in genetic terms, expressed). This is the phenotype—in this case the A blood type. It may surprise you to know that this actually refers to certain proteins on the surface of the red blood cells that carry oxygen in your blood. Another simplified example is that your father could have blue eyes and your mother could have green eyes. You carry the genes for both colors but may have only one color of eyes (usually!).

OK, I said we would talk about the nucleus, DNA, and genetics, so here we go. Let's peer inside the nucleus of a human cell and see what we might find. We are going to briefly look into the "story of life" and talk about the important discovery of the physical structure of DNA—what is known as the "double helix." DNA is the physical embodiment of the genetic code. The official scientific documentation of the structure of DNA was on April 25, 1953, when the science journal *Nature* published a series of three papers—primarily

Father or mother	O	A	B	AB
O	O	O, A	O, B	A, B
A	O, A	O, A	O, A, B, AB	A, B, AB
B	O, B	O, A, B, AB	O, B	A, B, AB
AB	A, B	A, B, AB	A, B, AB	A, B, AB

Figure 2.3. Different possible blood types and genetic inheritance.

written by James Watson, Francis Crick, Maurice Wilkins, and Rosalind Franklin—on this pair of molecules.

For a long time the science of life was considered to be the biochemistry of proteins and enzymes. Then, with the publication of these *Nature* articles, we were well on the way to the birth of modern molecular biology. The authors had used what was then a comparatively new technique of x-ray crystallography to show that the structure of DNA consisted of a double helix—its name comes from the fact that DNA is made up of pairs of nucleotides (see Figure 2.4). DNA consists of molecules called bases, which interact in specific pairs. The bases are adenine (A), thymine (T), guanine (G), and cytosine (C). They bond together only as A-T and C-G.

Only a hint of the paradigm-shifting implications of these discoveries for genetics appeared at the end of Watson and Crick's paper where—in possibly one of the most understated passages ever documented in the history of science—it was written: "It has not escaped our notice that the specific base pairing we have postulated immediately suggests a possible copying mechanism for the genetic material." This paved the way for our understanding of how DNA splits in two when an organism is being reproduced. Subsequently, the 1962

Nobel Prize for Physiology or Medicine was awarded to Watson, Crick, and Wilkins for this groundbreaking work.

Now that you have a basic understanding of genetics, how does it actually work and what does it actually mean for Batman, for his similarity to rats and bats, and for his extreme physical performance? To answer these questions, we turn to proteins and how they are made, which brings us to the field of proteomics. This is because that is the real role of your DNA—to provide instructions for the production of proteins. Proteins are very important to act as enzymes, to provide structure and act as biological "motors," and to help with

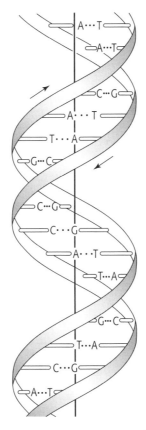

Figure 2.4. Physical structure of "double helix" of DNA, from the original model created by Watson and Crick. Courtesy Klug (2004).

movement of ions and products across the cell membrane. To construct a protein (you are making some right now) you use a protein "alphabet" composed of 20 elements. Instead of letters, your protein alphabet is composed of amino acids. When the 20 amino acids are combined in various groupings, you wind up with "words" that are the proteins. By the way, you have some pretty complex protein words since some can be made up of hundreds of amino acid "letters."

You may have noticed that I haven't yet mentioned where the letters come from. That is, how do you get the amino acids in the first place? This is where we return to DNA to answer the question of how protein is made. Sometimes protein synthesis is likened to printing a document from a computer. In this analogy, the hard drive is the DNA, the "copy" of the document displayed on the screen is the messenger RNA, the printout is the polypeptide, the printer itself is the protein-manufacturing ribosomal complex, and the paper is the protein. Recall that we have four bases (A, T, C, and G) and two base pairs (A-T and C-G). Putting three base pairs together gives us a codon, which is the signal for starting and stopping the making of a protein.

Making proteins this way requires a cousin of DNA called RNA (for ribonucleic acid). RNA is set up similarly to DNA in that it also has four bases. However, in RNA the thymine (T) is replaced by uracil (U). There are several kinds of RNA, but creating proteins involves three main types: transfer RNA, which selects the "letters" (amino acids); messenger RNA, which determines the order in which they will be sequenced; and ribosomal RNA, which manufactures the proteins.

RNA acts to create proteins through a series of steps. The first step is to transcribe the DNA coding. During this transcription, the DNA helix is unwound to reveal the gene segments. The transcriptional RNA then forms the proper base pairs that match those found on the gene segment. After a few more steps, messenger RNA binds to the protein-building ribosomes and with the aid of translational RNA (yet another kind of RNA), the new protein is created. This process occurs in the cells of all living organisms. Although fantastically simple in principle, the process leads to the immensely diverse and complex life that we see, hear, and feel all around us.

This brings us to the issue of genetic coding for an entire animal and the concept of the genome. Perhaps you have heard of the Human Genome Project, which mapped most of the genes of the human body. As a result, we now have a great deal of information about the role of specific genes in athletic and exercise performance. We will look at the Human Genome Project in more detail later.

Introducing . . . Bob Wayne

To help us figure out what Bruce really achieved en route to bathood, let me introduce you to Robert "Blocco" Wayne—Bruce's identical twin brother. Bob is an idler who does all the real partying that Bruce pretends to do, but he doesn't bother with any of Bruce's physical training. Throughout his life he didn't do much . . . at all. When you look at Bob and Bruce side by side, there really is a difference, particularly in how much sun they block out. Let's back up a few steps, though, and see Bruce and Bob together as kids. What could we learn about the potential each of them had for physical adaptation and skill development?

DC Comics once showed Batman with someone who could be considered a twin. In this case, it was an evil twin called "The Wrath," who appeared in the story "The Player on the Other Side" (Batman Special #1, 1984). However, unlike the idea we are exploring in this chapter about real twins and real genetics—and real-imaginary Wayne twins—The Wrath was the evil mirror image of Batman in an alternate universe. The same events that shaped Bruce Wayne's decision to be a crimefighter, the killing of his parents, motivated The Wrath to devote himself to a life of crime. As you probably anticipated, at the end of the story, the real Batman prevails and goodness is restored—in both universes, of course!

Let's make a brief stop to consider the whole area of "twin studies" mentioned in the last chapter. Twin studies represent the best scientific way to do an experiment that can tell about the inherent genetic predisposition for certain things. For example, how likely it is that someone will develop a disease or a disorder. Or, of more relevance to our discussions here, how likely it is that a person would be good at something. The ideal experiment to look into this would be to separate the twins from birth so that both can develop independently of one another. The way I've introduced Bruce's "lost" twin Bob here deliberately gets at this issue.

Above, I made reference to Bob becoming kind of a chubby, lazy, party boy in contrast to Bruce (as Batman) who became the most all-around fit human being to ever live! But is that realistic? If Bruce became something like "the Batman," why didn't Bob pursue something similar? Maybe even become another Batman, perhaps living on the West Coast?

We are beginning to move on to the effects of genetics or heredity as compared with that of our environmental conditions. How much of what is in our DNA defines our behavior and how much of our behavior is because of what we experience in our lives? This is often described as the "nature versus nurture" debate, and it doesn't have a clean resolution. A key thing to remember about Batman is that, as a young Bruce Wayne, he had the unimaginably horrific experience of having both his parents murdered right in front of him. As depicted in both the 1989 *Batman* and the 2005 *Batman Begins* feature films and as originally described, briefly, in "The Batman and How He Came to Be" (Detective Comics #33, 1939), this event was the defining "environmental" (it's a bit of a stretch to think of this as a "nurturing" event) moment of Bruce's life. So, we can suggest that, since Bob did not have this same experience (despite still losing his imaginary parents), he wouldn't have a "natural" inclination or desire to parallel Bruce's development.

Studies looking at families suggested that the likelihood of participating in exercise does have a component of heritability. However, environmental factors (like nutrition) play a huge role as well. The complex interaction among environment (what happens to you and what you choose to do), heredity (what your genes predispose you to), and how you perform athletically is shown in a simple way in Figure 2.5. The biggest issue contradicting the complete dominance of either nature or nurture is that genetics, environment, and exercise all affect one another. This is immensely useful but makes it difficult when trying to define relative contributions. A key thing to consider is that genetic influences are often quite specific and may be revealed or maximized only in certain specific situations. For example, if someone has an inherent capacity to respond to strength-training exercise, it may be only for a specific type of exercise.

We can get an interesting view of what Bob could have achieved by considering real-life athletes who are identical twins. As of 2006, 10 sets of twins were active in the National Football League. The most well known are probably Tiki and Ronde Barber. The most recent were Daniel Bullocks (drafted by the Detroit Lions) and Josh Bullocks (drafted by the New Orleans Saints). Josh is 6' (1.8 meters tall) and weighs 207 pounds (93 kilograms), and Daniel is 6'½" (1.8 meters tall)

environment genome

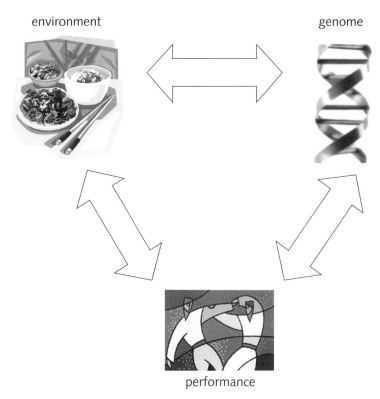

performance

Figure 2.5. The interaction between genetic predisposition (genome), nutrition (environment), and exercise performance.

and weighs 212 pounds (95 kilograms). These two really are similar in size and appearance. Because they followed the same physical activity choices and patterns, both maximized their potential to play in the NFL. Nancy Segal has documented an odd example of twins and skilled physical performance. In 2006, twin 62-year-olds were playing golf. On a 115-meter (128-yard), par 3 hole, each of them hit a hole in one. These examples demonstrate that genetic makeup is important. Also, important is that all these twins had lots of training—that is, similar environmental influences. The key thing about Bob is that he had the same genetic potential as did Bruce. However, since we are assuming that he never applied himself to the same dedicated training program as did his twin brother, he would never have achieved that potential or promise to become the West Coast Batman. Too bad. I think the "Dark Angel of Los Angeles" has a nice ring to it!

OK. So Bob and your newly found understanding of genetics and the nature/nurture debate gives you a pretty good idea about what might have happened if Bruce had lived his life differently. But a larger and very relevant question is: Would both Bob and Bruce respond to training the same way? Would you or I respond to exercise in the same way? Is adaptation to exercise stress one-size-fits-all? Scientists know quite a bit about how people respond and adapt to exercise, and much of the foundational concepts and information comes from lots of other critters . . . including rats!

Just how much can you learn about bats by studying rats? A whole lot, actually. It turns out that no matter what you do, you won't suddenly become Lance Armstrong or Hulk Hogan.

Before we look more closely at this issue, let's address a basic and relevant question: Why does something we learn from one animal species inform us about another animal species? When we are thinking about "nature," we are really wondering about how much of a genetic link there is between different animals, including that intelligent being known as *Homo sapiens* (that's you and me!). It is because of this tendency to share basic operational principles, such as how proteins are formed and how DNA is replicated, that fruit flies and mice can provide useful information for people. Therefore, studies of other species can have important implications for the development and function of humans.

Another reasonable question to ask is how much genetic material is shared across species? How much do we have in common with other animals? Answering this question has been made somewhat easier in recent years because of the tremendous work done to map the genetic coding for several different species. In living beings, from the humble bacteria to the human, genetic coding containing all heredity information is stored in the nucleus of the cell; this information is called the genome. For humans, our knowledge of the genome was greatly increased in recent years with the Human Genome Project, which mapped 92% of the human genetic code. This effort was achieved by both the public and private sectors operating separately. It may surprise you to know that this was accomplished by using genetic samples taken from less than a dozen people. In fact, the public portion of the project obtained data from only one individual (codename RP11, from Buffalo, New York).

What is of particular relevance for our discussion about Bob and Bruce Wayne, though, would be to know more about variation within the genome. In that arena, much work remains to be done. There are ongoing research projects entitled the International Hap-Mat Project and the Human Variome Project. The goal of these projects is to identify the extent of genetic variation across the human gene pool. This will have implications for human response to drug treatments, environmental conditions, and so on. It would also be quite useful for our own discussion about nature versus nurture.

Of importance for Batman and the issue of extreme physical performance is the extent of genetic contribution to exercise training response and physical fitness. In the 2004 update on the human gene map for performance and fitness phenotypes, almost 150 genes were identified that showed a relationship to variables around exercise performance and health. So, it seems that some important traits are inherited from our parents. Exactly how much of what your parents (and their parents, and their parents, going back into history) could do affects what you do? Many factors that are key to physical performance have about a 20 to 30% genetic contribution. Some factors may actually be closer to 50%. For example, as shown in Table 2.1, muscle strength and aerobic fitness both may have approximately 30% genetic contribution. What are the genes that are responsible for these differences? It has to do with mutations in one of the pairs of genes for a given trait. Remembering the alleles we discussed earlier, that means that changes in one allele may lead to the expression or enhancement of a certain phenotype. It is important to realize that this *may* happen, but it's not inevitable!

TABLE 2.1. Genetic contributions to physical fitness

Component	Function	Genetic contribution (%)
Maximal oxygen uptake	Aerobic fitness	20–30
Muscular fitness	Muscle strength and endurance	20–30
Resting blood pressure	Heart health	30
Habitual activity level	Exercise activities	30

Source: Data adapted from McArdle et al. (2005).

A key area of research that suggested genetic influences could strongly affect physical performance came from studies looking at twins and other closely related family members and contrasting those observations with unrelated people. The main focus was to examine the heritability of performance-related traits like endurance or muscle strength.

Some key factors that affect muscle growth and performance are linked to human genetic mutations. As is typical in molecular biology, they have some pretty fantastic names. We will briefly discuss one that goes by the name of myostatin (a.k.a. growth differentiation factor 8).

Myostatin has a history grounded in animal husbandry and selective breeding. Although it didn't go by the name myostatin back then, the effect of this growth factor was first described in cattle as "bovine muscular hypertrophy" by the British farmer H. Culley in 1807. A photograph of a thickly muscled bull is shown at the top of Figure 2.6. This is clearly an unusually muscular bovine, and its appearance led to the term "double muscled" as a descriptor. A cow that is double muscled has less bone, less fat, and much more muscle than does a typical cow. It should be mentioned that these animals don't really have twice the number of muscles, but rather more and larger muscle fibers than normal animals. It turns out that "double muscling" arises because of a deletion in a gene regulating the activity of myostatin, which normally inhibits the growth of skeletal muscle. The deletion of the gene allows relatively unchecked growth to occur and results in the extreme double muscling.

After first being detected in cattle, this mutation has been shown also in the mouse and most recently in the whippet, a racing dog breed (see bottom of Figure 2.6). In the case of the whippet, the increase in musculature allowed dogs with this mutation to run much faster than their normally muscled friends.

There has also been one reported case of myostatin gene mutation in humans, which is shown in Figure 2.7. In the figure you can see obvious increases in muscle tissue at the hip and calf compared with a typical infant. The figure also shows ultrasound images contrasting areas and sizes of the muscles for the child with the mutation (left) and a child of the same age without the mutation. This boy continues to develop normally but with greatly enhanced strength. At the age of four and a half years, this child was able to hold two 6-pound (3-kg) dumbbells with his arms held straight out to the sides!

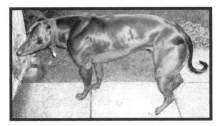

Figure 2.6. Double muscling in cattle and dogs. Courtesy Bellinge et al. (2005) (bull) and Elaine Ostrander (dogs).

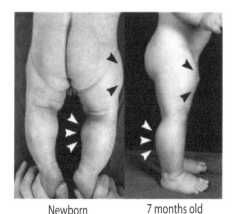

Newborn   7 months old

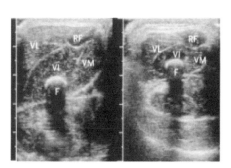

Mysotatin gene deletion   Control

Figure 2.7. Double muscling with myostatin gene deletion in a human child six days old (*left*) and seven months old (*right*). The black and white arrows point to increases in muscle tissue at the hip and calf. The ultrasound images below show the areas and sizes of the muscles for the child with the mutation (*left*) and a child of the same age without the mutation (*right*). Courtesy M. Schuelke et al. (2004).

The example of genetic differences of myostatin seems pretty extreme, and it is. What about the normal variation of genetic contributions? Given that you and Batman are both human beings, you share 99% of your genetic coding. So, how come you aren't Batman? I hope I haven't created too much emphasis on the nature part—that is, the genetic contribution. Even at the largest end of the spectrum we have discussed percentage contributions of 25–50%. That leaves 50–75% to be accounted for by other factors . . . like training! This book is after all entitled *Becoming Batman,* not *Born as Batman*! A very important role is played by the environment—the nurture part—in which someone grows up and develops as well as the kind of experiences one has.

Tom Brutsaert and Esteban Parra put it well when they said "elite athletes are those who respond in extraordinary ways to training in order to unlock an already present potential." So, an elite athlete like Bruce Wayne may have possessed a well-endowed genetic potential at birth, but to realize that potential required years and years of training to become Batman. Bruce Wayne made a choice to train to become Batman. In so doing, he made maximum use of his genetic potential while immersing himself in various environments that would support that potential.

Most traits are a complex mixture of many different genes and interactions with the environment. Height is a good example, as there is no single gene coding for it. Instead diet and genetics play strong roles together. The best way to consider genetics and environmental factors was captured in the Batman graphic novel *Child of Dreams* (2003). In this story an evil mastermind is taking DNA and creating clones to fight Batman. His ultimate objective is to create another Batman. But, as Batman says clearly, "A man isn't just his DNA . . . he's his intellect, his experiences . . . You're not Batman . . . You're not the things that I experienced, the events that shaped me."

Now that we've met Bruce's twin and seen the role of genetics, let's look at the role of another type of chemical found throughout our bodies: the hormone.

CHAPTER 3

The Stress of Life

HOLY HORMONES, BATMAN!

> Few fictional characters of any kind, let alone comic book characters, have enjoyed the kind of hold over their readers that Batman has exerted . . . More people have thrilled to the exploits of Batman than have ever heard of Hamlet or seen a play by Shakespeare.
>
> —*The Original Encyclopedia of Comic Book Heroes*, Volume 1: *Featuring Batman* by Michael L. Fleisher

Although we mostly think of puberty as the time when young adolescent bodies are awash in a sea of hormones, our bloodstreams are actually teeming with hormones at every age. This is not a bad thing! Slow- and fast-acting chemical signals are quite effective at communicating across distances within the body to affect multiple organs and organ systems.

Getting Stressed Out?

As a result of the genetic similarity among species, many basic physiological processes operate in common ways in different species. One such process is that of stress and stress response. The word "stress" has roots in the Latin verb *stringere,* which means to draw tight, strain, exert, or tax. The concept of stress seems to be everywhere in our society. As I write this in 2007, just typing "stress" in an Internet search engine yields over 197 million hits! In the field of science alone there is a staggering amount of research being conducted concerning stress. Basic filtering of the search results by including "physiology" brings this number down to a more manageable 10 million hits. A search of the U.S. National Library of Medicine and National Institutes of Health's PubMed search engine provides over 300,000 results. I hope you are getting the point that stress is a well-researched topic.

But why so much ado about stress? What is stress anyway? Are you getting stressed by all these questions? Although stress is a fundamental property of life—I mean that quite literally, as you will see—that has existed forever, stress as a scientific concept has its roots in the work of the great French scientist Claude Bernard (1813–1878). Bernard's contributions were so important that many consider him the father of physiology. The central issue for us to consider here with Batman is that having a functioning human body is a tricky business. Your body is composed of an enormous number of cells—on average about one billion cells per gram of tissue (about a third of an ounce) or about 100 trillion cells in an adult—and they all have their own internal environments (as we discussed in Chapter 2).

Maintaining order and concentrations of nutrients and wastes in the internal and external environments is a major function of cells. However, your cells are the ultimate nosy and envious neighbors. It really is all about keeping up with the Joneses. All your cells want to be the same. OK, that may seem fine. But it isn't quite so easy to keep the contents of each cell the same because the "walls" (membranes) of the cells are flimsy and allow movement of lots of things across them. So what happens in the external environment, held at bay by cellular processes and that flimsy membrane, has real consequences for each cell. This brings us back to Claude Bernard. He had the insight to observe that the most important issue for life that exists as a fluid environment independent from an external environment—that is to say, the life of our cells—was to have a very tight control or regulation of the fluid itself.

American physiologist Walter B. Cannon (1871–1945) picked up this concept and expanded upon it. In so doing he coined the term "homeostasis" to refer to the process by which the internal environment of the body is maintained within a range at which cells could function properly. The concept of homeostasis has embedded in it both changes and responses to change that all serve to drive the body back to its comfortable operating range. Body temperature regulation is a good example of this. Other examples include responses to extreme cold, hemorrhaging blood loss, traumatic pain, and emotional distress. These all essentially require responses related to hormones, which we will discuss shortly. Cannon also put forward the phrase "fight or flight" relating to hormonal responses to extreme stresses that challenged homeostasis. I think it is easy to imagine the relevance of fight or flight to a career as Batman!

Walter Cannon went on to say that the nervous system was very important in regulating homeostasis and that all systems were active at all times. This means that things in the body get turned up or down, not on or off. Consider the example of a thermostat. You would normally adjust the temperature up or down a little bit and not just full-blast hot or cold and then off! The best example in your body is that of your heart rate. Your heart beats constantly, but the rate is adjusted up or down depending on what you are doing. As long as things are intact and working well, homeostasis is maintained and the body is healthy. However, when failure to regulate homeostasis occurs, disease and death may follow.

Of interest scientifically and with regard to the rigors of Batman is Cannon's description of "shock" gleaned from his experience with soldiers on the battlefields of World War I. Cannon showed that hormones reacting to stress were very much a part of how soldiers responded to life-threatening wounds.

In addition to this extreme example, routine activities such as exercise evoke homeostatic responses. Although concepts related to stress have been around for quite some time, it wasn't until 1935 that the more modern notion of stress was clearly articulated by Dr. Hans Selye. Drawing from experiments on mammals of the order Rodentia and the genus *Rattus*—the common rat—Selye came up with the concept of stress.

Selye was born and trained in Prague and made his way to the Johns Hopkins University in Baltimore, Maryland, in 1931. Soon he moved on to Montreal and began his research in endocrinology at McGill University. With a background in organic chemistry and medicine, Selye was searching for new sex hormones. While testing the effects of a variety of extracts on rats, Selye was greatly surprised to discover that regardless of the extract used, a reproducible and devastatingly widespread negative response was observed—the catastrophic failure of several organ systems including the adrenal cortex (home of the adrenal glands) in the kidney and the intestines.

Selye extended this concept to something he called the general adaptation syndrome (shortened to GAS—I promise this is really the short form and that I didn't make it up). This syndrome was meant to embody the state of an organism in relation to adapting and responding to its environment. Within this framework the catastrophic organ failure observed in the rats was indicative of a failure to adapt to stress. There are three stages within the syndrome. The first is an "alarm reaction" that mimics the "fight or flight" response that Cannon described. In the second stage, adaptation occurs, and there is an adjustment and resistance to the stressor (see Figure 3.1). However, if this adaptation is insufficient, or if the stressor is too large, we enter the third stage, which is one of exhaustion and cell death.

We typically think of stress as something negative that needs to be "reduced" or "managed." In fact, without "stress" in a pure physiological sense, there would be no adaptation at all, no function, and life as we know it would not exist! Clearly, within a certain range—one that does not induce catastrophic organ failure, of course—stress is needed as a stimulus for biological activity. This assumption forms the backbone for most of our understanding about how the body adapts to exercise. The converse is also true: removing stresses can yield adaptations in the opposite direction to those that occurred in the presence of the stress. The key is to understand the process of stimulus and response shown in how Batman's (and your) cells adapt.

When there is a stimulus in our bodies, the body responds in such a way so as to remove or minimize the effect of the original stimulus. This is known as a biological feedback system. Let's look at a simple example of a biological adaptation to training stresses that Batman might experience: a callus on his foot. Suppose when he is training and working, his foot repeatedly rubs inside of his boot. If this action is not strong enough to form a blister, what will occur instead is that the superficial skin layers will harden and thicken. As these layers build up, a callus will develop. The adaptation of the increased layering of the skin serves to reduce the effect of the stimulus on the deeper layers of tissue. So, the callus winds up reducing the possible effect of the stimulus.

This basic example illustrates the underlying principle at work for adaptations to training and exercise stress for pretty much all our tissues. Basically, adaptations minimize the effect of the stress. The

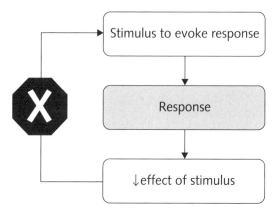

Figure 3.1. Basic negative feedback concept. The X indicates that the response to the stimulus stops the effect of the stimulus.

next thing to appreciate is the way in which physiological systems can adapt and change when exposed to a training stress. We will focus on this phenomenon as it relates to muscle, bone, and connective tissue, and the metabolic processes associated with each, in Part II, where we will specifically address each in turn. The overall message that I want you to take away from the discussion of stress is that it is a fundamental principle of life. Without stress and adaptation, we really would not have life as we know it. And we certainly wouldn't have a Batman or Bruce and Bob Wayne to talk about.

Turning our attention back to hormones, hormones can be defined as chemical messengers secreted into blood by endocrine cells or by certain special types of neurons. The eight major endocrine (or hormone-producing) glands of the body are shown for men and women in Figure 3.2.

Hormones from these glands act to regulate aspects of almost every bodily function. These encompass three general types of functioning. First there are things you have already experienced but paid little attention to, like the growth and development of your body. Second, there are things happening in you right now that you are not aware of, including water and electrolyte balance. And finally, there are things happening inside your body of which you probably are aware—at least indirectly—such as metabolism and body temperature control. If you feel cold, hot, hungry, or full right now, those sensations are direct outcomes of your hormones and of your homeostatic control systems at work.

Because many of these control mechanisms operate "silently" in the background, it is only when things go wrong that we pay much attention to them. A fairly simple example of dysfunction is one that may occur in thyroid hormone levels and results in goiters. Goiters are essentially a malfunction of the thyroid gland that causes a rather large lump to appear on the front of the neck, where the gland is located. The simplest form of goiter can be treated by administering iodine, which is needed to produce several thyroid hormones. The inflammation occurs—and here is an excellent example of the interplay

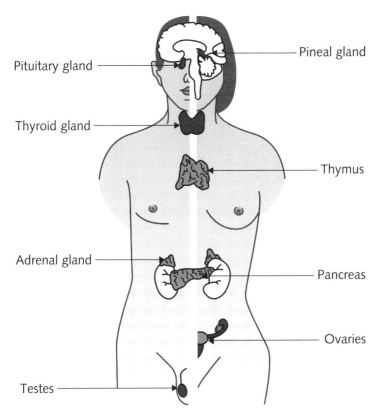

Figure 3.2. The eight major endocrine glands of the body for both men and women. Courtesy U.S. National Institutes of Health.

between different systems—because when low thyroid hormone levels are detected, the pituitary gland at the base of the brain releases a chemical to provoke the thyroid to produce more hormones. When the gland does this, a dramatic enlargement of the thyroid gland itself takes place. Physicians in ancient China, while unaware of the specifics of iodine, successfully treated goiter by prescribing the consumption of seaweed extracts, which happen to be high in iodine. The relation to thyroid hormone was what led to the present-day use of iodized salt. In addition, thyroid hormone is an important regulator of metabolism and protein building in the body.

When it comes to chemicals and scientific manipulation of bodily functions, a good example is one of Batman's most misunderstood foes: Man-Bat. Man-Bat first appeared in "The Challenge of the Man-Bat" (Detective Comics #400, 1970) and is truly more bat than man. In human form the creature is the zoologist Dr. Kirk Langstrom who studies bats. Because he was becoming deaf, Langstrom decided to create a serum from extracts of the blood of bats in the hope that he would gain some of the "sonar" (actually, echolocation) abilities from them. The good news was that, despite no scientific validity behind it—echolocation and hearing are not the same thing—the serum did improve his hearing. The bad news was that he was transformed into a real gigantic bat. Stories with Man-Bat (who never did lose the hyphen) involved numerous interventions by Batman. Some led to successful outcomes, some did not.

Batman always has another plan of action, another attack, or another defense prepared in case the first one fails. This parallels the general features of the endocrine system, where hormones tend to work together with other hormones. In this way the combination of several hormones has a bigger effect than any one hormone operating alone. Some hormones only work when other hormones are present, and some act in completely opposite directions (a feature called antagonism), like Batman versus Joker.

Hormones come in three types—this theme of threes recurs throughout the book, by the way—and can be amines, steroids, or peptides. Amines come from amino acids and include thyroid hormones and the hormones that respond to stress—epinephrine, norepinephrine, and L-dopa—which are also known as catecholamines. We will look at melatonin and adrenaline, which are also amines, later in the book. Steroids, by far the most discussed and most often found in the daily sports news, come from the adrenal cortex, gonads, and placenta. All steroids are derived from cholesterol. This is a telling reminder that despite the possible negative cardiovascular complications associated with high cholesterol, cholesterol is essential for life. Peptides are hormones that affect, among other things, insulin and testosterone production and certain functions of the heart and kidneys.

The main example I use here to illustrate the fantastic function of the endocrine system, and which is crucial for helping keep Batman working properly, is that of the regulation of the level of blood sugar—or glucose. We are going to talk about Batman's diet and energy needs a bit later, but before getting to that we will first chat a bit about the crucial regulation of blood glucose. First of all, why is it crucial? As I said, more will be revealed later, but for now the key point is that glucose is the only energy that your nervous system will accept and metabolize for its function. Your nervous system is the ultimate picky eater. It insists on a steady diet of a simple carbohydrate made from six carbon, six oxygen, and twelve hydrogen atoms. The tight regulation of this $C_6H_{12}O_6$ molecule in the blood is probably the best example of hormonal regulation that is of direct importance for maintaining energy in the body.

A further complication for the proper function of Batman's body is that the nervous system, in addition to being picky, doesn't plan ahead and store glucose for use later. A steady level of bloodborne glucose is therefore essential. To be fair, there really is nowhere to store glucose molecules in the brain and spinal cord anyway. The two main players in regulating the blood glucose levels are the hormones insulin and glucagon. You are probably familiar with insulin, especially if you are or know someone who is diabetic. Insulin is a hormone that has anabolic (to build something up) functions, while glucagon is catabolic (to break something down). By the way, we will return over and over again to the idea of anabolic and catabolic. Maybe a good way to remember the difference between the two is that when Catwoman (catabolic) is on the prowl, she is constantly breaking (break down) into banks to get money and jewels. If this doesn't work for you, think of your own way to tell the two concepts apart.

The anabolic hormone insulin builds up glucose in cells where it can be metabolized. Glucagon has completely the opposite effect, acting to release glucose into the bloodstream. You may hear concerns about proper levels of insulin, but it is in fact the ratio of insulin to glucagon in the blood that is the key issue for regulating blood sugar. They are both produced in the pancreas in a part known as the islets of Langerhans. Although this may sound like something straight out of *Pirates of the Caribbean,* the islets are in your own pancreas, which sits quietly in your abdomen tucked just under your stomach. You would also find a hormone called somatostatin in there too. Your pancreas is a busy place!

The full name for diabetes is "diabetes mellitus." We got the word "diabetes," meaning siphoning or moving through, from the Greek physician Aretaeus about two thousand years ago. The mellitus part (from the Latin word for honey) arises because it was known that when people have diabetes, their urine has a sweet taste from all the excess glucose in it. This name of sugar or honey urine disease has been consistent regardless of whether it was being described by ancient Egyptians, Chinese, Indians, Japanese, or Koreans. Ancient Indian physicians would observe whether insects were drawn to the urine of a patient and use that as a positive identification for diabetes. If left untreated, diabetes mellitus leads to wasting away of the body tissue, insatiable hunger, chronic thirst, and excessive urination. Damage to the nervous system can occur, causing reduced sensation in the hands and feet and visual difficulties.

Although the metabolic disorder of diabetes has been known as long as medical observations have been made, it was only fairly recently that the role of the pancreas and pancreatic hormones wa discovered. We can thank the German scientists Oskar Minkowski and Joseph von Mering for pointing out in 1889 the importance of the pancreas (which was later shown to be where insulin is produced). They established the link between the pancreas and excessive urination in diabetes. In 1922 Sir Frederick Grant Banting and Charles Herbert Best, along with colleagues James Collip and J. J. R. Macleod, at the University of Toronto created a pancreatic extract containing cells from the islets of Langerhans. This extract was shown to counteract diabetes in laboratory animals and led eventually to the creation of insulin injections that humans could use. For this work, the Nobel Prize in Physiology or Medicine was presented to Banting and McLeod in 1923. It is notable that these scientists did not patent their work for commercial gain and instead made the process and all its details freely available to the world. We thus have Banting and Best to thank for increasing our understanding of how the bodies of Bruce and Batman actually work!

What other hormones roaming around that batbody should we consider? We are particularly interested in ones that might be important for helping Batman adapt to exercise and training. Because of their significance in stress, exercise, and injury, we should also talk about testosterone, cortisol, growth hormone, insulin-like growth factors, and the catecholamines. The pituitary and the pineal gland come to mind here. These are very tiny formations at the base of the brain. The pineal gland was originally thought to have no physiological function. This is partly because it is very small in adults. It is large in adolescents but then shrinks, and it may often be calcified in adults. It secretes a hormone called melatonin, which is important for regulating our body clocks for many systems (we will talk much more about this in Chapter 12).

Let's look at how these other hormones affect Batman's training. We'll look first at cortisol. It has often been called the "stress hormone" because of its importance to both rapid and long-term responses to stress. Produced by the adrenal glands found on the kidneys, cortisol is important in regulating blood glucose levels, blood pressure, and the immune system. If you had a mosquito bite or a burn recently, the steroid cream you might have put on it to help reduce the itching would probably have been hydrocortisone based and would have had a similar chemical structure to the cortisol produced by your body. During exercise, cortisol levels can increase, suggesting the triggering of catabolic processes, which in extreme cases can lead to muscle wasting. It is a very interesting byproduct of steroids that, when taken orally or injected, they interfere with cortisol and reduce its release. Because cortisol is such an important overall homeostatic hormone (say that five times fast!) it is tightly controlled in the body. However, levels of cortisol in trained people like Batman aren't much different from those of the untrained—unless the person is overtrained and not functioning well.

Growth hormone is a protein hormone—here comes that clever naming procedure again—that is involved in regulating cell production and growth. Despite this being a book about becoming Batman and not Superman, growth hormone is part of a "super family" of related hormones. Growth hormone comes from the anterior, or front part, of the pituitary gland, and the levels are much higher during the busiest time for growth and development—adolescence. Too little growth hormone during adolescence can lead to extremely short stature. In adults, low growth hormone levels can lead to decreased energy levels and bone mass and to increased risk of cardiovascular disease. By contrast, too much growth hormone can lead to gigantism (acromegaly). During and after exercise, particularly the kind that is done during strength training (and which we will discuss more fully in Chapter 4), growth hormone levels rise. The increases are largest in the most strenuous exercise, the kind that Batman would engage in, and show a strong relation to the building up of muscle.

Testosterone is likely one of the hormones that you are most familiar with. It is a steroid hormone, like cortisol, and is made from cholesterol. Testosterone is associated with the testes, but it is also found in the ovaries, the adrenal cortex, and in the placenta. This hormone is closely related to stresses on the body as a result of exercise, and levels of circulating testosterone are elevated during and after exercise. As with growth hormone, the effects are largest with more strenuous exercise. It may be surprising that perhaps the most important role for testosterone may be how it interacts with and augments the effects of growth hormone and insulin-like growth factors rather than how it acts by itself. It may also be surprising that something called luteinising hormone, secreted in the pituitary, is the actual signaling molecule for testosterone release from the testes. The body synthesizes testosterone from cholesterol. The process of synthesizing and releasing this hormone has many steps. During the process intermediate compounds are created. These compounds are involved in the major problems for steroid abuse, because these intermediate compounds, such as androstenedione (made famous—infamous?—in major league baseball), can be taken in and used to boost this pathway.

Another important grouping of hormones is the insulin-like growth factors (IGFs). The chemical structures of IGFs are similar to insulin (hence the clever name) and generally work as anabolic triggers. So, they lead to increased muscle mass. All across our life spans, IGFs are necessary to help stimulate and maintain our muscle cells.

The Stress of Life

We have just outlined how important the hormonal systems are for adjusting the body to stresses and stressors. In the physiological response to stimuli that results in adaptations to exercise, there needs to be some way to convert the energy from all the bodies' stresses and strains into signals to which the biological organism can respond. Back in 1964 Geoffrey Goldspink showed that the cells in skeletal muscle tissue developed by laying down new cells in series with other cells. This adaptation minimized the stress of the muscle stretch.

Many types of cells respond to mechanical stresses. There are specialized receptors in skin and muscle, for example, that respond to mechanical stress including a wide variety of cells that provide support (such as bone cells or osteocytes) or covering (such as skin or epidermal cells), as well as produce movement (muscle cells). The term "mechanocyte"—from *kytos,* the Greek word for cell—is used to refer to these cells of bone, muscle, and skin. In many ways perhaps it is not surprising that these cells respond to mechanical stress and strain, as they are continuously subjected to such forces. The stress and strain experienced by the mechanocytes result in adaptation of the tissue. The main functional outcome of the adaptations is to reduce the negative impact of the stresses on the tissue, be it bone, muscle, or skin. This forms a common physiological system of negative feedback (see Figure 3.1), where the stimulus leads to a response that minimizes the initial effect of the stimulus. This fits within a general principle of physiology related to homeostasis described by Walter Cannon in 1932. Remember him from the beginning of the chapter? Recall too that homeostasis describes the way in which a biological organism maintains itself such that the "internal environment" remains within limits for proper function. This includes the concept of exercise and responses to exercise or training stresses with respect to the regulation of the endocrine system.

Too much training can actually lead to a cascade of events that leads to muscle wasting, fatigue, and malfunction. Think back to the third stage of Seyle's GAS, the stage of exhaustion and cell death. This is illustrated in Figure 3.3 where the normal regulation of body function is shown. A body can handle challenges to homeostasis if it is healthy. In a diseased state or in extreme stress, the body is too weak and failure of function occurs.

Batman hasn't found himself in that position too often. However, that was precisely where he was in the "The Broken Bat" (Batman #497, 1993). This was the part of the extensive Knightfall story arc in which Bane, Batman's steroid-laced nemesis, sets Batman up by releasing all the criminals from Gotham's Arkham Asylum. Batman has to sequentially battle them all, round them up, and send them back to prison. He does this night after night until he finally is exhausted—and would certainly be near stage three of the GAS. That is where he meets up with Bane and comes up against a very

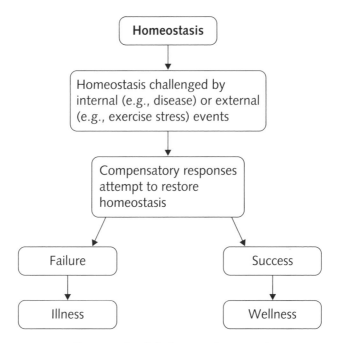

Figure 3.3. Different results of challenges to homeostasis.

atypical Batman fate—he is defeated (we will come back to this story arc in Chapter 13 when we discuss injuries). For now, the main point is that too much training can yield too much stress such that proper adaptation does not in fact occur. This is similar to extreme states of overtraining or "overreaching" in athletes and would be a real problem for Batman.

In future chapters, when we talk about how Batman's muscles, bones, skin, and metabolic machinery respond and adapt to exercise stresses, we will do so from the perspectives of stress responses and challenges to homeostasis that do not place him in a similar state of exhaustion.

So now let's look at the first of those body parts—the muscles!

PART II

BASIC BATBODY TRAINING

Laying the foundation for Batman's physical prowess to be later exploited by his skill

CHAPTER 4

Gaining Strength and Power

DOES THE BAT THAT FLIES
THE HIGHEST OR THE FASTEST
GET THE WORM?

What is the point of all those push ups if
you can't even lift a bloody log?
—Alfred to Bruce, while pinned under a burning
beam in Wayne Manor; from the film *Batman
Begins*

Think of the strongest person you know. Or know about. Or can imagine. Think about how much this person could lift physically—a breadbox? A car? Now, how fast do you think this person could move? Would you measure their fastest movement with an egg timer or a precision Swiss stopwatch? Muscles do lots of different things, and all of them involve producing forces. But producing large forces—being strong—and producing force while moving quickly— being powerful—are not exactly the same things. Would Batman need to be really strong or really powerful? I will show that Batman needs a base of batstrength but really he needs to be powerful. We will explore the adaptations that could occur in muscle as a result of specialized training to obtain strength and power.

To begin let's describe exactly what we are trying to understand here. How is it that we develop strength and get stronger in the first place? What physiological systems are "stressed"—used in the sense established in the previous chapter—and what are the adaptations? A useful way to proceed is to think of the stresses associated with exercise as being a challenge to homeostasis that requires some compensation to restore balance. As part of this exploration of how muscle adapts to exercise and training stresses, we need also to back up one step and consider how muscle is activated. That is, what are the effects of Batman's neural commands to activate his muscles? What is the process by which you activate your muscles now as you sit or stand and read this book? I will follow up later in Chapter 7 on the more complex issue of skill training and adaptation at various levels of the nervous system.

Making Muscles Contract

Let's look at how our muscles contract and generate the forces that then move our limbs around when we want to produce movement. It probably comes as no surprise that the trigger or command for voluntary muscle activity comes from the brain. Indeed, over three hundred years ago the Irish natural philosopher Robert Boyle (1627–1691), famous in chemistry for formulation of Boyle's law (which outlined the relationship between pressure, temperature, and volume of gases), described the case of a knight with a depressed skull fracture who was returning from battle. The knight had little movement in his arm and leg on one side of his body, and Boyle called this condition a "dead palsy." This suggested that some areas of the brain had a role to play in motor output—in physiological lingo, movement is typically described as "motor."

Boyle's work was followed by other scientists in the nineteenth and twentieth centuries. English neurologist John Hughlings Jackson (1835–1911) studied epilepsy and, based upon his clinical observations, suggested that some area of the cerebral cortex must be responsible for governing simple motor commands. These speculations were later confirmed in 1870 by G. T. Fritsch and Eduard Hitzig, who used electrical stimulation to map brains of cats and dogs.

A very important discovery was made by Wilder Penfield and Edwin Boldrey through their extensive survey of the human motor cortex: electrically stimulating cells in particular parts of the brain activated muscles in the body. From their work they generated a map of the surface of the motor areas of the brain that corresponded to the muscles of the body. The shape that this map took gave rise to a

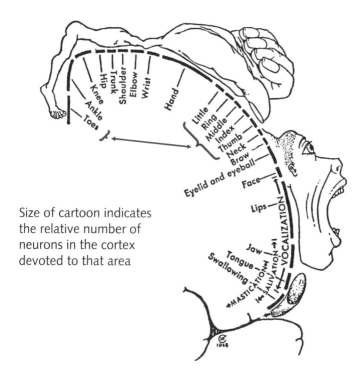

Size of cartoon indicates the relative number of neurons in the cortex devoted to that area

Figure 4.1. "Map" of the brain's neurons used for muscle activation. The "homunculus" (or little man) shows the relative numbers of neurons controlling particular body parts. For reference, the smaller cortical area for the toes is contrasted with that for the hand. Modified from Penfield & Rasmussen (1950).

"little man map" (called a "homunculus"; see Figure 4.1). Notice how large is the area of the map for the muscles controlling the fingers, thumb, and hand. This can be contrasted with the much smaller map area for the foot and speaks to the fine motor skill we humans have for the careful control of our fingers.

The Brain Says Go!

To begin let's think about some basic principles of how the nervous system and activation of muscle actually work. To signal for a contraction to occur, messages from the nervous system (as activity in nerve cells) are sent out to the muscles of our limbs. It's helpful to think about nerve cells as being a lot like trees. This might seem kind of weird at first, but the analogy actually works well. A typical nerve cell, or neuron, is composed of a cell body, an axon, and a receiving area made up of dendrites. The axon is really an elongated trunk relaying the output commands from the neuron and typically extends from one side, while the dendrites form a huge net of receiving posts on the other side. If you think of the tree analogy, imagine the dendrites (which are often described as a "dendritic tree") as being like the roots of the tree, the base of the tree is the cell body, the trunk is the axon, and the branches and leaves are the terminal connections where the neuron makes connections with other trees (neurons). Put your single tree in a dense rain forest where there is close contact between lots of leaves from different trees and you get the general idea.

So, to begin, you decide you want to do something. It could be a motion as simple as picking this book up from the bookstore shelf. Upon that decision, a relayed command arrives at the main movement output center of your brain—your primary motor cortex. Inside the primary motor cortex (from here on we'll refer to it simply as motor cortex) live the nerve cells, the neurons, which relay the command to activate muscle down into the spinal cord. This is outlined in the diagram shown in Figure 4.2.

These command motor output cells are often referred to as upper motoneurons—simply meaning the motor output neurons at the physically highest (uppermost) part of the nervous system. That relayed command arrives at the spinal cord level for the appropriate muscles and makes connection with some more motoneurons. This time we are talking about lower motoneurons—the cells that directly relay the electrical command for movement into activation of muscle. This is so because the lower motoneurons send their axons (trunks) out to connect with the muscle cells that will actually produce movement when activated.

The pairing of a motoneuron and the muscle cells (or fibers) it innervates is the basic functional unit of movement control. This was called the "motor unit" by Sir Charles Sherrington. Sherrington (1857–1952) was a pioneering British neurophysiologist who shared the 1932 Nobel Prize for Physiology or Medicine with Edgar Douglas Adrian for "discoveries regarding the functions of neurons." Sherrington is also my own favorite "science superhero." We will talk more about Sherrington's discoveries in later chapters.

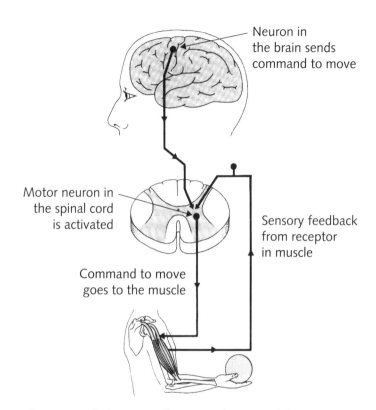

Neuron in
the brain sends
command to move

Motor neuron in
the spinal cord
is activated

Sensory feedback
from receptor
in muscle

Command to move
goes to the muscle

Figure 4.2. Links for commands to move, showing path from a neuron
in the motor cortex. Courtesy Sale (1992).

Figure 4.3 gives an example of a motor unit showing only a few muscle fibers. When the electrical signal to contract from the motoneurons arrives at the synapse between the axon from the motoneuron and the muscle fibers—conveniently called the neuromuscular junction—it changes to a chemical signal. At this "synapse" (also a term coined by Sherrington) a chemical neurotransmitter called acetylcholine, or ACH, is released that leads to depolarization of the muscle fibers. The signal is now again electrical and will trigger the release of calcium ions (shown in chemical terms as Ca^{2+}) that are directly involved in regulating the process of muscle contraction. Who knew there was so much biochemistry involved in moving your little finger!

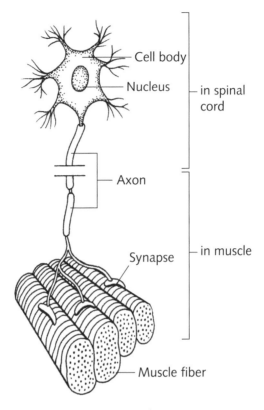

Figure 4.3. The motor unit concept, showing a motor neuron in the spinal cord, the axon in the peripheral nerve, and the muscle fibers innervated. Courtesy Noth (1992).

At this point muscle contraction will occur in all the muscle fibers of the active motor unit. It is all or none within the unit. Now let's pretend we have a microscope and are zooming in on just one muscle fiber within a motor unit. Batman's (and your) muscle fibers are composed of many different proteins, some that have an indirect role and some (called the contractile proteins) that have a direct role in producing muscle force. The contractile proteins come in two types only: actin and myosin molecules.

How actin and myosin produce force during muscle contraction can be thought of like pulling on a rope. The rope is the actin and your hands pulling on the rope are the myosin molecules. In the case of your actual muscles, the more ropes and the larger the ropes that you have within a muscle fiber, the greater the force that can be produced. This is often described for the whole muscle—which has lots of muscle fibers in it—as the cross-sectional area. So, if the cross-sectional area is increased with training (and it is), strength will go up.

The neat thing about these proteins is that they have the ability to bond together and to separate depending on the availability of an energy molecule called ATP (otherwise known as adenosine 5'-triphosphate, which we will revisit in Chapter 6). In this case you can think of the bonding between myosin and actin as being like the tightening and relaxation of your grip when you pull the rope along. An interesting thing is that the energy taken from ATP is needed for muscle relaxation, not contraction. This is why after an animal dies the condition of rigor mortis ensues. This rigidity is due to the lack of energy (in the form of ATP) to release the bonds between actin and myosin.

When Batman wants to change how much force he needs to produce—say, while fighting the Joker or Penguin—he has two main choices (although he cannot really choose them voluntarily). He can either bring into action more active muscle tissue by using more motor units by a process known as recruitment, or he can make the motor units that are already active become active at a higher rate. Both of these processes will result in increased muscle force.

To see why that happens, imagine that our ropes are now in a tug of war. Let's say you were in a competition that allowed 20 members on your team. To begin, though, you are so confident that your team can beat the first team you're facing that you let eight of your members sit out the first round. That leaves 12 to pull against the other team. As you get started, though, you notice you aren't doing well, so you add more team members. You recruit them to the cause, as it were. Well, each muscle that you have has a "pool" of motor units that can be recruited to become active and produce force. If you add more, you get more force.

As for increasing the rate of the motor units—called rate coding—the idea of tug of war also works here. Having learned your lesson from the first match—which you still won—you go to your next match with all 20 team members ready to pull on the rope. Now to get more force you have each team member pull more rapidly and frequently on the rope. This will mean more force is produced, and the rope will move toward your victory.

Where our analogy falls flat is that motor units aren't actually either just recruited or just altered in terms of their rate. Both of these actions occur in your nervous system. What is for sure, though, is that with higher and faster contractions you recruit more motor units and make them fire at higher rates.

One of the training adaptations that happens in the nervous system is that you are able to alter the way in which you can recruit and fire motor units. After training, Batman's motor units will be easier to recruit—they won't scuff and drag their feet when asked to join in—and will briefly fire at very high rates. This leads to the more powerful and stronger contractions that Batman produces. By the way, when someone begins a strength-training program, the initial gains in strength that occur over the first six weeks of training are mostly due to the adaptations the nervous system is making in activating motor units. It is only later, after the six weeks, that your muscle tissue—your muscle cells—actually change and become stronger themselves. What's really happening early on in training is a kind of change in coordination to give more strength and make use of your muscles more efficiently.

One last point to make about motor units is that they don't just come in one-size-fits-all form. In our tug-of-war analogy, think of your team as being composed of different-sized people. Just for simplicity let's say you have 10 small-sized and 10 large-sized people. Obviously, the large-sized people will be able to produce more force. Well, your motor units come in basically two types based upon speed of contraction and how long they can keep contracting (called fatigability). The types are called, rather unimaginatively, type I and type II, or slow and fast. The type II, or fast, units are broken down a bit further into fast fatigue resistant and fast fatigable. In contrast, type I units are all fatigue resistant. The strongest and fastest contracting units are the type II, and the slightly less strong and slower contracting units are the type I. If you have ever done something like tried to hold a bent arm chin-up for as long as you could, what was happening was that you had both kinds of motor units active during the contraction. Then, as you fatigued and slowly dropped to the ground, your type II units were dropping out but your slightly weaker type I units kept right on going! It is the type II units that are most affected by strength training.

Getting Warmer and Stronger

Now let's tie our discussion of muscles into one of our general themes: stress. Let's look at how, in the process of getting stronger and more powerful, biological tissue actually knows that it should respond to stress and how it detects mechanical stresses. First, we have lots of "sensors" in our muscles, tendons, and skin that inform the nervous system about things like muscle stretch and contact of the hands and feet with objects during our movements. In our explorations here we aren't yet concerned with these kinds of sensors—called proprioceptors. We'll talk about them more in Chapters 9 and 10. In tissue biomechanics, muscle, bone, and ligament have been described as mechanocytes (remember them from the last chapter?) since they can respond to mechanical stresses by altering gene expression. This can happen because although we obviously can't change the genes we were born with, what happens to us in life can alter our genes.

What sets muscles apart from other mechanocytes is that their cells respond to the mechanical stresses that are generated by their own activity. So, we can think of the adaptation that muscle has to produce as being a kind of self-inflicted challenge to homeostasis. This contrasts with other cell types like osteocytes in bone, which respond to mechanical stresses that are induced by activity of other cells . . . like muscle. Anyway, when muscles are subjected to mechanical stresses that exceed their accustomed levels, a whole host of properties—such as speed of contraction and activity of enzymes—are adapted. The result of the adaptation is to minimize the overall effect of the same stress when applied again to the muscle. This process is really very much like the negative feedback system described before (see Figure 3.1). This concept of adaptation to applied stress was originally presented by Hippocrates (460-370 BC) when he wrote "that which is used develops, and that which is not used wastes away." We might paraphrase that nowadays as "use it or lose it." But right now we don't have anything to lose and are instead trying to ask, how do we get it in the first place?

Let's go from this general discussion of muscles to a young Bruce Wayne just beginning his long journey to become Batman. He wants to increase his strength, so he does something simple like buying a set of barbells and some free weights. Bruce could choose to purchase a set of weights and follow a program such as the one advertised in many comic books back in the days of his (and my) youth. The Charles

Atlas ad showing a "weakling" getting sand kicked in his face was very prominent when I was first reading comics as a kid. Maybe you have seen similar ads in comics or on television. Bruce then performs many different exercises with the weights. He would have no reason to perform the exercise shown in the second panel of Figure 4.4. Holding a heavy weight overhead with one hand is really not a very useful part of Batman's actual required training regimen. In fact this is contrary to the main point of specificity in training. This example is one panel from the story "The Legend of the Batman—Who He Is and How He Came to Be!" (Detective Comics #33, 1939; Batman #1, 1940). This story, while obviously very much ridiculously simplified, was the first comic book documentation of the physical training Bruce Wayne had to undergo to become Batman.

To take a more realistic example of what a person can do to train his or her muscles, concentrate on a very clear and simple bicep curl exercise which involves elbow flexion. To get the idea, stand up and straighten your arms with your palms facing forward. A bicep curl is when you flex your arm by raising your hand. Your body (and that of Bruce Wayne) is calibrated for the mass of your limbs and has been adjusting to your daily activities for your entire life. We could say that your muscles are adapted already to the level of mechanical stress that you subject them to with whatever movement and activity you already do. Now, if you want to make your muscles stronger, you have to provide a mechanical stress that exceeds this already adapted level.

Bruce could do lots of flexion movements with no weights each day if he wanted to. He would get tired, for sure, after doing hundreds of empty-handed bicep curls. However, he wouldn't really get stronger. That is because a key principle for adaptation to increased training stress is something called overload. Overload means pretty much what the name implies. Muscle needs to experience a load over and above the previously adapted level in order to trigger a new adaptation.

Bruce, therefore, needs to put some weights on the barbell. This is often described as increasing the load or resistance against which muscles contract. It will result in his having to produce more force when he flexes his elbows. If we cast backward to Greece in the sixth century BC, we might find the story of wrestler Milo of Croton instructive. Legend has it that he trained by carrying a calf on his back each day until it grew into a fully grown cow. This is a very clever application of the overload principle, to be sure.

Figure 4.4. The first description of Batman's training regime from "The Legend of the Batman—Who He Is and How He Came to Be!" (Batman #1, 1940). *Left,* the sole documentation of Bruce's scientific training in which Bruce stares at a test tube of unknown material. *Right,* Bruce is shown lifting a barbell above his head, which would not have been a likely part of his training.

You might wonder why muscle (or other tissue) needs an overload to respond with an adaptation. If you are going to do some exercise to increase strength, why not just have your body start adapting right away to provide responses for increased strength? The bottom line is that our physiological systems are essentially lazy. Many physiologists would actually say that a bit differently and call it "efficiency," but it really comes down to the same thing—your systems will generate large and meaningful adaptations only if they have to. You and I operate in the same way. Often when we have to do something, we may try to do the minimum needed first. If that works then everything is fine. If it doesn't, we then ratchet up our efforts to the next minimally more difficult or least costly next step. We will continue doing only what is necessary until our objective has been achieved.

Your cellular responses are similar. Cells are more thrifty than lazy, because every cellular adaptation has a corresponding physiological cost that has to be paid. So, a minimum level of training stress for a certain duration of time needs to be experienced to trigger physiological adaptation. Also, we have a bit of a buffer in our responses, as most systems tend to generate a safety margin when they adapt. This is to ensure that the applied stress plus a little bit more can be handled without damage to the body.

To return to our example of the young Batman early on in his training for increased strength, we can now appreciate that to keep gaining in strength he will have to incrementally keep increasing the load or resistance against which he is forcing his muscles to contract. This process will continue on and on until Batman stops at his desired level or reaches the adaptive physiological limit.

So, Batman Lifts Some Weights, Then What?

When Batman does strength training, stresses on his muscle result in his muscle fibers getting stronger because of increased contractile proteins inside them. Muscle cells are really quite good at this and have some very specialized features. For example, unlike most other cells, they have many nuclei. So, more actin and myosin proteins need to be synthesized and inserted. This process is called muscle hypertrophy. Hypertrophy sounds like a bad thing, but it just means that muscle cells are increasing in size.

Think back to the interaction of the contractile proteins actin and myosin being likened to pulling a rope. Imagine more hands on the rope and increasing the strands on the rope and you will get the general idea that more force can be generated and larger forces tolerated with hypertrophy. If the muscle has been severely damaged, such as can occur with extremely high loads during exercises that cause muscles to lengthen, it may be that a normally dormant undifferentiated muscle cell comes into play. This has been called the satellite cell and was discovered almost 50 years ago by Alexander Mauro. Mauro discovered a kind of stem cell in skeletal muscle that he suggested "might be pertinent to the vexing problem of skeletal muscle regeneration." This was quite an understatement, as it is now known that satellite cells can be fully activated to regenerate damaged muscle tissue and participate in the process of hypertrophy. However, the extent to which satellite cell populations are "activated" in response to exercise training is still mostly uncertain.

A puzzling issue about the response of skeletal muscle to exercise stress has been this: exactly what is the necessary stimulus for hypertrophy? To answer this question, let's think back to Bruce's preparation to become Batman for a minute (see Figure 4.4). Bruce knew that he would have to both understand the science of his body and work hard physically if he wanted to achieve his full potential. We cannot grow stronger unless specific chemical and genetic changes take place. We all know that we are born with certain genes, but remember from Chapter 2 that our cells are constantly being created anew and that RNA is always in action in our bodies.

Having said this, let's look at what happens during hypertrophy. It was well established that stretching muscle (such as occurs during contraction) can lead to hypertrophy. It turns out that stretch-activated ion channels (that relate to movement of calcium ions) in muscle cells appear to be involved in this action. So, strange as it may seem, you get stronger because the cells in your muscles increase in size from the chemical activity of calcium. Another reason that we should all drink our milk!

Another element of hypertrophy is that messenger RNA in muscle cells increases on a very short time scale. In fact, the elevation of transcriptional activity (creation of new RNA) occurs within hours of the training stress and can remain elevated for days. When this process is completed, the same stress that induced the adaptation will no longer cause the same relative stress to the muscle fibers.

So, when Batman subjects his skeletal muscle to overload stress while doing his weight-lifting exercises, his muscles undergo a sequence of molecular-level events that lead to increased creation (anabolism) of contractile proteins. This process also increases the size of his muscles. In this way the stress from the adaptation is spread over a larger surface area of muscle protein and, just like the concept of pressure, leads to a smaller stress on the muscle. Because the increase in contractile protein is an expression of the capacity to produce forces, muscle strength is often expressed relative to its cross-sectional area. It is important to note that the cross-sectional area of muscle fiber has limits beyond which no further increases in size will occur.

Last, during Batman's training a host of hormone and signaling chemical cascades are triggered. These include many growth factors that trigger the anabolic muscle-building phase of training response. These chemical actions along with the direct mechanical stresses of strength training lead to increased muscle hypertrophy. It should be clear from this that, while training does eventually make Batman stronger, the immediate effect is to make him weaker! The training stress is induced during the training, whereas the adaptation occurs later. It is therefore important for Batman to not train on days when he will be saving Gotham from evil hordes.

Now, in Batman's case, he doesn't really want to be at the limit of his strength adaptations. He does need to be *near* his power limit, though. Let's now look more closely at the difference between strength and power.

Are the Strong Always More Powerful?

Strength and power are often incorrectly thought of as identical. We might see an extremely strong athlete and assume that the athlete also possesses great power and vice versa. Strength should be understood as the capacity for gross muscular effort. Having great strength means having the ability to generate large forces regardless of the speed of contraction. Think of the task of lifting an extremely heavily weighted barbell during an Olympic dead lift (where you hold the bar and stand up). That is a feat of great strength. Power, on the other hand, should be thought of as effort at high speed. In this case, let's use another Olympic example and imagine a 100-meter sprinter exploding out of the blocks and streaking down the track toward the finish line. That is an example of great power. It is possible to be strong and yet not that powerful, but to be powerful requires a certain base of strength.

The real reason that Batman wants to get strong is not merely to lift up heavy objects. That is not a well-established virtue for winning fights against criminals! He isn't going to be a very effective crime-fighter if all he can do is perform feats of strength. Batman needs to be strong but also quick and agile so that he can perform powerful martial arts techniques and acrobatics. The proper performance of fighting techniques and acrobatics necessitates very high velocity movements. So, power is vitally important to Batman's training and practice and is more important to excellent performance than is strength. However, it is absolutely necessary to have a certain strength base before, or developed along with, power training.

Batman understands the subtle difference between strength and power. In the story "Daughter of the Demon" (Batman #232, 1971),

Batman is fighting one of R'as al Ghul's main henchman, who is a huge man and very strong. Using typical bad guy banter, the henchman says to Batman, "I shall dance on your corpse!" Batman responds by saying, "Not likely! Oh sure, you're large and powerful . . . size and strength don't count for much! Skill is the item. Agility helps too! And those things you lack! You're clumsy!" Batman correctly tells him that skill and agility are needed for fighting, which is just what we have been discussing.

Strength and Power Training

Although there is a major distinction between the concepts of strength and power, the principles underlying training for each and physiological adaptations for each are very similar. Let's discuss, then, some of the basic principles underlying any resistance-training program that would lead to increased strength and power. Two foundational principles are overload and specificity. The overload principle can easily be understood with reference to the stimulus-response model proposed earlier. In order to bring about an adaptation, a certain stimulus must be applied. In the case of strength training and the overload principle, one must apply a stimulus to the muscles that is greater than that normally experienced. The overload principle can be understood as simply applying a stimulus to the body and gradually increasing this stimulus as the individual responds to the stimulus by getting stronger.

The principle of specificity must also be considered under the umbrella of the stimulus-response model. Any stimulus that is applied to the body will cause some response. This response is simply a protective one in that the body is attempting to minimize the stress that is being experienced and to regain homeostasis. It should come as no surprise that the response the body exhibits is quite specific to the stimulus applied. This specificity of response applies to movement pattern, velocity of movement, type of muscular contraction (lengthening or shortening), and frequency of contractions or movements. Therefore, to bring about a training adaptation that will be useful to Batman's job performance, the training stimulus must be as close as possible to the movement pattern, velocity, and type of contraction that he uses.

Based on the principle of specificity, Batman should try to train with the same movement patterns for which he wants his strength and power gains to be used. It is extremely difficult to exactly replicate fighting movements with conventional strength training equipment. However, concentrating on a rough approximation of martial arts movement patterns would be his focus. Training exercises could be done with fixed-weight machines or free weights. For example, squats and calf raises would be done with free weights to simulate springing and lunging, while leg extensions and curls could be employed to develop kicking and jumping power.

The emphasis in training for Batman's strength should be on 12 to 15 repetitions to failure, also known as repetition maximum (RM), or the amount of weight a person can lift in one repetition for a given exercise. It is vitally important that the execution of the movement be performed as quickly as possible. In total, the actual number of repetitions of any particular strength training movement is therefore only going to be about 30 to 60 on any given training day. Studies show that this level, which means using a weight that is about 60% of the maximum load that could be lifted once, is good for making muscle stronger.

Obviously, if free weights are used, training with a partner to act as a spotter is extremely important for safety. Alfred or Robin would be fantastic in this role . . . Well, Robin, anyway, Alfred is pretty slight after all. Batman and his crew would train with strength exercises at least twice per week and probably more like three times per week. This would cause his muscles to increase in cross-sectional area by about 0.2% per day in less-trained muscle like the elbow flexors and about 0.1% per day in muscle like his knee extensors. When training for power, the same exercises can be performed. But now the weight used should be reduced to a load such that 20 to 30 repetitions can be performed before failure, and the exercises must be performed ballistically. "Ballistic" comes from the Greek word for throwing and indicates movements that are as rapid and forceful as possible.

As a further wrinkle into how our physiological systems respond to stress, the adaptations to strength training appear to change while the systems themselves adapt. Put another way, there is a changing "dose-response" for building strength. What this means in practice is that just incrementing the load against which Batman works his muscles as a constant percentage of his maximum will not be effective in producing corresponding increases in strength. If we consider Batman as moving through three categories—untrained, recreationally

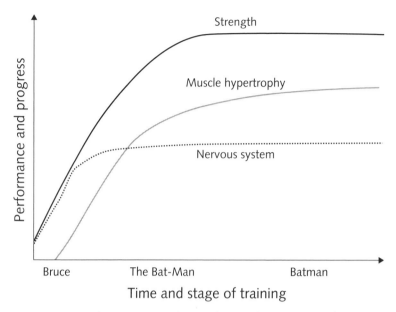

Figure 4.5. The time course of strength gains due to training. Shown are the contributions from changes in the muscle and changes in activity in the nervous system. Modified from Sale (1988). "Bruce" refers to Batman at the beginning of his training, "The Bat-Man" refers to the in-process Batman, and "Batman" to the finished product. This reflects chronological changes in Batman's name in his own comic book.

trained, and then highly trained athlete—the way he has to go about his training will need to change. This performance progress is shown in Figure 4.5. I will refer to the untrained Batman as "Bruce Wayne," the in-process Batman as "The Bat-Man," and the finished product as "Batman" to reflect chronological changes in Batman's name in his own comic book. A key issue is that Bruce will start off as "untrained," and he could make maximal strength gains by training three days per week using a load equal to 60% of his 1 RM and doing about four sets of exercises each day. When he moves to "recreationally trained" ("The Bat-Man" status), he would need to train two days per week using a load equal to about 80% of his 1 RM. This means that the benefit of exercise training varies as the training status changes and fits with the overall framework of challenges to homeostasis and

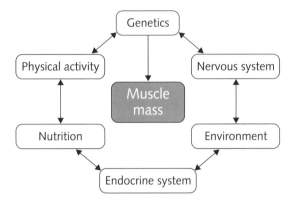

Figure 4.6. Influence of multiple factors on muscle hypertrophy. Data from McArdle et al. (2005).

stress mentioned before. Finally, as "Batman" he needs to perform more sets at higher loads just to make any progress.

Bear in mind that, as mentioned, the development of strength comes first, followed by power training. Another thing to remember is that the training for strength can be of a more general nature, while that for power must be as specific as possible.

In addition to the very important mechanical signals associated with performing high-force contractions, the Ca^{2+} levels, metabolic byproducts, and circulating hormone levels will all be changed. These can significantly affect the hypertrophy response. We will return to this complex chemical interaction later.

How Strong Can Batman Become?

Overall there are a number of factors that contribute to Batman's ability to get strong and powerful as a result of his training. Most of these are summarized in Figure 4.6 and relate to things we have already touched on, like nervous system activation, environment, the endocrine or hormonal system, and genetics. Other factors, related to metabolism and nutrition, will be discussed in future chapters.

There is an interesting story in the graphic novel *Batman: Venom* (1993) in which Bruce Wayne is pushing himself to train harder and get stronger after his "weakness" prevented him from saving a little girl from drowning. Bruce tries to lift 288 kilograms (635 pounds) in a "dead lift" (where you hold onto the bar and then stand up) and then tears his shoulder muscle in the process. Later on in the story, Bruce lifts 690 pounds in a clean and jerk (where you pull the bar up to the chest and then jerk it straight up over your head). It is reasonable at this stage to ask was that a realistic weight to lift, and how strong should and could Batman actually be?

As a reference for this, the current (as of 2007) Olympic record for clean and jerk in the closest weight category Batman would find himself (105-plus kg category) is 263.5 kilograms (about 580 pounds). This record was set by Hossein Rezazadeh of Iran on September 26, 2000, at the Sydney games. The world record for the dead lift is 455 kilograms (about 1,000 pounds) held by Andy Bolton of the United Kingdom. Maximum strength for weight lifting is roughly equal to the height of the person doing the lifting in meters squared. This calculation gives the total sum of the weight that could be lifted when combining two world weighlifting categories of the snatch and the clean and jerk. Using this for Batman gives him a maximum of about 223 kilograms (496.3 pounds). So, not quite Olympics but pretty good!

His muscles are not the only thing Batman needs to strengthen. Next we'll next look at surprising ways Batman can build up his bones.

CHAPTER 5

Building the Batbones

BRITTLE IS BAD, BUT IS BIGGER BETTER?

I choose this life. I know what I'm doing. And on any given day, I could stop doing it. Today, however, isn't that day. And tomorrow won't be either.
—Bruce Wayne, in the graphic novel
Identity Crisis

No matter what Batman does, it involves some sort of movement. Fast or slow, a lot or little. All of that movement can only happen because Batman's muscles pull on his bones. In the last chapter we looked at how muscle generates force. Now we will look at how force must also be transferred across the bones. This means that bones are subjected to both the stresses arising from active muscles and those created by the body's interaction with the environment. Think of the forces that affect your skeleton when you run. Your muscles are pulling on your bones, and your bones also experience large forces every time your feet hit the ground. Let's explore how bones work and how bones adapt to what we do.

It's likely that you haven't spent much time thinking about how your bones can change or even considering the complicated job that our bones actually do for us. This isn't surprising since we don't really pay much attention to our bones generally, unless we injure them! Bones are, after all, buried deep in the body and can be felt or their appearance guessed at only by looking at the shape of the skin and muscle that cover them.

You were probably aware of your bones changing in size as you grew up, and you may be able to think back to that one summer you grew three inches in three months. (For those of you not yet in your teens, don't worry. Your time is coming!) You may have also have had some experience with an elderly friend or family member with osteoporosis who broke a hip from a minor fall. The word "osteoporosis" means porous bone. You can imagine that porous bones would be weak and break easily. Batman certainly wouldn't want that to happen while he was fighting criminals! Weak bones have another disadvantage. When bones weaken they are said to demineralize, losing essential minerals such as calcium, and then they don't have the structural content they need to support the body and its movements.

In this chapter we examine bone and bone mineral density. Before we consider the mineral content of bone, let's think about the stresses that could maintain and change bone. Remember that biological tissues respond in a compensatory way when subjected to stress.

An example used in the last chapter had Batman beginning to do strength training exercise. We talked about the bicep curl, which begins with the arm extended straight down to the front and holding a weight (or weights). Batman flexed his arm by generating motor commands that led to the excitation of his muscles. His contractile fibers interacted and generated force; this force was transferred throughout the muscle to the tendons at either end. The tendons are connected to bones and cross over joints—in this case the elbow joint. Because joints are really a kind of lever, activation of the muscle causes rotation of the forearm about the elbow, and this leads to bending stress to the bone because of both the weight and the force of gravity acting on the forearm. In many ways this bending stress arises following on the third law of motion formulated by Sir Isaac Newton (1642–1727): for every action there is an equal and opposite reaction. When muscles produce force to move parts of the skeleton, forces are acting on the skeleton.

So, what are bones good for anyway? Or, more grammatically correct, what is the function of our bones? Well, the bones in our skeleton provide a rigid frame upon which all our other body tissue is laid. In other words, bones give our bodies a shape and structure and provide the actual framework for our muscles to move. Bones also help protect internal organs—think skull and brain here—from impact forces in the environment. Although impact protection is only occasionally called into use, a more imperative feature of bone is to be strong and resilient so that it won't easily fracture or fail during normal use. Your skeleton is repeatedly subjected to stresses every time you move. Even while you sit here reading this book, the force of gravity is providing a strain load on your bones. Repetitive bone loading during physical activity and exercise can lead to bone damage at the microscopic level, and that damage must be repaired, as you will read more about later in the chapter.

As long ago as during the life of Galileo Gallilei (1564–1642), physical activity was known to affect bone. Galileo suggested an association between mechanical forces and the structure of bone when he noted that bone size was related to body weight and activity. It turns out that key issues for bone are the stresses generated by forces occurring during muscle contraction as well as the force of gravity acting on the skeleton. This is a crucial problem when gravity is reduced—during spaceflight, more than 10% of bone mineral density can be lost after a six-month mission.

The concept of physical activity changing mineral content and therefore structural properties of bone was suggested in a formalized way by Julius Wolff (1835–1902). Wolff stated that, in a healthy animal, bone will adapt to the loads that are applied to it. This was actually articulated in what has become known as Wolff's law: every change in the function of bone is followed by certain definite changes in internal architecture and by external confirmation in accordance with mathematical laws.

Without going into specifics about what Wolff meant by "mathematical laws," one thing has proved true: bone remodeling—or modification of the bone over time—increases the strength of bone specifically related to the stress and strain applied to it. (By the way, now might be a good time to remind you that stress and strain are not the same. Stress is the reaction of the body to forces that affect its balance, whether they are physical or chemical. Strain is when a part of the body is injured by overuse.) Conversely, if the loading pattern and stresses are reduced or changed, the bone will remodel to the lowered demands as well. So, the general adaptation response of bone fits well within the framework already established for muscle.

This regulation of bone remodeling is quite specific. We first encountered the concept of specificity of physiological changes with Batman's adaptation to strength training. It is a theme that will recur again and again.

The skeleton is a very interesting structure to consider from the perspective of mechanical loading and forces that act upon it. Compared with muscle, there is a much larger range of structural and mechanical loads that our bones must bear. For example, I mentioned the skull as an example of a bone (22 bones, actually) that protects an internal organ from impact loading. In the case of Batman, that means getting hit on the head. The bones in the skull are not normally subjected to repeated strains or stresses during daily activity and the skull doesn't really accumulate much mechanical microdamage. The skull of Batman, however, experiences impact loads seemingly on an almost daily basis. As with many other things, Batman might be an exception!

For most of us, the bones in our legs are subjected to thousands and thousands of "cycles" of loading and unloading each and every day. The specific load that a bone experiences relates to where it is located in the skeleton and what its job is during movement. This tends to mean that changes in bone remodeling really depend on the site where the mechanical stresses are applied.

Let's think back to the previous chapter on muscle. If you do a lot of strength training with your arms, your leg muscles aren't going to get much stronger. Similarly, bones that are subjected to strain loads get stronger and those that are not, do not! That is not the whole story, though. Sometimes bones that are not subjected to the loading strains get weaker. This is because bone remodeling is a response to mechanical loads. The physiological adaptation depends heavily on the availability of materials, specifically calcium, to change bone structure. To understand this better, let's look at the cellular process for bone remodeling.

How Does Bone Remodeling Actually Work?

Bone has a certain cellular structure that is altered by the actual minerals inserted into it. Let's break that sentence down and consider each part of it. Figure 5.1 shows the basic structure of bone, using the example of a bone similar to one of the long bones of the

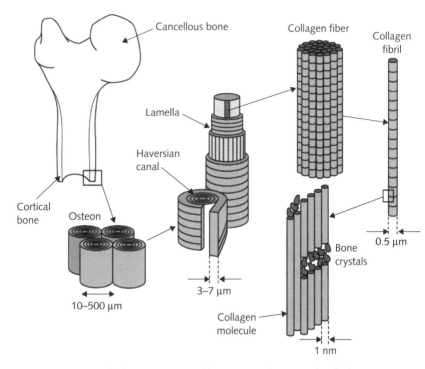

Figure 5.1. The basic structure of bone, using the example of a bone similar to one of the long bones, like the femur. Moving from *left* to *right* in the figure we go from the basic functional unit of bone, the osteon, all the way down to individual collagen fibers at the far right. Courtesy Enoka (2002).

leg, such as the femur in your thigh. The basic functional unit of bone is the osteon. If you were to peer at a slice of compact bone (like that found in your leg or arm) under a microscope, it would resemble a bunch of plant stalks or tree stumps. The osteon is made up of rings (called lamellae). In the center of these rings, you would see a tubelike section, called a Haversian canal. These canals, named after English physician Clopton Havers (1657–1702), provide nerve and blood to bone.

At the smallest level, bone is largely composed of collagen, which is the main protein found in connective tissue throughout your body. This collagen is then embedded with minerals. We can think of bone as being composed of three types of cells that all have slightly different jobs but all begin with "osteo" (for bone). Osteoblasts—think *b* for building—are the cells responsible for the formation of bone. They lay down the unmineralized matrix that forms the main bone content. The primary activity of the osteoblasts occurs during periods of bone modeling and remodeling. Modeling, which is the period of growth that occurs in childhood and adolescence, is not relevant to understanding Batman's adult bones. Instead, we are focusing on the remodeling process. After the matrix is formed, osteoblasts eventually reduce their activity and either retire to the bone surface or become entombed in the mineralized bone matrix itself.

Osteoblasts that are entombed in the matrix are called osteocytes, which are the most abundant and also the longest-lived of the three bone cell types. Osteocytes are linked together by microscopic interconnecting canals (called, not surprisingly, canaliculi, or little canals) that make up the Haversian canal system discussed above (see Figure 5.1). (So remember *c* for canal.) Their main purpose is to sense and signal responses to mechanical inputs, such as those during loading.

Osteoclasts are the last cell type. The job of the osteoclast is to clean up the bone as part of maintaining bone integrity. Think of the *cl* in osteoclasts as the *cl* in cleaning. Picture the video game Pac-Man, and you will have the basic concept. Osteoclasts dissolve the organic and inorganic parts of the bone mineral. This occurs as part of the extensive remodeling that is always going on in bone.

In bone remodeling, osteoclasts and osteoblasts work in tandem. When bones are loaded, they experience microdamage—tiny cracks—that need to be filled and strengthened. In resorption (or dissolving of bone or other tissue), osteoclasts come along and break up very thin bits of bone in the microdamaged areas. Right after this, osteoblasts fill in the little divots left behind by the dissolving action of the osteoclasts.

This is followed up by mineralization of the newly created organic matrix. In a way this whole process of activation, resorption, and formation is a bit like seeing a smallish hole in the drywall of your house. You first need to smooth out the hole with some sandpaper. Then the hole can be filled and will cure while it dries. The curing process (really, the hardening of the fill) is like mineralization in bone. Events of bone remodeling are really sensitive not only to mechanical loading but also to hormones. Two essential hormones that can influence the rate of bone remodeling are parathyroid hormone and estrogen.

Now that we have some grounding in the basics of how bone as a tissue works to remodel itself, let's visit what mechanical loading events might occur during the kind of exercise that Batman would experience in his training.

Physical Exercise and the Bones

When Batman is performing his training exercises or when he is leaping, cavorting, and energetically fighting any of the members of his rogue's gallery, he is constantly subjecting his skeleton to many "loading events." Large impacts will be experienced when he jumps down from a height and the large forces he needs to generate with his muscles require strain on his long bones, such as the thigh bone (femur) and upper arm (humerus). This means his bones are experiencing tensile (bending) and compressive (squishing) strains. These strains give rise to changes in fluid pressure within the bone that trigger specific adaptations for bone strength.

When we think of Bruce Wayne beginning his journey to become Batman, we want to know what led to the strengthening of his bones that would have occurred during his training. Well, let's start with the scenario in which the strains are very large, causing small microfractures of the bone matrix. These microfractures are like little fissures in the bone, and they wind up separating and isolating some of the osteocytes embedded in the bone. This starts a cell death cycle for these osteocytes, initiating the cycle of bone remodeling described above. When the loading strains are lower, the pressure changes within the bone fluid stimulate the osteocytes to release hormonal and biochemical signals that activate the remodeling process.

The size, frequency, and repetition of the strain events are important for bone remodeling. Just as with muscle, a general principle is that the extent to which bone will remodel depends really on how much it is strained. And Batman not only has lazy muscles, as we learned earlier, but his bones are also lazy! To stimulate the bone remodeling process, we have to exceed some limit of strain size and repetitions. It is really important for the strain to be repeated and above a certain frequency. Just applying large loads to bone will not trigger the bone remodeling process. In fact, a problem with trying to stimulate a change in bone remodeling as an exercise adaptation is that bones typically have a very large safety factor. Batman's bones (or anyone else's for that matter) are able to withstand loads that are two to five times larger than the loads typically experienced every day. Great, you might say, that means my bones are safe from injury most of the time and that is why Batman hardly ever seems to have broken a bone. Well, yes, this safety factor helps keep the bones safe. But it actually means that training to make the bones stronger means significantly exceeding the daily loading cycles and pushing near the upper limit of the safety factor. This is why minor or trivial loading doesn't yield a huge change.

What Kinds of Bone Are There?

Bone in Batman's skeleton (and yours) comes in two types: compact (sometimes called cortical, which I described above) and trabecular (sometimes called cancellous). About 80% of Batman's skeleton is compact bone, while about 20% is trabecular. Compact bone is found in the walls of long bones (like your humerus) and on the surface of flat bones (like those found in your skull). If you were to look at a close-up of compact bone, you would see that it is made up of tightly packed concentric layers of fibrous mineralized material as part of an interconnected network of osteocytes.

Trabecular, or cancellous, bone is found at the ends and inside of the long bones and, in contrast to the makeup of compact bone, is made up of a spongy-looking lattice. This lattice (shown in Figure 5.1) is composed of what look like supporting struts, and these struts orient themselves and thicken in the direction that will resist the loading patterns to which the bone is exposed.

Another example may be helpful. We subject our legs to many daily stresses and the long bones of our legs adapt accordingly. But the adaptation of the bone strength is still very much specified by the structure of the bone and what it does. The femur is strongest in compression (which is the main type of loading that happens during walking), three times weaker for shearing (imagine a sideways force applied to your femur to get the idea), and intermediate for tension (think bending forces).

At this stage it might be reasonable to wonder if the kind of training Batman needs to engage in could reasonably be expected to affect his bones. The answer is yes! And there are some pretty inter-esting examples of the specific way these adaptations occur. Let's consider two kinds of athletic groups that face many of same the physical demands behind Batman's prowess—martial artists and rock climbers.

Martial artists typically have much higher bone density than do untrained people, but you may be surprised to know that where this density is found in the body depends very much on the martial art. Training in judo, which involves a lot of grappling and throwing, and in karate, which involves a lot of punching, kicking, and strik-ing, results in higher total bone density. Remember that your body responds and adapts in a very specific way to stresses. Given the main emphasis on grappling and throwing in judo and on kicking and striking for karate, these adaptations are specific and make a lot of functional sense.

This brings us to the other athletic group I mentioned above—rock climbers. Now, rock climbers also closely approximate one of the main activities Batman excels in and trains for: scaling buildings. This was something emphasized very early on in the Batman chronology. The panel shown in Figure 5.2 is from "The Batman Meets Doctor Death" (Detective Comics #29, 1939). In this story—and often throughout his adventures—Batman has to do a great deal of covert nighttime sur-veillance. We can see that Batman needs to do a fair bit of climbing to accomplish his tasks. Specifically, he needs to strongly grip the suction cups he uses for climbing. Compare this with the kind of climbing and gripping that rock climbers (maybe like you?) use routinely. Examples of these grips are shown in Figure 5.3. The main thing is that these activities require putting a lot of strain on the fingers. Advanced rock climbers commonly expose their fingers and hands to extreme stresses when using their fingers to support all of their body weight.

As you might guess after everything we have talked about to this point, mechanical loading of the fingers in rock climbing and boul-dering should lead to increased bone density in the fingers. And yes, Climbers do have much higher cross-sectional bone areas than peo-ple who don't climb, which corresponds to what you might predict. The mechanical stresses of these activities stimulate increased bone deposition, or the forming of new bone. We can rest assured that Batman's skeleton adapts to the unique mix of loads he provides during training practice and while prowling the streets—and scal-ing the buildings—of Gotham City.

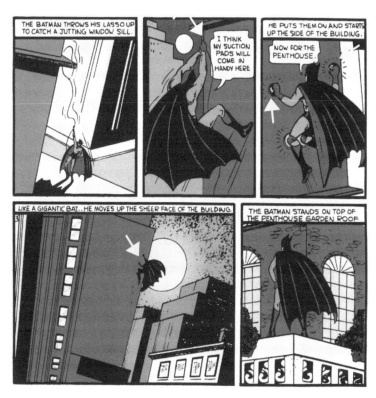

Figure 5.2. Stresses on the bones of Batman's fingers and hands while climbing from "The Batman Meets Doctor Death" (Detective Comics #29, 1939). Batman needs to strongly grip the suction cups he uses for climbing (arrows).

The Work of the Joker: Bone Stealing from Bone?

There is one more feature about bone metabolism that should be of great interest—actually concern—to Batman. It turns out that while bone density goes up in a very specific area as a result of exercise training, bone density may also go down in other regions. That's right. I said go down, not just stay the same. When athletes aged 18 to 40 have been contrasted with untrained people, they exhibit the increased bone density described above. Runners, weightlifters, and dancers all have increased density in the long bones of the legs. Surprisingly, in addition to these useful adaptations, athletes may also

Figure 5.3. Examples of stresses on the bones of the fingers and hands during rock climbing and bouldering (arrows). Courtesy Sylvester et al. (2006).

have lower bone density in areas of the body not subjected to exercise loading. For example, athletes may have lower bone density in the bones of the skull than do untrained people.

Although this isn't much of a problem for a runner or a weight-lifter, it actually represents a big problem for a fighting machine like Batman! This finding may not seem to make much sense. One speculation is that when bone resorption is activated, there may be an overall "zero-sum game," meaning that the body may maintain an overall level of bone density. So strengthening some regions may lead to corresponding weakening elsewhere. This is not always the case and, in fact, it may not apply to other physical activities like rock climbing. But Batman better protect himself from falls!

Now we will look at another part of Batman's training, one that is very important even to us non-crime fighters: how much he needs to eat to maintain his strength scaling walls and otherwise battling bad guys.

CHAPTER 6

Batmetabolism

*WHAT'S FOR DINNER
ON THE DARK KNIGHT
DIET*

He was never blessed with instant super-powers—it took him fifteen years to hone himself into a physical marvel and scientific and deductive genius.

—*Tales of the Dark Knight: Batman's First Fifty Years: 1939–1989* by Mark Cotta Vaz

How much energy does Batman use in a day, and how much food does he need to eat? Even if you have pondered the activities of Batman, have you ever considered what would be the real energy costs in a day spent fighting crime as the Dark Knight? The answers to these questions depend on how much and what type of activity he had that day. Was it a big training day or a big "fight-an-entire-squadron-of-henchmen-single-handed" night? The bottom line is he uses up more calories than you or I do. Oh, also, in case you are wondering, Batman *does* take his vitamins.

Let's start with the concepts of energy balance and metabolism. Many people make comments about their metabolism. We have all heard someone say something like "I have a low metabolism but my wife has such a high metabolism that she can eat anything." Certainly there are lots of misunderstandings about metabolism and metabolic rate. Metabolism is defined as the sum total of all the chemical reactions occurring in the body. This means all of the processes that are occurring in all cells of the body. Metabolic processes can be categorized as either those that result in building up (anabolism), or in breaking down material (catabolism). An example of anabolic metabolism is building skeletal muscle proteins as a result of exercise stress (as discussed in Chapter 4). An example of a catabolic metabolic process is that of taking energy from food to provide energy for our cells to function. It is tempting to think of anabolic processes as "good" and catabolic processes as "bad." However, both occur continuously in our bodies, and both must be in balance for healthy function.

The balance part I mentioned above has to do with a very simple fact: in a physiological energy system (a.k.a. your body), total energy taken in must be balanced by total energy expended. We have come back to the concept of homeostasis and also take on a new concept that "energy in equals energy out." This concept adheres to the first law of thermodynamics, as laid out by the English physicist James Joule (1818–1889). Joule's research was originally on the relation between mechanical work and heat. In fact, the international unit for work—the joule—was named after him and is used as the measure of energy in all fields . . . except metabolism and food energy. For various historical reasons, the term "calorie" (literally meaning heat) remains in use for energy expenditures in the body.

The first law of thermodynamics comes from what is more commonly described as the "theory of conservation of energy." The main point is that energy is constant and only changes forms within a fixed system. In a physiological fixed system like Batman's body, this means that there is a direct relation between energy input and energy output. Energy input really means stored energy taken in the form of food and drink matched with energy expenditure in terms of work performed in the body.

By "work" here I don't mean tasks. I also am not referring to what scientists or engineers might call work—mechanical work. The concept of "work" in biology is a bit less obvious. For example, if you take a break from reading this book (probably a very short one) and lay down the book, you clearly have used some force and moved the book some distance. It wouldn't be difficult to realize that you performed both mechanical and biological work in putting the book down. However, if you are just sitting and reading the book, you clearly aren't doing much mechanical work at all. In both cases, you are actually doing a lot of biological work. Even when you sleep tonight, and think contentedly of all the interesting things you have gleaned from this book, you will still be doing lots of biological work. In fact, while you are alive your body never stops working.

The work that is going on in your body can be basically grouped into chemical, transport, and internal mechanical work. The chemical work involves activities like the growth and repair of your cells (including protein synthesis and wound repair) and the continual struggle to maintain homeostasis, such as continuous regulation of body temperature. Transport work includes the continual movement of ions, molecules, and large particles across cell membranes. The internal mechanical work that you are doing right now includes moving cellular organelles and contracting muscles needed to hold the book, maintaining your posture as you do so, and moving your eyes to follow the words in this sentence as it unfolds majestically across the page.

This comparison between mechanical and biological descriptions of work also extends to the concept of energy. In mechanical systems we can think of energy of motion and stored energy. The usual way this distinction is made is to ask you to think of a simple task like rolling a big ball up a hill. As you start at the bottom of the hill, the ball has no energy. When you begin to move, it has energy of motion—kinetic energy—and slowly gains stored, or potential, energy. When you get to the top of the hill and come to a stop, the kinetic energy will be zero but the potential energy will be high. Then, when you let the ball roll down the hill, the potential energy will be transferred into kinetic energy. This goes on until the very bottom of the hill, where the ball is on a flat surface, full of kinetic energy and with no potential energy. That's a simple mechanical example.

For our biological example, the energy of motion is contained in chemical bonding, transport across cell membranes, and the mechanical work that occurs in muscle contraction. Potential energy is found in the chemical bonds created in storing foodstuffs. In metabolism, cells transfer the potential energy of chemical bonds into kinetic energy for growth, maintenance, reproduction, and movement. So, work always involves movement, and energy can convert forward and backward from potential to kinetic. It is important to note—and this is especially relevant to you if you are sitting in a cool room—this conversion is never 100% efficient. That means energy is lost in the conversion process. For example, lots of heat is generated when energy is used (and lost) during muscle contraction.

For muscle contraction, as with other processes in the body, this means taking the energy in the molecule ATP, adenosine 5'-triphosphate, which you might recall from Chapter 4, and adding water. If you remember any chemistry you studied in school, combining chemicals often results in their changing into something else. In this case, ATP has three phosphate groupings. After water is added, one of these groupings splits off. This leaves ADP (adenosine 5'-diphosphate, with two phosphate groupings) and one phosphate grouping by itself, which is used to power muscle contraction. But also during this process, energy is released as heat.

We can trace the roots of ATP back to famous French scientist Louis Pasteur (most known for giving us safer milk to drink, through what we now call pasteurization). In the late 1860s Pasteur noted that yeast was able to convert the energy in sugar to create carbon dioxide and alcohol. Continuing this research, in 1929 the German biochemist Karl Lohmann discovered the energy source for cellular breakdown of sugar in the presence of yeast. He found that a substance called adenine was linked to the sugars and to three (there's that number again) phosphate groups. This brings us to adenosine triphosphate (or ATP). The high energy bonds between adenine and the inorganic phosphate groups store the energy that we liberate for use in our cellular processes and energy that is evident in every living system. So, Batman has a lot in common with actual bats beyond his wing-like cape.

The Dark Knight Diet

What should be in Batman's diet? An overview of his optimal diet is shown at the top of Figure 6.1. The numbers I provide for the "Dark Knight Diet" are based on the 2007 recommendations of the Institute of Medicine of the National Academies of Science. As such, the "macronutrient" (that's the official way to describe what's in the food you eat) breakdown in the typical diet should contain 40–65% carbohydrate, 10–35% protein, and 20–35% fat. The numbers for Batman—60% carbohydrate, 25% protein, and 15% fat—reflect the

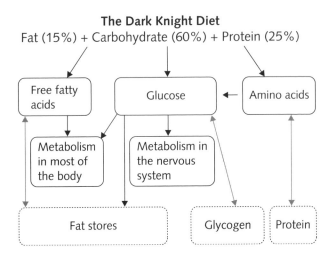

Figure 6.1. The Dark Knight diet and the fate of food intake.

values within these ranges that are closer to those for trained athletes, which Batman clearly is.

Carbohydrate is very important as a fuel source during exercise. Because the body has a low storage capacity for carbohydrates, they make up a larger proportion of the diet of an athlete than for the average person. Athletes may need some slightly higher ranges of protein in the diet as well, which shows up in the Dark Knight Diet. Batman definitely doesn't eat a high-fat diet.

What are macronutrients, exactly? You no doubt read at the detailed food labels on cans, boxes, and wrappers when you are shopping. Given carbohydrates should make up the bulk of your diet, let's start with them. Depending on their biochemical structure, carbohydrates are classified as simple or complex. Simple carbohydrates include fructose, sucrose, and lactose and are found in foods such as fruits and milk products and in sugar. Complex carbohydrates are starches and glycogen and are found in foods such as grains, beans, and potatoes. When carbohydrates are eaten they must be changed into the simple form to be absorbed. That is, they must be broken down in your body to the smallest, simplest chemical structure.

When proteins are consumed, you are really eating something made from chains of amino acids (called polypeptides). There are twenty amino acids to be concerned with. (Do you remember the amino acid "letters" we talked about in Chapter 2?) Nine of them are considered essential. You have to get them from your diet because your body cannot make them from other amino acids or proteins. This group of nine is isoleucine, leucine, lysine, theonine, tryptophan, methionine, histidine, valine, and phenylalanine. These nine (and the other eleven) amino acids are essential because the body needs proteins to perform almost all cellular processes. If not getting them from the diet, the body will attempt to get them from its own muscles and other tissues. So, eating these proteins is a good idea for Batman and for you!

The last macronutrient to consider is fat. The "fat family" includes triglycerides (which form by far the largest percentage of fats), cholesterol, phospholipids, and fat-soluble vitamins. Fats are divided into four essential fatty acids and also classified as either saturated or unsaturated. An easy way to tell the difference is that saturated fats typically are solid at room temperature, whereas unsaturated fats are liquids.

No discussion of diet would be complete without vitamins and minerals. We have already seen how useful calcium is for muscle and bone. Vitamins and minerals are also needed to ensure that all the energy pathways work properly. They act as facilitators (actually as enzymes and catalysts of reactions) of your metabolic pathways. You get most of them from your dietary intake. Some key fat-soluble vitamins (A, D, E, and K) are absorbed with fats. Many of the vitamins that Batman's body needs and must be in his diet are shown in Figure 6.2. This figure also shows some of the main functions of the vitamins. Minerals such as iron and calcium are absorbed and linked to the needs of the body. If you look at food labels when shopping or eating, you will see vitamins listed. For example, niacin is found on breakfast cereal labels. When you eat niacin, remember that it is an important vitamin for energy production, the function of your muscles, and the health of your skin!

Figure 6.3 shows how minerals help with metabolism for both catabolic and anabolic activity. (Recall that anabolic activity creates and that catabolic activity breaks down. I wonder what batabolic activity would do.) Some minerals, like magnesium, potassium, calcium, and manganese, are dual workers—they are involved in both building up and breaking down. By the way, Batman seems well aware that he needs these vitamins and minerals in his diet. In a

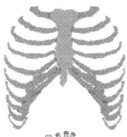

Bone: A, D, C

Blood: K, E, B_6, B_{12}, folate

Hormones: A, B_6

Muscle & nerve:
A, B_6, B_{12}, thiamine,
niacin, pantothenic acid

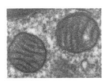

Cell & energy release:
E, thiamine, riboflavin,
niacin

Figure 6.2. Some of the functions of vitamins in the body. Data from McArdle et al. (2005).

Anabolic metabolism

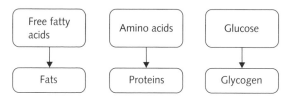

Some minerals involved in anabolism:
Magnesium, Potassium, Calcium, Manganese, Chlorine

Catabolic metabolism

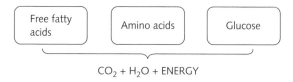

$$CO_2 + H_2O + ENERGY$$

Some minerals involved in catabolism:
Magnesium, Potassium, Calcium, Manganese,
Copper, Iron, Zinc, Cobalt

Figure 6.3. Utility of vitamins and minerals in anabolism (processes that build up) and catabolism (processes that break down) in the body. Data from McArdle et al. (2005).

panel in the graphic novel *Batman: Venom* (1993), Batman is talking with Commissioner Gordon, who comments on the increased "muscling" of Batman's build. Gordon actually tells Batman that he looks "Bigger. Beefier." Batman makes an off-the-cuff joke about switching cereals: "I'm eating the kind that's fortified with vitamins and minerals." Unfortunately, as we will discuss later in Chapter 13 in the context of steroid use in athletes, the reason for the change in Batman's physique is much more sinister. However, don't worry about any enduring transformation in the Dark Knight's character—the change is temporary!

At this point, I have probably convinced you that a fair amount of work actually goes on inside your body at all times. You may be wondering where the energy for the biological work comes from. It may come either from absorbed nutrients that we get from eating food or from stored nutrients that we packed away earlier from anabolic processes. Usually the metabolic state of the body is broken into two modes: fed or fasted. Now, fasted doesn't necessarily mean "fasted," as in not eating for days on end. Rather, it defines the period during which you aren't eating and nutrients aren't being absorbed into the body.

In the fed state, nutrients from whatever meal Batman has just eaten are being digested and absorbed. The fats, carbohydrates, and proteins that were in Batman's food are initially broken down into their basic components (refer back to Figure 6.1). This is an anabolic state in which energy is transferred from the components of the food into something your body can use directly in metabolism—that is, free fatty acids, glucose, and amino acids—and then used up or stored away. This contrasts with the fasted state in which nutrients from the meal are no longer in the blood. This occurs typically within a few hours of eating. The fed state is a catabolic one in which larger molecules and their stored energy are converted into smaller ones to be metabolically used for energy. A superficial overview of what happens to molecules in our food is that they are metabolized quickly (as in blood glucose used by the nervous system), used in the creation of other molecules, or stored primarily as glycogen and fat. As you saw in Figure 6.1, most of the carbohydrate winds up as glucose and is used up throughout the body and in the nervous system. In fact, about 30% is used for liver metabolism and the remaining roughly 70% is used for nervous system, muscle, and other tissues.

The liver is very important because it is the great carbohydrate "storage tank" in the body. Actually, your muscle tissue is an even bigger tank for storing carbohydrates. Much of the excess glucose gets packed away as glycogen and stored in the liver for use later. In addition, glucose is stored in all of your muscles as glycogen. If you look back at Figure 6.1 again, at the bottom the boxes with dotted lines show the "storage" fate of nutrients. The trick is that the glycogen in your muscles can only be broken down and used up by that same muscle, whereas your liver breaks down glycogen when it needs to and releases glucose into the blood to go everywhere. Whatever glucose remains is stored away as fat.

Proteins are absorbed and broken down into amino acids. Amino acids are sometimes used as cellular energy but typically only when glucose levels are extremely low. Starvation represents probably the best example of a time when protein would make up the bulk of the energy needs. Excess protein beyond that needed for cellular building and repair is stored as fat. Fat is stored as fat in liver and in adipose tissue.

The key trigger for the fasted state is a drop in glucose levels in the blood, which signals the end of the fed state. This is kind of like the fed state being the eating of a meal plus the full cleaning up after. As soon as everything is put away and cleaned up and every last scrap of food—including leftovers on dirty plates—is taken care of, you are entering the fasted state. This is a state of catabolism. I mentioned that the level of blood glucose was so important because your nervous system needs it, and your nervous system is so important because one of its main functions is to maintain homeostasis. And without homeostasis, life isn't possible for very long. So, the drop in glucose is something your body closely monitors. In the fasted state the liver is the primary source of glucose. In fact, byproducts of other metabolic activity in muscle are sent to the liver to be made into glucose.

Our systems work mostly in balance. In biology this energy balance is reflected in the amount of oxygen our cells consume. You may be surprised to know that this brings us to the question of how much energy is there in the food that we eat. This is similar to asking how much energy is in the gasoline we use for fuel in our vehicles. Indeed, the process of consuming fuel in a car engine is similar to the principle of consuming foodstuffs to run our cellular engines. Both involve a kind of burning known more properly in chemistry as "oxidation." Measures of overall metabolic energy content can be made directly using a technique called "bomb calorimetry," described in detail below. This name refers to the unit used in describing the energy content of food: the calorie, which is defined as the amount of heat energy needed to raise one gram of water by one degree Celsius. This definition isn't particularly useful for metabolic calculations and nutrition however. In nutritional applications, energy is instead calculated from the composition of the foodstuffs consumed. In these calculations a calorie (or kcal) is used, which is equal to approximately 4.18 kJoule, if you are keeping count.

We typically think of the energy content of food we eat as coming from protein, carbohydrate, or fat (remember Figure 6.1). Conventionally, proteins and carbohydrates have been described as having about 4 kcal per gram (which is about a third of an ounce) and fats as having about 9 kcal per gram. Soon we'll tackle the question of why there are 9 kcal in fat and only 4 in carbohydrate or protein. But the precise measurement of energy content of food can be taken using the bomb calorimetry mentioned above. This involves placing the material inside a chamber and burning it while measuring the total heat energy released. You could do this with everything you wanted to eat or drink, if you had a bomb calorimeter. However, by convention we use the estimates of energy content in food based upon the approximately 4 or 9 kcal per gram given above. In that case, all we need to know is the mass of the food and the relative proportions of fat, carbohydrate, or protein it contains.

So now you have an idea of how to measure the energy we take in when consuming food. How do we get a handle on the energy we use just being alive? Answering that question will guide us further toward answering the question we are actually most concerned about. How much energy does Bruce Wayne expend while being Batman?

To find the answers we need to know about metabolism in our cells and in particular about the concept of cellular respiration. Respiration is the process by which biochemical energy in the food we eat is transformed into energy that can be used in our cells. In addition to producing energy, respiration produces carbon dioxide, water, and heat. Above we started discussing energy in food and the caloric content of foods that we consume. Energy in the foods we eat is in the wrong format for our cells to use. To transform the energy sources from food into cellular energy means turning those carbohydrates, fats, and proteins in our dietary intake into a form that our cells can understand—molecules of ATP, the high-energy compound that we were introduced to in Chapter 4 and saw again earlier in this chapter.

A currency exchange analogy is good to use here. As such, ATP is the local currency of our cells. However, your body takes in "tourists," who "pay" with carbohydrate, protein, and fat, which then have to be converted into ATP dollars. There's a different but fixed exchange rate for each one—that's where the 4 versus 9 kcal per gram part comes in—but the end objective is always to get that conversion into ATP. Throughout both the plant and animal kingdoms—from the bat flower *Tacca chantrieri*, to flying bats, and then onto Batman—ATP is the universal energy currency. The reason that the exchange rates are not the same for the three main types of food has to do with the biochemical makeup of protein, carbohydrate, and fat and their basic elements: amino acids, glucose, and fatty acids, respectively. Fatty acids are the most complex and contain the greatest number of chemical bonds. Because potential energy is stored in the chemical bonds, more energy is found in fat. In contrast, protein and carbohydrate are simpler molecules with respect to their chemical bonds. Because of that, less energy can be stored or extracted from them. Regardless, we can still consider all of them to be consumed in cellular respiration in generally the same way that gasoline or diesel fuel can be consumed in the engine of a vehicle. In both cases oxidation occurs, and the oxidation liberates the energy contained in the biochemical or petrochemical bonds. Unlike an internal combustion engine, such as the one you have in your car that relies on oxygen, cellular respiration can proceed both with and without oxygen. The terms aerobic (with oxygen) and anaerobic (without oxygen) respiration or metabolism are used when describing these two sets of pathways.

Aerobic metabolism occurs in cellular structures called "mitochondria," which are our cellular engines and power-generating stations and produce the bulk of our energy needs. These mitochondria create large numbers of ATP molecules by the oxidation of glucose (mostly), fatty acids, and amino acids (not as much). Despite the fact that mitochondria are found inside our cells, they have their own DNA and genetic history independent from the genome of the cell nucleus. Some evidence suggests that mitochondria were once independent single-celled bacterial organisms that were incorporated into our cells about two billion years ago.

Anaerobic metabolism occurs also inside the cell, but it occurs outside the mitochondria in the spaces around all the other organelles. Anaerobic metabolism is extremely fast but much less efficient than aerobic metabolism. In muscle, one glucose molecule can provide up to 36 ATP molecules from aerobic metabolism, but only two ATP molecules are generated from the same glucose molecule during anaerobic metabolism. By the way, your heart muscle does even better with aerobic metabolism, yielding 38 ATP molecules in the same process. Overall, anaerobic pathways are supplements to the bulk of energy production obtained during aerobic metabolism. To return to our car engine analogy, consider fuel economy. If you went around in your car always accelerating to top speed after every stop, you would have very poor fuel economy. In contrast, gradually increasing speed to some constant is much more efficient. Well, of course you cannot always gradually accelerate your car. Nor can Batman slowly move around all of the time. All of us need to produce extreme bursts of high-speed maximal effort from time to time. The point is that if maximal efforts are all that is done, we will run out of fuel very quickly.

Carrying on with our theme of threes that runs throughout this book, we can think of there being three related but functionally different energy systems. They are related to the anaerobic and aerobic concepts mentioned above and can be thought of as immediate, short-term, and long-term energy systems. These descriptions refer to the time period over which you might do an activity and which energy system would be most used in that activity. Immediate energy comes from the splitting of ATP-CP (the CP here refers to creatine phosphate, an energy source found in skeletal muscle), short-term from the anaerobic breakdown of glucose (called glycolysis), and long-term from the aerobic metabolism of glucose, fatty acids, or amino acids.

Why have all these different fuel stores? It might seem to be easier if the analogy to the tank of gasoline was actually easier to deal with. You don't have special immediate, short-term, and long-term energy tanks to supply fuel in your vehicle, so why do you have that kind of setup in the body? The answer lies in how the energy systems work and the immediate capacity each has for energy production.

The contribution for each system is as generally shown in Figure 6.4. The duration of exercise activity is shown at the bottom of the figure going from seconds up to five minutes or more. A quick glance will tell you that for maximal efforts, like running as fast as you can, much of the energy comes from the immediate energy system, which mostly uses anaerobic metabolism. At the far right you can see that if you go for an eight-kilometer (five-mile) run (which will take much more than the five minutes indicated) you will use primarily the long-term energy system, which mostly uses aerobic metabolism.

To put this in a frame of reference for Batman's activities, let's talk about "The Lazurus Pit" (Batman #243, 1972), drawn by the great artist Neal Adams. In this story Batman is—once again—fighting for his life against a misguided henchman of R'as al Ghul. They close to grappling and fighting distance and Batman succeeds in disarming the semi-evil bad guy. I say semi-evil in this case because the henchman

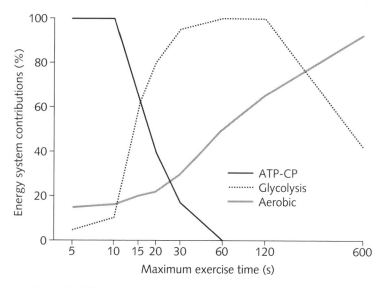

Figure 6.4. Physiological energy systems and their contributions over time (in seconds). ATP-CP = Adenosine triphosphate—creatine phosphate (an energy source created by the body). Data from McArdle et al. (2005).

has been coerced into attacking Batman. We read at the bottom of the panel that it has taken exactly four seconds for this exchange. The length of time Batman needs to fend off evil and semi-evil bad guys was also nicely described in the 2003 graphic novel *Trinity*, which was the first Batman, Superman, and Wonder Woman combined story. In that story Batman is shown dispatching a small gang of about six punks. The caption reads that it took "thirty-two seconds to dispatch a roomful of armed and dangerous men." This is an accurate assessment of the time that Batman would spend on directly fighting individual attackers. This means he makes frequent use of his immediate and short-term energy systems and anaerobic metabolism.

To further help understand the interactions of the different energy systems for Batman's activities I have broken down three fighting scenarios of different durations in Figure 6.5. For Batman against Killer Croc, I have estimated a time of 10 seconds, and for Batman versus Bane I reckoned on 60 seconds. Fighting Catwoman was right in between at 30 seconds. The thing to notice is changes in the various

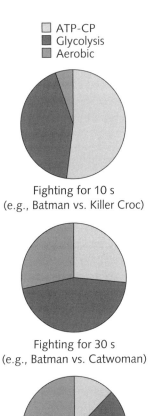

☐ ATP-CP
■ Glycolysis
■ Aerobic

Fighting for 10 s
(e.g., Batman vs. Killer Croc)

Fighting for 30 s
(e.g., Batman vs. Catwoman)

Fighting for 60 s
(e.g., Batman vs. Bane)

Figure 6.5. Breakdowns of the likely energy sources for fights between Batman and Killer Croc, Catwoman, and Bane for 10, 30, and 60 seconds, respectively.

proportions of the different energy systems being drawn upon as the exchanges become longer.

In these examples Batman is using both aerobic and anaerobic metabolism and will be using up much of his energy stores, or fuel. While amino acids can be used as fuel, generally the typical fuel supply for Batman's body would come from fatty acids and glucose. The fatty acids are stored as body fat either around the body organs—where it is called visceral fat—or underneath the skin—where it is called subcutaneous fat. The trick with body fat is that it is stored away so well that our bodies don't like to use it up. It is harder to access and takes longer to metabolize. Really, fat is an awesome energy reserve in that it contains no water and is a very concentrated high energy storage system.

Glucose floats around in our bloodstreams in its original state but is converted to glycogen when stored in the body. Glucose is stored as glycogen because it is more compact and requires less water for use. In a way it is kind of like a concentrate for glucose. Glycogen stores are found in the liver and in skeletal muscle, as we talked about earlier. Muscle is so important for our functioning that each muscle gets its own storage tank of glycogen. The liver holds the glycogen for use throughout the body, for example, in other organ systems like the brain. The tricky thing about glycogen stores, as we learned earlier in the chapter, is that the liver likes to share and liberates glucose for use throughout the body. However, our muscles do not share their glucose. The molecular formation of muscle glycogen is slightly different from liver glycogen and because of that must stay in the muscle.

You might wonder how much energy Batman could have stored up in his body. If he doesn't take in any additional energy, he would have about four hours' worth of glycogen, or enough for four hours of hard, continuous exercise. In contrast, Batman has about one month's worth of fat stored away to be used in aerobic metabolic pathways. (You and I would have about two months' worth of stored fat, depending on how much we eat and exercise.)

Because the dominant way the body produces energy is through aerobic metabolism, we can estimate cellular metabolism by measuring the volume of oxygen consumed and volume of carbon dioxide produced. This will help us determine the energetic demands of Batman and Bruce Wayne. To do this we could use a technique called "indirect calorimetry," indirect because direct would mean having the ability to measure what is actually coming in and out of each cell on a moment-to-moment basis. Instead, we can get an overall view of the sum of metabolism by monitoring the exchange of gases (mostly carbon dioxide and oxygen) from the lungs.

This measure of expired gasses makes use of equipment called a "metabolic cart" and requires the person to wear a mask or two-way valve device (called a Rudolph valve) that is essentially the reverse of a scuba regulator. In a scuba regulator the intake is from a pressurized gas cylinder (the scuba tank), and the outlet is simply to the surrounding water. In a standard Rudolph valve setup, the intake is simply the ambient air and the outlet is to a gas analysis system. Such a setup is shown in Figure 6.6 from an older experiment that I did to find out the metabolic cost of performing martial arts techniques.

By comparing the percentage concentration of oxygen and carbon dioxide in the room air and in the expired gas, we calculated the amount of oxygen consumed and carbon dioxide produced during very vigorous karate movements simulating fighting. By the way, during these kinds of activities, energy use can be as high as 90% of the level used pedaling a bicycle at maximum speed for ten minutes! Obviously, Batman doesn't fight people for ten minutes, but the point is that the peak of the energy used can be very high.

Before the arrival of modern metabolic carts and portable measurement systems, a simple reversal of scuba was used for gas collection. Created in 1911 by British physiologist C. G. Douglas, this technique involved collecting all the expired gas in a big sealed canvas bag. Given the hugely creative talent scientists display in generating colorful names, you won't be surprised to learn this was called a "Douglas bag." The Douglas bag technique was originally developed to help gauge respiratory and cardiovascular fitness in advance of the 1911 joint U.S.-U.K. Pike's Peak expedition. It was subsequently used in hundreds of studies and was crucial for advances in understanding of the metabolic cost of many tasks.

Using indirect calorimetry we know that for the consumption of every liter (or about a quart) of oxygen approximately 5 kcal of energy are used. This allows the calculation of the basal metabolic rate (BMR), which is the minimum metabolic rate needed just to maintain your body's basic functions. The overall daily metabolic rate consists of three—here we are with the threes again!—main components: the BMR, the amount of energy related to activity, and the amount related to food and eating. For the general person, the BMR accounts for

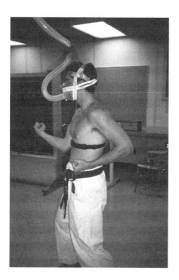

Figure 6.6. A Rudolph valve measures the amount of oxygen and energy used to perform karate by calculating the oxygen taken in and the carbon dioxide produced.

60–70%, activity 15–50%, and feeding 10% of the total daily metabolism. Many factors can affect the BMR including genetics, age, gender, amount of lean tissue, diet, hormones, and activity level. The BMR can be roughly estimated for men as 1.0 kcal/hr/kg body weight. For women, the value is slightly lower at 0.9 kcal/hr/kg body weight. As such, the BMR for Bruce Wayne/Batman is about 2,400 kcal. Now, added to that is the effect of activity, which for Batman can be up to 50% of his total. By the way, metabolic activity varies in different animals and adheres roughly to a principle called "allometric scaling." The simple point is that basal metabolic rate increases with mass. Despite that, the very low-mass bat has a very high metabolic rate. In fact bats have a metabolic rate that is among the highest in the animal kingdom and is just behind the hummingbird!

The amount of energy expended in activity can be expressed in units of calories, just as with food consumption. Daily energy expenditures vary widely among people and activities. Cyclists in the famous Tour de France may use up to 5,000 calories on fairly flat stages and up to 8,000 calories a day on the mountain climbs. Assuming that

Batman isn't gaining or losing weight, and given Batman's activities, he probably tops out about 3,500 to 4,000 calories daily. His brother Bob sits at around 2,800 calories. What we really want to know is a more tangible estimate of how much energy Batman expends while actually being Batman.

To give you some indication and frame of reference for this, I watched the 2005 Warner Bros. movie *Batman Begins* and kept track of the activities of Batman and Bruce Wayne. I categorized and timed the main Batman activities as fighting (approximately 18 minutes), climbing (approximately 6 minutes), driving (approximately 6 minutes), swimming (about 1½ minutes), and calisthenics, hiking, and his machine work to build his gear (about a minute each). I did all that so we could compare how many calories of energy Batman/Bruce used during the roughly 130 minutes of the movie. Calculating the energy requirement during these special categories yielded about 520 calories over the 30-some minutes of Batman activities. Bruce spent about 315 calories over the remaining 99 minutes of the movie, which gives us a total of around 835 calories. You can compare that with the number of calories expended simply while sitting there watching the movie itself. For men with body weights between 74 and 83 kilograms (165 and 185 pounds), these values would be 170–190 calories, and for women between 58.5 and 72 kilograms (130 and 160 pounds) the values are 130–160 calories. Batman expended a lot more than you or I would have just watching the movie!

We started off part of this discussion with the concept of having a high or low metabolism. Well, how much can a person's metabolic rate change with training? A way to look at this is to consider what a sustainable metabolic rate is. Given the principles underlying homeostasis, your body tries really hard to maintain an energy budget that keeps body mass constant. This means that energy intake will equal energy expenditure. We already discussed how the BMR is a main contributor to energy expenditure and how exercise and work can dramatically affect metabolic rate when we are exercising.

What is the long-term effect of activity on metabolic rate? Many studies suggest there are definite limits to maximal metabolism. That means we cannot just do more and more on an ever-increasing scale. Sustainable energy expenditures are based upon the physical activity level and can be as high as two and a half times the BMR. When someone begins an exercise program—like when Bruce Wayne began to train to become Batman—the physical activity level goes up. For example, if an untrained person, such as Bob Wayne, began a training program—finally, after all these years—for a half marathon, his physical activity levels could increase from about 1.7 (completely sedentary is 1.5; this number is not zero because of the energy involved in just being alive) to 2 after eight weeks. In highly trained and highly active people, like soldiers during field training, this can get as high as 2.4. However, body mass losses will often occur and can be as much as five pounds per week. This would be the likely result of acting as Batman. Those Tour de France cyclists can get as high as 3.5 to 5.5 times the basal physical activity level but there will be body composition changes. The use of supplementary high carbohydrate foods and drinks like Gatorade help reduce these negative effects. These athletes also tend to eat many small meals throughout the day. High performance athletes seem to be able to maintain their the basal physical activity level at much higher levels probably because of those genetic factors we talked about earlier.

As far as adaptations to training are concerned, the changes all happen in systems that drive the metabolic pathways themselves. Aerobic exercise leads to an increase in mitochondria, which in turn helps with aerobic metabolism. Anaerobic activity leads to increased enzyme activity in the glycolytic pathways and an increase in storage of ATP-CP. This all follows very logically in the stress-response framework I have used elsewhere in the book. Batman's body experiences a stress (such as exercise) and responds with a compensation to minimize that stress. It all seems so simple that it is easy to forget about the effort needed to provide the stress in the first place!

Don't Be Nervous About Metabolism

As with almost every function, Batman's nervous system is intimately involved in regulating food intake, digestion, and metabolism. There are two general kinds of "tone" for the nervous system control of metabolism, both of which work together but in antagonistic ways, a feature of homeostatic control, of course! During the fed state (discussed earlier in the chapter) there is dominance of what is called "parasympathetic tone" related to insulin release. This is a state of "wine, dine, recline" where the idea of relaxation and low stress is captured. In contrast, the opposite tone is called "sympathetic;" it reflects high stress "fight or flight" and stops insulin release.

To sum up, metabolic activity is fundamental to biological function. Put another way, no metabolism equals no life at all for dear Batman. Biological function is intimately regulated by homeostatic control mechanisms, as you might have guessed. It is therefore to be expected that we humans have some pretty cool control over endocrine function of metabolism. As you recall, metabolic rate is related to glucose levels in the blood. It may surprise you to know that hormones we met in Chapter 3—cortisol, catecholamines, thyroid hormone, and growth hormone—are all involved in this process. As a point of trivia, thyroid hormones are catabolic in adults like Batman but are actually anabolic in children. This makes sense if you think about it, as children are still growing (building up). So when Robin as Dick Grayson first met up with Batman their endocrine response was opposite for this particular function!

An Internal Battle Besieges the Batbody

By reading through the last few chapters and this one, you have really had a good look at what is going on within Batman's body. Are you wondering how much is too much, though? How much change can he really undergo, and do all the changes get along with each other without causing damage to the body? I explained that power, strength, and endurance occur separately, but obviously even in your own activities of daily living you wind up doing things that combine the needs of all three. Well, Batman needs to be really good at all these things. Can he be the best at everything, though? Can he be the strongest, fastest, and go the longest?

The short answer is "no," and there is a relatively simple explanation. If you keep in mind the general principle of adaptation to stress that permeates this book, you will probably realize that the kind of stresses that result from trying to be the strongest (and needing very brief but maximal muscle activity) are quite different from those that result from trying to go the longest (and needing low-level muscle activity repeated over and over again for long periods). Because of this we say there is conflict between adaptations for endurance and power. There is a reason why NASCAR drivers aren't out there driving their pickup trucks! The pickup truck is the wrong tool for the job. Similarly, the metabolic adaptations arising from the different metabolic stresses are trying to create two different kinds of tools.

A better example is thinking of track and field. You find runners who do, say, the 200- and 400-meter races. These races require mostly power and short duration activity. You don't find any runners who compete in the 200-meter and in the 10-kilometer or marathon. The physical look of the runners—reflecting the body composition needed for success in those different races—is quite different as well. Within a framework of stress and strain and challenges to homeostasis, it is not possible to maximize adaptations to all responses! A good training program—and certainly one Batman would have followed—includes strength and endurance training. You can do them together; you just cannot expect to push the adaptations in a maximal direction for both.

In the next chapter, we will look at how Bruce Wayne put his muscle, bone, metabolism, and hormones to work together and began training his body in the movements needed to be one of the world's best crimefighters.

PART III

TRAINING THE BATBRAIN

Batman on the path to mastery of the martial arts

CHAPTER 7

From Bruce Wayne to Bruce Lee

MASTERING MARTIAL MOVES IN THE BATCAVE

Experience teaches slowly, Robin. And at a cost of many mistakes.
—Adam West as Batman, from the ABC TV series *Batman*

Rare because it is one of the few times that Batman has come close to losing control. Revealing because it shows the awesome physical strength of an unleashed Dark Knight.
—*Tales of the Dark Knight: Batman's First Fifty Years: 1939–1989* by Mark Cotta Vaz

Batman seems to have an extensive repertoire of movement at his fingertips. So in becoming Batman, Bruce Wayne had to learn all the movements for some pretty complex skills. This means quite a bit of plasticity, or flexibility, must have been going on in his brain. He had to learn a lot and his body had to accept that learning and demonstrate it as skill at martial arts. You might watch a Batman movie or read a comic and say he has good reflexes. In this chapter we look into this concept of reflexes and what it means to learn a skill so well

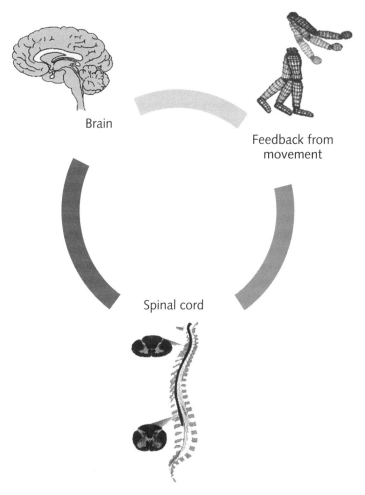

Figure 7.1. Seamless relationship in the nervous system between the brain, the spinal cord, and feedback from the moving limbs.

that it seems you can do things automatically and almost on "autopilot."

Before we learn about learning and fine-tuning movements, we need first to discuss the basic way our movements are controlled. This means reviewing the different parts of the nervous system and their roles in movement or motor control. Movement is a basic characteristic shared by all animals, including us humans. Sir Charles S. Sherrington wrote in 1924 that "to move is all mankind can do . . . whether in whispering a syllable or in felling a forest."

The nervous system controls muscle activity and subsequent movement. It does so by means of a three-part system composed of the brain, the spinal cord, and sensory feedback. This system is illustrated in Figure 7.1, where the three parts are shown endlessly interacting with each other. In this system, commands within the brain and spinal cord interact and are shaped by sensation generated by movement itself. We are going to discuss these bits separately, simply as a convenient way to describe the flow of information. Certainly, all these parts are intimately linked and communicate during real movement. However, we can separate them to lay down some basic concepts.

The Cortex Is in Charge

Let's begin, as we did back in Chapter 4 when talking about the activation of muscle, by starting in the brain. Keeping on with this idea of three-part systems, we going to talk about three sections of the brain: the cerebral cortex, the cerebellum, and the basal ganglia. The relationship between these parts is shown in Figure 7.2.

These three parts interact on many levels, but probably the easiest way to think about them is to picture the nervous system as a kind of huge company with the cerebral cortex as the CEO of motor control. In fact, let's make the cortex the president and CEO. Following on from this, the cerebellum and basal ganglia are vice presidents of movement planning and execution. The spinal cord circuitry represents the local district managers who oversee implementation of plans from head office—and some plans of their own. Feedback arising from movement represents information from actual agents in the field. The main point is that the VPs get to give lots of advice to the president, who has an "open door" policy with his advisors. However, the president gets to make his own choice on matters of strategy and output related to movement and doesn't have to listen to the advice he is given. The general idea is that we have the cerebral cortex coming up with a plan of movement based upon advice from loops in the basal ganglia and cerebellum.

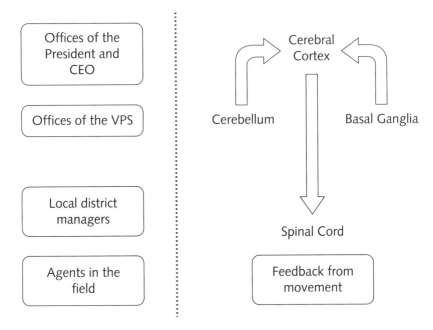

Figure 7.2. A corporation compared to the nervous system.

Let's consider some details in the cerebral cortex. Most brain regions are organized with relation to the main function that occurs in that part of the brain. Think back to the motor cortex, which I described earlier as the place where the final motor output cells in the brain are found. This area is highly organized and even holds a loose representation of the map or plan of the body (remember Chapter 4 and what Penfield called the little man, or "homunculus").

I want to switch analogies at this point and bring up the concept of upstream and downstream. When we trace the action in the body from where the thought to move occurs and the action of movement takes place, those actions farther from specific movements can be referred to as upstream. In the case of our corporation, the VPs are upstream from the agents in the field and the CEO is even farther upstream.

Now that we have defined our terms, let's address where plans to move arise and what they mean. To do so requires thinking about two other parts of the cerebral cortex: the supplementary motor and premotor areas. The main thing about these two areas is that they are anatomically close to the primary motor cortex but are a bit upstream from the final motor commands that issue from the motor cortex to activate muscle. Activating the motor cortex uses that mini-map of the body's muscles and is related to a clear, single muscle representation. Stimulation of the supplementary motor area produces activity instead in groups of muscles. Let's say we were to stimulate Batman's cerebral cortex (or really Bruce Wayne's brain, as we would need that mask and cowl out of the way!). If we were right over the part of the motor cortex for the hand muscles, we could evoke small twitch movements of just, for example, the index finger. However, if we stimulated the supplementary area, we would get activity of many related muscles. We might find Batman's index finger curling along with flexion of his wrist and bending of his elbow. So, motor activity still results after activation of the supplementary motor area, it is just more complex than that from the motor cortex.

There are two additional things about the supplementary motor cortex that are worth commenting on. This part of the brain, being related to planning, shows lots of activity when movements are imagined but not performed. For example, if Batman were thinking about, or rehearsing, certain movements but not actually doing them, his supplementary motor area would be active but his primary motor cortex would not. That is because if his primary motor cortex were active, he would actually be doing the movement! If you tap your right index finger against this page while you read it, both your motor cortex and your supplementary motor area for your right finger flexor muscles (found on the left side of your brain) will be active. If instead you just think about tapping your finger but don't actually do it, only the supplementary motor area will become active.

Related to the supplementary motor area, but even more upstream, is the premotor area. In the premotor area, more abstract features of movement than muscle selection and coordination are planned. For instance, preparation for a general direction of movement or response to a certain cue. So, if Batman is perched above an alleyway waiting to swoop down on Oswald Chesterfield Cobblepot (a.k.a. the Penguin) as the bird-brained bad guy emerges from a side door, Batman is really waiting for a cue. As soon as the door opens, activity in Batman's premotor cortex will signal him to strike. Of course, in order for us to see these he would have to be OK with wearing the necessary scalp electrodes under his cowl. In some movements changes in electrical activity within the brain can be detected almost a second before movement occurs.

This premovement brain activity was originally discovered by German scientists Hans Kornhuber and Luder Deecke in 1965. They recorded electrical activity from the supplementary and premotor areas as people made voluntary finger flexion movements. This discovery was the first hard evidence of detectable brain activity that was directly related to voluntary movement. It was called a "readiness potential" (in German, *Bereitschaftspotential*) and has been studied a great deal ever since.

This activity is curious for two main reasons. Events in the nervous system operate on a millisecond (thousandths of a second) timescale. So, a change in brain activity directly related to movement but happening before movement actually occurs is very puzzling. Studies have shown that these potentials occur not only before movement is detectable but also before a person is even aware that he or she will move! That means we could record these changes in Batman's brain activity before he even started thinking about swooping down on the Penguin. This kind of observation has provided much study for scientists trying to investigate the issue of what "voluntary" really means and what "conscious will" is, but all this is a bit beyond our focus here.

If we now move even farther upstream, we come to a fork that goes in one direction to the cerebellum and in the other to the basal ganglia (have another look at Figure 7.2). Both of these VP advisors for movement provide support to the CEO for producing movement. The information that they convey and the kind of support they provide to the cortex are not the same. Generally we could say that the cerebellum is a bit more related to sensation and body movement itself, while the basal ganglia is a bit more related to internally generated movements.

When the Batbrain Doesn't Function as It Should

We know a lot about how certain parts of the brain work from older research in clinical neurology. Through many years of observation, neurologists were able to piece together certain deficits in movement that some patients had and correlate those deficits with obvious damage to the brain (for example, from a gunshot wound) or upon dissection in autopsy.

For the cerebellum, sadly, gunshot wounds played a very important role in explaining just what this brain area does. The Irish neurologist Sir Gordon M. Holmes (1876–1965) was a pioneer in this work. During World War I, Holmes saw many soldiers with head injuries from gunshot, and this spurred on his study of the cerebellum and its functions related to balance and movement control. The cerebellum is heavily involved in assisting ongoing movement and coordination of the moving limbs and posture of the body. The cerebellum, although it takes up only about one-tenth of the volume of the brain, has more than 50% of the neurons.

Combining this with the dramatic suppressive effect that alcohol has on the function of the nervous system provides the underlying basis for the roadside "checkpoint" tests that the police will use when they pull over a driver under suspicion of driving while intoxicated. The tasks of standing upright with feet together and eyes closed, of reaching out and touching the tip of the nose with the index finger, and of walking a straight line all require cerebellar input and regulation. That is, the cerebellum in its VP role gives very important advice to the cortex in these tasks. The "sleepiness" of cerebellar neurons from alcohol consumption makes these kinds of tests very relevant for inferring impairment. Of course, any inferences require confirmation by breath or blood analysis. To relate this back to our analogy of motor control relationships in the brain, we could consider this an example of when the advisor provides very poor advice that may or may not be ignored by a truculent president!

The basal ganglia, the clumps of neurons at the base of the brain, are very important in helping to initiate or trigger movement. Following on from the description of cerebellar activity above, a main role for the basal ganglia can be best understood when they aren't functioning properly. An exallent example of this is in the serious neurodegenerative disorder known as Parkinson's disease. James Parkinson (1755–1824) was an English physician who wrote a book describing a "shaking palsy" based on his experiences with many of the patients he had seen in his career. The "shaking palsy" was so named because of the obvious tremor that Parkinson's patients demonstrate even when no movement is attempted.

Other characteristics of Parkinson's disease include slowness of movement and a difficulty in starting movements. Parkinson's disease arises because of problems with the part of the complicated neural circuitry that keeps the basal ganglia functioning and that is supported by neurotransmitters. The cells that produce the neurotransmitter dopamine slowly die off. Because these cells function as a supply route within the basal ganglia, the overall function of the basal ganglia slowly degenerates and weakens. The upshot is that the basal ganglia eventually fail to provide the needed advice for voluntary movement and therefore movement becomes more and more difficult to perform. Sadly, this is often paired with unintentional and unwanted twitching movements.

Thinking of how badly things can go wrong when the advisory roles of the cerebellum and basal ganglia are disrupted speaks to how finely tuned the nervous system is in someone like Batman. Movements are called upon with great ease and produced according to desired specifications. Looking at Figure 7.2, it is easy to notice that the command for movement has to be relayed to the spinal cord—that is, to the level of the local district managers and agents in the field. It is at this level that the actual output command to make muscles become active occurs. The neurons at this level are really concerned with implementing the movements brought into action by the spinal cord motor neurons. These are the cells that actually command muscles to contract and that we discussed in Chapter 4. As such, all inputs eventually funnel (the actual physiological term is "converge") onto the motor neurons, which Sherrington called "the final common pathway" for movement control. The neurons in the spinal cord are also charged with adapting the motor output based on what is occurring—that is, making use of feedback—during the movements that are already under way.

For example, lots of information about what your arms and legs are doing during movement comes from the movement of skin across joints, the stretch of your muscles, and the tension in your tendons. Together this information about the movement of the body parts is called "proprioception." This term means perception of our body and our movements. It is contrasted with the perception or sensing of what is happening on the outside of our bodies.

It appears that the Batman writers (in the guise of the Penguin) know the importance of proprioception for motor control. In "Hidden Agendas" (Detective Comics #598–600, 1989), Oswald Cobblepot is shown using a fancy device—not grounded in any actual science, in case you are wondering—called a "synaptic field disruptor." He sets it to "full blast" so he can incapacitate and control the bad guy goon Moraga. When I read this story I really wished that I had at least one piece of equipment in my own lab that had a full-blast setting, but no such luck. The best I could do was "maximum output." In addition to telling the spinal cord and the supraspinal structures like the cerebellum and cerebral cortex about movement and the state of the arms and legs, sensory information carried in proprioceptive pathways can also be used to cause immediate and rapid corrections to movement.

At the level of spinal cord motor control, we have therefore entered the territory of what constitutes "reflex" control. This is the level of the agents in the field indicated back in Figure 7.2. The term "reflex" is actually a fairly problematic one. It seems like it should be very straightforward, though, since we hear expressions like "knee-jerk response" as a way to describe a predictable response to something or a "reflex reaction" used to describe a fast response in sports. And many Batman stories describe him as responding with "instant reflexes." Can reflexes be instant? (No, they can't, as we'll explore in a bit.) What is a reflex really? If you pick up a dictionary, you might find that a reflex is defined as "an automatic or involuntary response to a stimulus."

The earliest known reference that I have found (and, mind you, I have looked pretty hard!) is from David Hartley, who in 1748 described "reflex actions." A reflex seems to be something that reflects or is a consequence of something else. Even before 1748, the great natural philosophers Jean Fernel (1497–1558) and René Descartes (1598–1650) described similar concepts without using the word "reflex." My favorite definition of a reflex is something that is "best defined as responses evoked with great probability by particular stimuli," which was articulated by Vernon Brooks in 1985.

So a reflex is something that can be fairly automatic and can happen very rapidly. Why is that? Reflexes are so fast because they typically operate in defined (yet also quite complex) terms around sets of neurons that provide positive or negative feedback (think back to Chapter 3). The basic outline of the negative feedback for reflexes is shown in Figure 7.3. The flowchart shows the idea that the stretching of muscles activates receptors in the muscle itself. These receptors send nerve impulses (action potentials) back to the spinal cord. In the spinal cord they activate the motoneurons that are in the same muscle. This means that the feedback from the stretch makes the muscle contract more. This might seem weird, but if you think it through, it is a good way to remove the stress. The stress is stretch of the muscle. If the muscle contracts and the body part (the foot in this case) moves, then the effect of the stretch is reduced. It really is negative feedback. That is what the big stop sign with the X in it indicates in Figure 7.3.

To give some more context, let's think about a reflex pathway that you use every day. Have you ever misjudged the depth of a step while walking upstairs? Usually, your foot is placed far enough forward on a step so that when you put your weight onto that leg, your ankle doesn't give and you are able to keep stepping with no interruption. Sometimes, however, we don't get one of our feet far enough into the step when the weight shift onto that leg occurs. When that happens the ankle gets overstretched.

You have little spindle-shaped receptors (propriocepters, such as those the Penguin was trying to disrupt earlier) in your muscles. It is

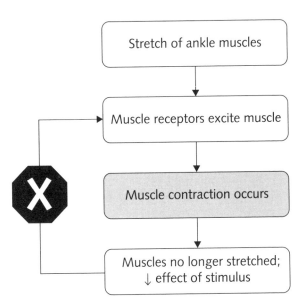

Figure 7.3. Feedback concept in reflexes. The X shows that the response of muscle contractions stops the stimulus.

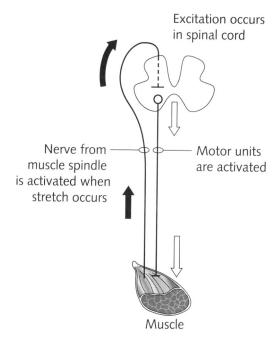

Excitation occurs
in spinal cord

Nerve from
muscle spindle
is activated when
stretch occurs

Motor units
are activated

Muscle

Figure 7.4. Basic spinal reflex. Courtesy David Collins.

their job to tell the spinal cord and brain about the length of the muscles—from which the nervous system computes joint angle—and how fast changes in muscle length are occurring—from which the nervous system computes speed of movement. When activated by stretch, these muscle spindle receptors send a signal back to the motor neurons in the spinal cord causing them to strongly and rapidly increase contraction levels. This is cleverly termed the "stretch reflex," by the way, and it is rapid because there are no other synaptic connections that need to be made. Not all reflexes work with this few synapses, but the idea is basically the same anyway, as is shown in Figure 7.4.

Returning to the example of overstretching because of foot misplacement on the stairs, one of two things would occur. You may have, in your lifetime, experienced both of them. First, the best-case scenario is that the stretch reflex increase in muscle activity at the ankle is large enough to help overcome the stretch, and you carry on stepping. Only after a few seconds have passed will you likely even recollect that something odd happened while you were going up the stairs. That is good; your reflexes did their job well. Second, the worst-case scenario is that the reflex correction is too weak or the stair possibly too slippery, and your foot slides right off the step. This likely would send you crashing forward and force you to either grab the railing (if there is one), or the higher steps (if you can), or to violently bash your shin into the next step (often this is the outcome).

Instant Reflexes

So, can you train reflexes? Well, more highly trained and physically fit people have shorter movement times. Movement time means (again, don't be surprised by this) the overall time taken for a movement to occur. It is often used in the context of evaluating how fast someone can respond to something, for example, if you had to decide when to move to a target when given a "go" signal. Movement time is the elapsed time from the onset of the signal to when you actually complete the movement. It is composed of your reaction to the signal (your ability to detect when to move, your choice to move, and your neural command to your muscles) and your actual physical movement. With training, movement times can be much reduced. This is particularly true in martial arts where maximum speed ("ballistic") movements are common.

This improvement is not largely due to a change in the reaction time. It is instead due to a faster physical movement. So, while the responses of Batman are very fast, his reflexes aren't instant! However, some kinds of reflexes, like the muscle stretch ones we have been talking about, do become stronger and more reliable with training. Scientists would say that excitability in reflex pathways is increased. This again makes sense because the whole nervous system is trying to work together and reinforce movement. So, it would stand to reason that feedback would improve after more training. This is really the case for the sort of strength and power and martial arts training that Batman has to do.

Teaching an Old Bat New Tricks

Now that we have a general understanding of how Batman's move-ments are produced, let's explore how he actually learns new skilled movements. This is the process usually described as motor learn-ing. To begin, take a minute to think about what it was like for you to learn how to do some special sport or movement skill. Maybe it was learning how to swing a golf club, to throw a spiral with a foot-ball, or to hit a baseball. What was it like while you were learning? What kind of mistakes did you make? Probably many! It was also probably very frustrating. While you were learning how to hit that ball, many changes were taking place in your body. These changes aren't the ones related to your increasing frustration levels, by the way, but there is a link to those too. What I am talking about are actual changes in how your brain and spinal cord—the central nervous system, or CNS—were working to make your muscles do what needed to be done. Scientists who study the nervous system call these changes plasticity because it gets at the idea of "change-ability." When thinking of Batman we are really starting to ask how it is he learned the skills to become such a proficient martial artist and dark knight avenger. What changes actually occurred in the CNS of the Caped Crusader when he did all his training? Why do we get better at motor skills when we practice them over and over again?

To achieve the high level of crime-fighting skill that we all know Batman has attained, he would have had to move through three levels of motor learning: cognitive, associative, and auto-matic. Keeping the basic idea of progression that I described ear-lier, we will refer to our protagonist as Bruce in the cognitive stage, the Bat-Man in the associative stage, and Batman in the automatic stage. Details on these stages can be found in Figure 7.5. The first level, cognitive, is where someone is just learning how to perform a physical skill. Let's take doing a front kick, for example. While in the cognitive level, Bruce Wayne would use information on how the skill should be performed to develop a motor plan, also called a motor program. This plan represents the basic organization of what needs to be accomplished to actually do the task. At this stage, a lot of conscious thought would go into the movements, and Bruce would have to pay close attention to the sequence of motions he must perform. For the front kick, that sequence of motions might

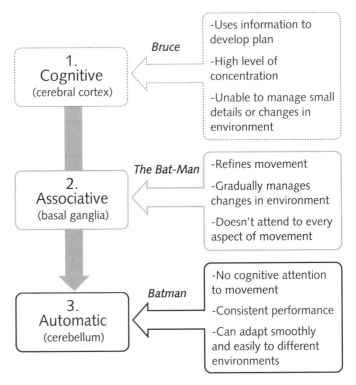

Figure 7.5. Stages of Batman's motor learning. Modified from Fitts and Posner (1967).

be lifting the knee, pulling up the ankle, kicking by extending the knee, and then pulling the toes up and back while hitting the target.

At this stage Bruce would keep in mind the big picture of the skill and be unable to deal with small details of the movement or cope with performing the movement in different settings—like when under attack, for instance. Bruce would likely not get that much specific feedback from his teachers at this stage. Henri Ducard, a main teacher of Bruce Wayne and one who was central to the "Blind Justice" story arc (Detective Comics #598–600, 1989), would know to let Bruce work on developing his motor programs for movement. Without establishing some kind of program for a task such as a front kick, it would be difficult in the next stage to refine that program.

The next stage is the associative one. Here, the Bat-Man would begin to concentrate on a more refined approach to his skills. Instead of just worrying about picking up his foot to do his kick, he would begin to do things like timing the movements within the kick and refining his motions. When to pull the toes up, when to extend the knee exactly, and how to time those actions most efficiently would be his main focus. The Bat-Man would be in this stage for a long time and would have a lot to gain from feedback. During his front kick practice, Ducard might urge the Bat-Man to quickly pick up his knee by pulling through his hip and trying to fling out his leg to strike a target. At this level, the Bat-Man would gradually learn to more efficiently perform the skills and deal with the environment in which he is training. The Bat-Man would not need to attend to every aspect of the performance at this stage and would be fine-tuning his skills.

The third and last stage is the automatic one. Batman would no longer pay much direct attention to the movements. His performance would be very consistent now and could be adapted to different settings. So, he would be able to apply his skills in any environment and against real attackers. It is really at this stage that we would call Batman highly trained. This is the point made in a story in the 1961 Giant Batman Annual called "How to Be the Batman." As a result of taking a drug given to him by a ne'er-do-well, Batman has lost all memories of his prowess and crime-fighting skills. Robin takes him through a refresher program hoping to jog his memory. Robin comments to Batman, "Your muscles are so well trained that they respond automatically! It is only your mind that doesn't remember." What is interesting is that Robin does realize Batman is aiming to regain automaticity. He clearly appreciates how well-trained Batman is and was and how well ingrained are the "automatic muscle responses." Regrettably, this also corresponds with the popularized idea of "muscle memory" that you hear trotted out on almost any television broadcast for any sport. Muscles don't have a memory in this sense, but by now you know that your spinal cord and brain certainly do!

What Channel Are Those Programs On?

You might ask at this point just where all that training "lives"? How is it remembered and where does the remembering occur? To answer those questions we must refer back to the cerebellum and introduce another brain area called the hippocampus, which is the brain's main home for memory formation and storage. The hippocampus is found under the frontal part of the cerebral cortex (cleverly named the frontal cortex!) and was named from the Greek words *hippos* and *kampi*, meaning "horse that is curved," from the anatomical shape of this region. The role of the hippocampus in memory formation and storage was brought to light in the 1950s by the study of an individual known by the name of "Henry M." or more commonly only by his initials. HM had intractable epilepsy and underwent neurosurgery involving sectioning through the hippocampus on both sides of his brain. After that, HM could recall events from before his surgery but was unable to make new memories. Researchers concluded that the connections through the hippocampus are critical for memory formation. The exact way in which this occurs involves activity in many neurons firing at the same time. This simultaneous activity leads to an enhancement of information flow across certain synapses because of a mechanism known as long-term potentiation, or LTP. LTP is the process by which memories are laid down and stored, and it requires input from multiple sites within the hippocampus. LTP is now known to occur in many different sites in the brain, including the motor cortex, but it does not occur after damage to the hippocampus. If the hippocampus is damaged, memories cannot be stored as before.

The importance of the hippocampus has really been demonstrated in experiments in which rats have learned how to navigate through mazes. If the connections in their hippocampi are disrupted, rats have great difficulty learning to get around. A really neat human comparison is that of London taxi drivers. To become a licensed taxi driver in London requires being trained for two to four years, learning all the 25,000 routes in this huge city. This is called "The Knowledge" and is strictly evaluated by an examination given to ensure that all drivers can navigate the city by memory. You might guess that the size of the hippocampus in these taxi drivers is somewhat larger than normal, and you would be correct. There is an interesting study of a London taxi driver who had a rare syndrome leading to damage of the hippocampus on both sides of his brain. He had worked as a taxi driver for over 40 years and thus had a very old and well-stored memory of "The Knowledge." He could still get around London but became easily lost when going off the main routes. This again provides an example of the crucial role of the hippocampus in memory formation and storage. It will probably not be a surprise to learn that the neurological disorder Alzheimer's disease, in which the formation of new memories eventually becomes impossible, arises because of degeneration in the hippocampus. We will come back to Alzheimer's disease in Chapters 13 and 15.

So, memory formation while Bruce, then the Bat-Man, and eventually Batman was performing his training partly occurred in the hippocampus. For motor skills the cerebellum, our trusted VP of sensation and movement, plays a major role. In the cerebellum the reverse process of LTP occurs—wait for it, you know this will be good since scientists are so fanciful in naming things—by means of long-term depression, or LTD. The cerebellum receives information about what the cortex plans to do for movement as well as feedback related to what actually occurred. Therefore, the cerebellum is uniquely situated to act as a mediator during movement control and learning. Output (advice) from the cerebellum is used by the cortex to continually update and adjust the motor plans that are enacted.

A neat experiment that clearly shows how important the cerebellum is during motor skill acquisition involved people throwing darts at a target board while wearing prism goggles that shifted the visual field to one side. This meant that they perceived the target to be in front of them, even though it wasn't. Let's say you tried this. Over time, about 30 minutes or so, if you have no damage to your central nervous system, you would adapt to this shift and begin to throw the darts so that they hit the target (even though it would still appear to be in the wrong place). If the goggles were then removed, you would now "overshoot" in the opposite direction and miss the target just like you did when you first put on the goggles. Again, you would adapt to the new target over another 30-minute period. However, someone who has damage to the cerebellum would not make any adaptation and would always miss the target. This means the cerebellum is needed for motor learning required to adapt to new conditions.

An umbrella term is used to describe many neural processes related to things like motor learning or just changes in activity in the nervous system. That term is "adaptive plasticity," and it refers to the remolding of neural circuits as a result of activity that has occurred. The basic principle behind this was suggested in 1949 by the Canadian neuroscientist Donald Hebb, who coined what is known as Hebb's postulate. This states: "When an axon of cell A is near enough to excite a cell B and repeatedly takes part in firing it, some growth process or metabolic changes take place so that A's efficiency of firing B is increased." The shorter version, and one which is easier to remember, is "neurons that fire together, wire together." This explains why it is so important for Batman to have good practice conditions while he is learning and building his motor programs for martial arts and other skills. If nerve cells are wiring together by firing together, you want the correct stuff firing at the same time. That is, sloppy practice will generate poor motor programs. In a way this is the neural basis for the old expression "practice doesn't make perfect, perfect practice makes perfect."

This is also related to the neural basis for adaptations to strength or power training (which we discussed back in Chapter 4). Training responses can occur either at the muscle level or at the level of the central nervous system (within the brain and spinal cord). At the muscle level, changes will happen to mirror the stimulus that is applied. That is, if the stimulus involves forcing the muscle to perform small numbers of high-force contractions, the adaptation will be different from times when the stimulus involves high numbers of low-force contractions. Within the central nervous system, differences in the motor program or movement command are sent by the brain when similar movements are performed fast or slow, with greater force or with lesser force. Try this yourself. Stand up and move your hand. Repeat the movement faster and slower. Then try a different movement with the same hand. Did you notice having to think about it? If you had repeated the same simple movements over and over, you could have done them more automatically.

These factors underlie the previously mentioned principles of overload and specificity in training. Because of the very nature of the training response in human beings, it is vitally important that the training stimulus be as specific and similar to the technique as possible. That explains the way in which Batman learns the motor skills he needs to have at his disposal for fighting crime. However, when we think about applications for full-blown combat in martial arts or military applications, we really have entered the arena of what is known as overtraining or overlearning. That is, to go beyond just performing a task adequately, making the task and skill so ingrained as to really and truly be automatic. What we are talking about now is learning a skill so well that it is part of the individual. This is a basic approach of martial arts training, as I will further describe in the next chapter, as well as military training.

How Much Is Too Much?

This issue of overlearning was originally described by William Krueger from the University of Chicago back in 1929. He did experiments not on motor skill learning but rather on memorizing lists of words. The term "learning" describes the ability to remember the lists accurately, and the term "retention" indicates the ability to remember those lists after various set intervals. With a bit more relevance for motor skills, he performed another set of experiments in 1930 involving a maze-tracking task. The term "overlearning" was used to mean how much extra practice was required after a task or skill was learned. So, if it took 10 trials to do a certain maze-tracking task, 50% and 200% overlearning would occur with 15 trials and 30 trials, respectively. Now, with complex movement skills such as those with which Batman would need to be familiar, 10 trials would not likely approach reasonable skill. In fact, many old tales of martial arts mastery suggest that thousands or more repetitions of a form or pattern are needed for mastery. Tsuyoshi Chitose (1898–1984), the founder of one of the karate styles that I studied for 25 years, wrote that his teacher would not teach a new movement form until basic proficiency had been obtained in the previous form. Chitose recommended three thousand repetitions as the minimum to achieve this proficiency. I am not sure where I am in this count, but after more than 25 years I have some forms (*kata*) that I have now practiced more than ten thousand times. I still find something new every time I do one! Maybe I am a slow learner?

The kind of movement skills Batman uses in his nighttime prowling and crime-fighting activities are procedural skills. Procedural skills are tasks that have a series of discrete responses chained together. A discrete response is one where there is a well-defined beginning and end. A continuous response is one which, not surprisingly, continues. So, Batman on foot and running after Catwoman is performing a continuous skill—walking or running. However, once he catches up to Catwoman and they begin fighting, he will perform discrete actions—kicking for example—added together in a series, and this would be procedural skills.

It turns out that procedural tasks are ones that are the easiest for us to forget. For the U.S. Army, this was a major problem for the essential skills that the infantry learn in basic training. For example, it is critical that soldiers know how to assemble and disassemble their firearms. However, this is but one among a large set of motor skills and tasks that recruits are required to master during basic training. There is therefore only limited time to devote to each task or skill. This is not unlike the situation encountered in the basic training of essential public service providers such as police officers and firefighters. In the example of the U.S. Army, it was known that the amount of practice devoted to skills such as the assembly and disassembly of the M60 machine gun was sufficient to gain mastery during training. But, this mastery was rapidly forgotten in the weeks that followed basic training. It is quite costly and unwieldy to conduct refresher courses at regular intervals, so therefore the U.S. Army Research Institute explored overlearning as a way to mitigate the effects of forgetting. Soldiers typically could reach acceptable criterion performance of this skill in about 30 minutes of continuous practice. Overtraining of 100% past this criterion skill level resulted in improved performance at an eight-week post-training test.

Overtraining combined with refresher courses is an efficient way to store and restore procedural skills. It is now known that the effect of overtraining has a "half-life" of about three weeks. So, after five to six weeks, if no additional refresher course or training is implemented, the benefit of overlearning may be reduced almost to zero. What this means is that regular practice, even just a little bit, dispersed over weeks is critical for maintenance of the learning of procedural skills. I tell my martial arts students that even five to ten minutes of practice each day can make a huge difference in their ability to remember and improve on basic movement skills.

Batman cannot, therefore, expect his skills to be maintained if he just sits around (or runs around, or whatever he might do that is not practicing his important martial arts skills). Gichin Funakoshi, an Okinawan karate master who pioneered the development of karate on the Japanese mainland, wrote that "karate is like boiling water: without heat, it returns to its tepid state." This metaphor very nicely captures the underlying science of motor skill learning and retention.

A question that you might be framing even now in your head is why is this so? If learning these skills fits with the concept of motor program and motor learning mentioned above—and it does—then why don't these programs just sit there nicely and wait to be used? I am telling you that Batman's skills will degrade if they aren't used or practiced. However, if you have a certain software program on your computer and don't use it for one year, you know it will work just the same now as it did a year ago. It hasn't degraded, so why do the biological motor programs degrade?

A probable explanation can be seen when considering motor learning in light of the overall stress-response model established in Chapter 3. We have to consider the overall metabolic cost of learning—synapse formation and maintenance do require increased metabolic cost. The act of learning a skill and then constantly trying to use that skill can be considered the environmental stress needed to keep those skills and the underlying neural connections strong and efficient. We can think of practice and attempts to remember during practice as the stress for maintaining learning.

This is even more of an issue for Batman's tools. His batarangs, his gliders, his weapons are all "tools." It turns out that learning and remembering motor skills with tools can be even more difficult than without tools. In Batman's case that really means that remembering how to use all his weapons is harder than just doing empty hand fighting. This is also why learning to play something like golf is so difficult. This is probably because the tools that we use are not "calibrated" as parts of our bodies. Remember the homunculus concept? Well, you have had those maps of your body in your brain since you were a baby. The map has been recalibrated over the years to reflect your changing body size and activities. However, your body has always been there. Well, tools aren't with us all the time and we use them usually quite intermittently. It turns out that our homunculus can include parts of the way we use tools. But it seems these changes in the maps are very weak compared with those for our actual body parts. That means they need much more "maintenance" than do our other maps. I can testify that in my own martial arts experiences, empty hand karate techniques and patterns are much easier to learn and remember than are weapons techniques and patterns. Also, it is much, much easier to forget or "get rusty" with weapons than it is with karate technique.

Although both require continual practice, empty hand fighting is more forgiving. This is why, as with almost every aspect of biological and physiological systems, motor skill learning for you, me, and Batman is absolutely a case of "use it or lose it."

Now let's look at how Batman would have taken these methods of learning skills and made himself a master of martial arts.

CHAPTER 8

Everybody Was Kung Fu Fighting

BUT WHAT WAS BATMAN DOING?

> I don't have to explain that he has conditioned himself to the peak of physical perfection . . . and . . . is a master of the martial arts.
> —*The Greatest Batman Stories Ever Told,*
>   Volume 2: *DC Comics,* from the introduction
>   by Martin Pasko

Batman is the most highly trained martial artist of all DC Comics superheroes. It could be argued that he is the greatest pure fighter in the history of comic book heroes. In fact, I am arguing that right now as you read this. So there. Batman has been shown doing many different fighting techniques over the years. A memorable panel appears in the story "This One'll Kill You Batman" (Batman #260, 1975). Batman, described in the panel as "a master of unarmed combat," is shown doing kung fu, judo, aikido, and "plain old fisticuffs."

What type of martial arts training would best suit Batman? In *The Ultimate Guide to the Dark Knight,* Scott Beatty—a true master of all things Batman—says the Caped Crusader has studied 127 martial arts. First, I doubt that there are that many truly different martial arts. There are many subdivisions of martial arts, though, that could easily reach into the hundreds. Second, even if there were that many, could a person really study all of them? The idea that training in many different martial arts is the way you attain superior skill and mastery is false mythology. Studying four martial arts for one year each does not result in the same skill as having four years of training in one discipline. Instead it is more like going to ninth grade at four different schools and then asking for a high school diploma. You never really gain any deep understanding or competency with this approach. This is certainly the "jack of all trades, master of none" route. And master of none means a very short career as a costumed crimefighter.

Before further discussing the type of martial arts Bruce Wayne might have studied while he was studying to become Batman, let's start with what "martial arts" means. Do martial artists create pictures or sculptures that then fight each other? I hope not! I am a reasonably accomplished martial artist, but I cannot draw a decent picture to save my life. This idea of martial and arts put together is admittedly a bit confusing. The confusion comes from the Western translation of the Chinese characters that are used to write out this term. The martial part is pretty straightforward. It relates to fighting and combat (in Japanese and Chinese the written characters actually mean "to stop a spear"). The arts part is more properly translated in English as "technique" or "method." The term "martial arts" means the technical knowledge to stop physical confrontation. In Japanese traditions these are sometimes called martial ways, or *budo*.

You might suspect there are lots of physical confrontations going on since, if you open up your yellow pages, you will find many entries under "martial arts" or "self-defense." You probably would find karate, tae kwon do, judo, aikido, and t'ai chi. You might also find wing chun, hapkido, savate, capoeira, and many others. Do the choices really matter or are they all the same things anyway? Deciding which martial arts might be better is relative and depends on what you are doing. It is similar to a language metaphor I use in this chapter. Can one ask "what is the best language?" The answer to that question kind of depends on who you want to talk to!

Historical origins of martial arts are hard to sort out. Details are sketchy, and often an oral history (frequently a suspect one) is the only record available. Given these cautions, let's look at where martial arts can be said to have originated. Keep in mind we are discussing here the systems of empty hand fighting and associated weapons, not the history of warfare generally. When we say "martial arts" we almost always mean Asian or Eastern traditions. Draeger and Smith suggest that Western martial arts traditions date back to the Greco-Roman period. Plato wrote of fighters practicing *skiamachia,* or "fighting without an antagonist," and of a kind of shadow boxing very similar to the practice of solo forms and patterns found in Asian martial arts. Also, some of the actual techniques used in the West were similar to those found in Asia. In 400 BC at Nemea there was a battle between Creugas and Damoxenus. In this fight Damoxenus killed Creugas with a "spear hand" strike, a kind of open hand technique commonly associated with Eastern martial arts.

As the origin of Eastern martial arts is almost impossible to determine for sure, let's look at the stories that do exist. Some suggest an origin in India spreading to China and from China to all of southern Asia. Since really the best documented part of the trail can be traced back to China, that is as far back as I want to go. This takes us about three thousand years into the past to the Chou dynasty between 1122 and 255 BC. In this chapter I briefly mention many different martial arts. However, a key thing I want to get across here is that what specific martial arts Batman studied is largely irrelevant. It isn't the specific tradition from a specific place that is the most important thing. It is what is contained in that tradition and who is studying it that is! This will make more sense as we go along, trust me.

For now let's study a few examples that illustrate how martial arts traditions may have had unique starts in different parts of the world but were heavily influenced by only a few dominant places. Since martial arts have been so thoroughly dominated by Eastern traditions, I am going to focus on China, Korea, Okinawa (separate from Japan when martial arts developed), and Japan for the time being.

As I mentioned above, somehow martial arts traditions sprung up in China. Some old stories suggest that Bodidharma, who is credited with bringing a type of Buddhism to China in the fifth century AD, came up with early martial arts exercises and techniques to help Buddhist monks keep up fitness levels to allow for more meditation! Historically there have been very strong links between philosophical and religious traditions and martial arts.

Everyone Wasn't Always Kung Fu Fighting

When asking what martial arts Batman did, should, or would need to study, we also need to ask what time period we are talking about. Martial arts reflected in Batman comics have depended on the cultural dominance of different martial arts traditions in North America. Back in the 1930s and 1940s, judo and jujutsu were very popular and found in many movies and magazine articles. The term "judo chop" was commonly used, and the artwork in Batman comics from that era clearly reflects Batman doing judo and boxing.

In the story "Introducing Robin, the Boy Wonder" (Detective Comics #38, 1940), Batman (as Bruce Wayne) teaches Robin all about fighting. At that time he used boxing punches and the throws from jujutsu (then called "tricks"). By the late 1950s and into the 1960s and 1970s, karate and "kung fu" were popular both with the general public and in movies with martial arts actors such as Chuck Norris and Bruce Lee. These influences blended in the 1980s and into the 1990s where the synthetic martial arts traditions such as seen in "mixed martial arts" and ultimate fighting have now come to the fore.

Flavors of Martial Arts

Martial arts can be categorized in a variety of ways. First, they differ in the cultural and political aspects of the martial art within the country of origin. For example, martial arts practiced in China, Malaysia, or Brazil all have aspects common to each region. Second, martial arts differ in focusing more on particular aspects of combat—such as punching and kicking, joint locking (defined as forcing an opponent's joint to extend past its normal range of motion), and throwing—or on weaponry and weapons fighting. I would label these as different types of martial arts. Third, they differ in methodology, tactics, or philosophy even within a given type. These represent stylistic differences. For example, there are distinct styles of karate or wu shu that someone can train in or study.

This brings up a related point. It is much like the old joke about a physician "practicing medicine"—no thanks, I'd like a doctor who doesn't need the practice. However, when serious martial artists describe what they do the words they will use are typically "practice," "study," or "train in." There isn't typically a convenient end point specified. That is because martial arts training is a process. The analogy of mountain climbing is often used in this context. No matter how high you climb in a range of mountain peaks, there is always a higher peak to be scaled. This isn't to be interpreted as defeatist—you do celebrate your accomplishments—but it should serve as a strong counterpoint to egotism.

What's in a Name?

By the way, even the terminology used to describe the different martial arts is confusing. The Chinese martial arts were originally translated into English as "Chinese boxing." However, most people think of them as kung fu. I even used that term in the title for this chapter (and in partial homage to Carl Douglas for his great lyrics). Kung fu is a Cantonese expression that is commonly used to describe hand-to-hand fighting. However, kung fu really means the "dedication that one puts into a task or any kind of physical effort." That could be anything—from painting a picture to housework like vacuuming. The most appropriate term for the performance of Chinese martial arts is actually *wu kung*. That means martial (*wu*) expertise. I guess musical lyrics such as "Everybody was wu kung fighting . . . those cats were fast as lightning" probably wouldn't have been nearly as popular or danceable! Also, the most accurate term is actually *ch'uan fa,* meaning "fist method." Anyway, kung fu has become the accepted term, so we'll just go with it. While it is important to use proper descriptors for things, I think a famous English playwright wrote that "a rose by any other name would smell as sweet."

This is probably a good time to explain something else about modern martial arts. Some aren't very martial anymore. Let's use judo and t'ai chi chuan as examples. Judo was once a formidable martial art but is now simply a sport. T'ai chi chuan is still practiced by small numbers as a serious martial art but is mostly done as a health exercise.

Let's start with judo. Judo has its roots in Kito-ryu jujutsu and was developed by the great martial arts master Jigoro Kano, who was a jujutsu expert and dedicated teacher. He wanted to create a martial activity that many people could practice safely. The last part is key: how do you take a martial art that has inherent in it deadly force and make it safe for lots of people—including children and young adults—to do together? I think you can probably guess that what you would do is take out the really dangerous stuff. In the case of judo that means mostly the open hand striking and kicking.

Remember earlier when I mentioned that the kind of martial arts training Batman was said to do varied across the history of his comic books? Well, in the 1940s the term for what you now might call a "karate chop" was "judo chop." This change reflected the slow disappearance of the striking techniques from the judo curriculum. Nowadays there isn't any of the striking left, and most of the extremely dangerous throws and locks have been deleted. This allowed for mass participation and even inclusion as an Olympic sport. However, a natural and unavoidable result was a severe weakening and dilution of the fighting aspects found in jujutsu.

By the way, something similar but not as extreme also happened when karate was brought from its home in the island of Okinawa to mainland Japan in the mid-1930s. Gichin Funakoshi, founder of what is now known as the Shotokan style of karate, tried to broaden its appeal. Many of the more deadly aspects of karate were removed, including the joint locking, throwing, and break-falling found in many Okinawan and Japanese karate styles with strong Okinawan ties. This also included the deletion of most associated weapons techniques.

The end result was a karate that was much more palatable to the broader Japanese population, still had a superficial form of warrior tradition, and was good exercise. These modifications also allowed judo and karate to fit into the more common bracket of "martial ways." This really means former combat arts now not so much used for combat but good for exercise and philosophical grounding. This is essentially what happened to most Japanese martial arts at the end of the samurais' reign in the late nineteenth century. A last comment here is that this road of diluting the martial elements of the practice is also being followed in the Korean martial art of tae kwon do. It is moving rapidly—and in all honesty I should say it has moved—along to becoming purely a sporting activity.

T'ai chi chuan ("grand ultimate fist"), or simply t'ai chi as it is more commonly known, is a Chinese martial art with a long history. It is often seen in mass practice, and its hallmark is probably the long extended and graceful movements performed at a very slow pace. People of all ages—including the elderly—can and do practice this form of t'ai chi. However, the real martial arts form encompasses full speed defenses, attacks, and takedowns. Teachers of this form of t'ai chi are difficult to find but do exist. However, the main point here is that t'ai chi was a martial art but is now mostly a health activity, which is good for many aspects of general fitness but not of much utility for fighting.

All this really means is that the martial arts were and are influenced by the society in which they flourish. Most martial arts came from systems that involved real and effective combat techniques. Historically, whether we are talking about warring periods in China, Japan, Korea, or wherever, martial arts were used in altercations with real consequences. However, as those warring periods passed by, the value of the martial arts shifted to one of pursuit of other objectives. These included health and philosophy but still had the martial self-defense aspects. Now, in today's culture we are swinging back again to a more combat-oriented focus. Sort of. There is a real popularity to ultimate fighting and mixed martial arts that fits in with what I am saying. However, this is a kind of combat light, I guess. I am not demeaning the mixed martial arts when I say this. What I mean is that in real combat there are no rules, but in any competition there are rules. So, activity approximates but never really reaches real combat.

Here is where I insert my disclaimer! Please, please note that what we have been discussing here are the kinds of martial arts Batman would study to gain fighting prowess. He might get some sporting enjoyment from whatever he does, and surely the activity would have an exercise component. However, those are not the main objectives. My disclaimer is that I am not saying you shouldn't do judo or t'ai chi chuan or tae kwon do. However, Batman would not gain much direct fighting prowess from them in the form they are in now.

The Batchoice?

So now we have a basic idea about where martial arts came from and what we mean by the words "martial arts," but we are no farther ahead in trying to figure out what would be the best one for Batman. Should he train in judo, aikido, wing chun, karate, or tang soo do—or a combination? To determine the answer, I am going to turn this around and think of it in completely the opposite way. Instead of thinking about what the differences are, let's talk instead about what is the various martial arts have in common. The main common element is protecting the self and others from attack. The technical elements of any martial art can be understood from this perspective.

To build up this concept I want to look closer to the analogy of language I brought up earlier in the chapter. In the case of language, the objective is communication with others by learning words, phrases, intonation, sentence structure, and other parts of speech. You are making an effort to be able to talk to a group of people on as broad a range of topics as possible. Would it make any sense to ask what language is the best to learn? Of course not. The answer depends on who you are trying to talk to. Having said that, the number of people who speak a language does help guide effective choices. Selecting Latin as the only language you could speak, for example, would really trim down the potential number of people you could talk to.

Does it make sense to learn more than one language? The answer here is of course "yes." The more languages you speak, the greater number of individuals you will be able to communicate with. In the same way if Batman "speaks" only one way of fighting he will have a limited ability to "communicate" with the criminals he is trying to subdue. When I say "way of fighting" here I mean it in the sense of having expertise in only one fighting range, such as only knowing how to do long-range striking. Of course, this analogy breaks down quite a bit now. If Batman cannot "communicate" effectively it doesn't mean just not understanding someone as in language, it means failing to stop a criminal or, worse, getting pulverized! Since Batman doesn't always know who he is going to have to interact with, having more options at his disposal means an increased chance of success in combat.

Martial arts can be distinguished by the kind of attacks and defenses that are usually emphasized. There are many different ways to categorize martial arts, but I prefer to focus on distance. Fighting is all about manipulating distance. That is, the physical space that separates two (or more) opponents. This is because to attack someone you have to close the distance between you and that person. This is the case whether someone uses a long-range weapon like a staff or is trying to position for a throw and choke hold. The distance will change according to what strategy one is trying to implement.

I'm going to admittedly make things overly simple here and lump a few things together, but so be it. Let's say you had five kinds

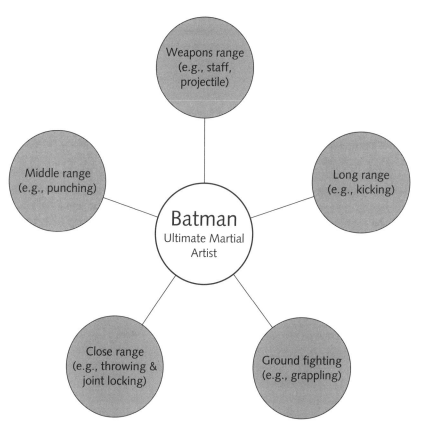

Figure 8.1. Components of martial arts at different engagement distances.

of attacks you could do. You can also do the reverse example and think of five kinds of attacks you were good at defending against, by the way. These five, moving from longest to shortest distance, include a weapons range attack (with a six-foot stick), a long-range attack with a kick, a middle-range attack with a punch, a close-range joint lock for a throw, and a close-range ground fighting attack with grappling. I have also summarized these in Figure 8.1. If you were good at all five of these, I would say you were a superb all-around fighter. That is what Batman must be and why he is placed in the center of the diagram in the figure. However, if you are only good at one of them then you will have problems unless you can do the whole fight at that range. Real fighting typically involves rapid closing of the distance to throwing and grappling range. If all a person is good at is doing kicking from a long range, then he or she will be really limited at the close range. This is why Batman, like any fighter, must have skill at all ranges.

What martial traditions cover all of these ranges? It is probably safe to say that none do. Many weapons systems, like the Ryukyu Kobujutsu that I study, provide a synthetic expertise at long distance with most classes of weapons. It also has closer ranges such as kicking and punching. However, there are very limited close-fighting techniques. Most karate styles have some limited weapons-range techniques and may or may not include close-range joint locking and throwing. However, grappling is usually not emphasized. Tae kwon do (Korea) and capoeira (Africa and Brazil) have fantastic and devastating long-range kicking techniques. However, again, short-range techniques are not as emphasized. Aikido provides lots of techniques for defense against punching and kicking and does joint locks and throws that move to close range. But in this case, there is no grappling. Judo has good throwing and grappling but no striking. Classical jujutsu was the style of fighting used by the samurai. It included striking, kicking, kneeing, throwing, grappling, joint locking, and choking, and also some weapons applications. the important thing to remember here is that different traditions focus on different things.

For example, karate styles nowadays rarely have very much in the way of weapons techniques. This is despite the fact that many of the old masters who laid the foundation for the modern karate styles also had extensive training in weapons. Instead, modern karate styles will have at best a few forms for maybe one (usually the staff) or two weapons. At the other end of the spectrum you might find kendo, a sporting martial art that uses the simulated (bamboo swords are used) long sword but has no empty hand techniques at all.

Maybe looking at popular culture movie actors who are also martial artists will help you visualize some distinct martial arts traditions. The five I would like us to consider, and who each represent slightly different main traditions of fighting, are Bruce Lee, Chuck Norris, Jean-Claude Van Damme, Jackie Chan, and Steven Seagal. All of these five have extensive training backgrounds in traditional martial arts. No doubt you have seen at least one of them in action.

Although you can't glean much about the essence of a given martial art by examining what kind of fight scenes a certain actor performed on screen, it is safe to say each one demonstrates techniques that play to his main strengths.

These strengths are certainly the result of their backgrounds. Bruce Lee trained originally in t'ai chi chuan and wing chun, both of which are Chinese martial arts. Chuck Norris learned mainly tang soo do, a Korean martial art, but also some Shito-ryu karate. Jean-Claude Van Damme began his martial arts training in Shotokan karate and also studied some muay thai kickboxing and ballet. Jackie Chan began his wu shu training at the Chinese Opera Research Institute and the Peking Opera School where he learned acrobatic fighting skills. Steven Seagal is mainly an aikido stylist but also has studied some karate, judo, and kendo.

So now we have outlined different types of martial arts and shown some examples of what they look like in action. Now let's pick the one for Batman!

Is Batman a Ninja?

I probably have convinced you by now that as long as Batman trained in some martial art that encompassed all aspects of fighting (remember that means striking, throwing, joint locking, grappling, and weapons) it really is irrelevant what specific traditions he picked. Batman could have achieved this with a few different martial arts or by sampling at most half a dozen. This is nowhere near the estimate of 127 we talked about earlier. However, I did promise I would give an example of my take on Batman's best choice. So, if Batman were stranded on a deserted island in the South Pacific and could only take his favorite book, one CD, one special keepsake, and one martial art tradition, that tradition would be ninjutsu. This was nicely hinted at but not specifically stated in the movie *Batman Begins*, when Bruce Wayne is shown being trained essentially as a ninja. If you watched the "ninja movies" of the 1980s, you probably don't have a very accurate idea of what ninjutsu really was, by the way! I watched all those movies too, but sadly, ninja demons that can teleport across vast distances or become invisible don't exist and offer a poor representation of actual ninja. These martial artists were highly trained and could achieve some fairly amazing feats.

So if ninja don't bear any resemblance to the way they are depicted on the silver screen, what are or were they? Ninjutsu includes many martial arts techniques and methods at every range. Martial arts historians Donn Draeger and Robert Smith define ninjutsu as both a method of protection against danger and a feudal system of espionage. The last bit springs from the fact that ninjutsu also has elements of spying, harassing, and confusing an enemy. One of the main homes of the ninja was Iwate province in the village of Iga Ueno in Japan. Not surprisingly, a major influence was from Chinese military spying techniques.

Ninjutsu is thought to date from the reign of Empress Suiko (AD 593–628) and a war between two factions that occurred during her reign. A main warrior at that time, Otomo-no-Saijin, was awarded the nickname Shinobi for his role in the conflict. In fact the Japanese character from which "ninjutsu" comes has the root of "shinobi," which means to "steal in." This is clearly reflective of how Batman, that detective of the dark night, operates. A main role for the ninja was to work as spies hired by the feuding warlords in Japan. Ninja trained in empty hand fighting involving all aspects of combat and also used almost every kind of weaponry. These included short swords, staffs, blowguns, and explosives.

The ninja were also were famous for the use of thrown weapons. These could be either dart-like (*shuriken*) or in discs in the shape of stars (*shaken*). This is where the throwing stars that pop up in pretty much every martial arts movie come from. These have a striking similarity to the batarang that Batman uses. Ninja also had to scale many castle walls, using special climbing gear that included metal "claws" that they wore on their hands and feet called *shuko*. If you look back at Figure 5.2 showing Batman using suction cups to climb a wall in Gotham City, all you have to do is replace that building with a castle and the suction cups with shuko and you have a ninja!

Another parallel between Batman and ninja is the element of concealment. Ninja sported black full-body coverings and masks on their stealthy nighttime missions. Can you see a connection to Batman's dark clothing, Batcave, secret identity, and nighttime prowling activities? Also, ninja like Batman left nothing to chance, carrying their six essentials tools on them when they were about: a short length of bamboo, a rope, a hat, a towel, a stone pencil, and medicine. Doesn't that remind you of Batman's utility belt, his "silken cord," and his grappling hook? You could look at ninja as the equivalent of modern-day special forces and secret operatives in the military. By the way, and this will have more resonance when we get to Chapter 14, women were commonly trained as ninja alongside men.

1868 was the year that marked the end of the Tokugawa feudal system in Japan and the rise of Western influences. This was when Western weapons began to arrive in Japan and to supplant the ninja and the samurai. Over time these warrior and martial traditions were handed down and, in times of peace, became pastimes. This is essentially what happened in Japan where the fighting traditions of the samurai became martial ways for the perfection of the character of participants. Drawing the sword (*iaido*), using the sword (*kenjutsu* or kendo), archery (*kyudo*), among other things, have all become their own traditions.

There are still practitioners of traditions containing these elements of ninjutsu. However, they do not exist as an espionage network anymore. Fujita Seiko was a preeminent twentieth-century martial artist within the Koga style of ninjutsu. Fujita learned from his youth with his grandfather as his teacher. In addition to ninjutsu, Fujita also mastered grappling, fighting with the short staff, and dart throwing. His prowess was so well known that he was employed as a bodyguard for a former prime minister of Japan. Fujita was one of the teachers of Inoue Motokatsu, who was the founder of the martial arts weapons (Okinawan weapons, Ryukyu Kobujutsu Hozon Shinkokai) and empty hand (Yuishinkai) systems that I study. Apparently, Fujita was skilled at throwing just about anything, and he fought with a very aggressive style involving low kicking and attacks to the eyes, groin, and neck. In other words, he used an effective method for real fighting. This is the kind of fighter that Batman would need to be. The way that Batman fights in the movie *Batman Begins* clearly reflects this.

In Table 8.1 I have summarized some of the key similarities (as well as one main difference) between Batman and ninja. The big difference is in the use of bladed weapons. Batman has used bladed weapons in combat extremely rarely. A notable example of when he did can be found in the 2005 graphic novel *Superman/Batman: Supergirl,* in which Batman uses a giant battle-ax in combat. A key distinction is that Batman isn't fighting ordinary criminals here. Instead, he and Superman are fighting hordes of supernatural extraterrestrials on the villain Darkseid's home planet of Apokolips. This was no-holds-barred, out-of-control action, and the normal batarang, empty hand, and staff fighting just weren't going to be enough! So,

TABLE 8.1. Comparison of Batman, ninjutsu, and other martial arts

Feature	Ninja (18th c.)	Batman	Judo	Tae Kwon Do
Stealth and concealment	√	√	X	X
Multiple forms of combat	√	√	√	√
Bladed weapons	√	X	X	X
Projectile weapons	√ (throwing stars & darts)	√ (batarang)	X	X
Masks and full body covering	√	√	X	X
"Utility belt"	√	√	X	X
Climbing and agility	√	√	√/X	√
Use of lethal force	√	X	X	X

even though Batman doesn't use all these weapons all the time, he is skilled in how to use them.

To be a versatile martial artist and to be able to defeat attackers of all types—armed and unarmed—really means understanding deeply armed and unarmed fighting. This exact point was brought up very early in Batman's history in the story "Blackbeard's Crew and the Yacht Society" (Batman #4, 1940). This story has Robin and Batman (actually pictured as Dick Grayson and Bruce Wayne) training in fencing. Dick asks Bruce "What's the good of our knowing how to fence? We don't use foils to fight with today!" Bruce responds by saying "True, but fencing teaches you quickness of movement . . . and besides, in our business it helps to know the use of all weapons." This is a very important point. Even if Batman isn't going to use all the weapons—including guns—or all the hand-to-hand techniques, he certainly will have to defend against them all. He must be well versed in how to use them in order to understand their weaknesses.

The last thing to comment on takes us back to the language analogy I used above. Learning different fighting techniques and patterns and so on may seem kind of abstracted from real combat.

And it is, to a certain extent. That is a bit like learning set phrases when studying a new language. You may never actually say to a real person in a German town "Wie ist das Wetter heute? Der Himmel ist blau und die Sonne scheint." That is, "How's the weather today? The sky is blue and the sun is shining." But it does help to practice those phrases so that you can have an extensive repertoire of responses to draw upon in a real conversation. My favorite Batman example of this is from the story "Eyrie" (Detective Comics #568, 1986), in which Batman finds himself facing, you guessed it, hordes of evil henchmen—again. This time he has a broken rod in his hands which he uses as an "impromptu version . . . of a bo stick." He improvises to use the Okinawan long staff—or bo—with something that is not a staff. This is an example of understanding a general way to use tools like weapons that can transfer to other tools. It is a realistic example of the actual practical utility of martial arts training. By studying many different weapons you learn the way different tools move and the weaknesses and strengths of each. Then, essentially everything becomes a weapon.

So, lots of practice in many different fighting methods is what Batman would need when it comes time to "communicate" with Killer Croc and others. The key point is that there is no fixed huge number needed. It is possible that Batman could get most of his needed skills in one place. As I said above I would put my money on his having been trained as a ninja, as long as this training occurred back in the early twentieth century. He may need training in three martial arts or in five, whatever would provide the experiences at the different ranges and ways of fighting. However, 127 styles of combat are neither necessary nor possible. It does sound impressive, but it would result in a Dark Knight who would be incapable of having a decent conversation in any language.

Batman has the physical skills to justify his martial arts renown. However, less than half of the benefit of Batman's martial arts training is related to his physical prowess. Anyone can be trained to produce adequate physical skills in a few years. However, the main point is that "grace under pressure" that real experts display in times of stress and urgency. Batman needs to be able to produce responses to situations of extreme stress. That requires 6 to 12 years of training to forge such strength of will and calmness of mind and body. It is this mental forging that forms the basis of what we will address in the next chapter.

CHAPTER 9

The Caped Crusader in Combat

CAN YOU KAYO WITHOUT KILLING?

We wondered if Batman might not be passé, because for all of his dark mien he will not inflict more pain than is absolutely necessary, and he will never take a life.
—*DC Comics: A Celebration of the World's Favorite Comic Book Heroes,* by Peter Milligan

Too many Bessarovian Cossacks around here, Robin. If I'd joined you in the fight, some of them may have been injured.
—Adam West as Batman, from the ABC TV series *Batman*

One key to Batman's success in fighting legions of evildoers is that he never really loses his temper, blows his cool, or even gets distracted. He remains calm and mostly detached in his actions and takes out the criminals with precision. OK, OK, he also "cracks wise" from time to time, particularly in the more jovial late 1950s and 1960s, but I'm going to ignore that. That stuff usually happened well after everything was under control anyway and was part of his act to unsettle his opponents. For the most part across the entire history of Batman, he has had that "dark mien" referred to in the quote from Peter Milligan that led off this chapter. Batman represents a blend of high octane fighter with a strong ethical streak.

There is something about the philosophy and way of thinking that flows under the surface in martial arts training that gives Batman this combination of traits. We will also examine Batman's ability to respond to different highly stressful life-and-death scenarios with the ultimate in control. Batman defends himself and Gotham City without using lethal force. So what do you think? Can the Caped Crusader really kayo without killing?

Don't Think of a Pink Elephant

Let's begin with the idea of the dispassionate and calm mind-set that is often a product of martial arts training. A great example of this is a scene in the motion picture *The Last Samurai* (2003), in which a samurai and an American soldier are training together. The samurai is educating Captain Nathan Algren (played by Tom Cruise) about how to think—or actually how not to think—during combat using the Japanese long sword. He mentions, in broken English, that the student "has too much mind."

This may not make much sense when you first hear it. How can you have too much mind? Can "mind" really even be quantified at all? This is actually a very good description of a concept in most martial arts that refers to detachment in combat. In Japanese martial arts this term is called *mushin* or *mushin no shin*, meaning "no mind" or "mind of no mind." This means to be able to focus on the task at hand with no distractions. By the way, don't equate "no mind" as meaning mindless. These aren't the same thing. No mind means not paying any specific attention to anything while simultaneously being ready for everything. Although it seems paradoxical, when you actually focus on one particular thing you close off appreciation or the ability to respond to something else. And, since you cannot predict with perfect certainty what technique will be used in a combat attack, focusing just on one thing will work out well only if you guess correctly!

For example, if Batman were to try to anticipate only a high punch from an opponent, he wouldn't be as ready to respond to a low kick. However, if he remains in a state where he anticipates an attack of some kind—including the possibility of a high punch and a low kick—then he is well placed to respond to any attack from any direction.

When Tiger Woods is lining up a long—which in his case usually means all of four feet—putt to finish off another major tournament, he is in a state related to mushin no shin. Batman would need this same ability to focus on defeating his attackers. This concept is also very similar to what people mean or experience when they "focus" on a task. However, there is a key difference for martial arts and combat, where, unlike sports like golf, Batman could be attacked at any time. This means having to be focused with general attention on someone or something but also having the ability to be aware of other threats. Batman has to be aware not just of threats to himself but also of the safety of the people he is trying to protect or people who just happen to be around when a crazy event is unfolding.

A good example of this appears in the opening panel from the "Hush" story arc (Batman #608–619, 2002–2003). The setting is at an opera that Bruce Wayne had been attending. Suddenly pandemonium ensues when Harley Quinn, an associate of the evil Joker, tries to steal jewelry and money from all those in the audience. Batman suddenly appears, leaping through the orchestra pit and taking in all that is happening around him. Despite the chaos of the scene, he remains calm and detached and thinks strategically about minimizing damage and loss of life. He is the consummate professional peacekeeper in this instance. Right in the first caption his thoughts show he is aware of everyone when he says, "My first responsibility is the safety of the patrons." He is then shown trying to maneuver so that the fight stays localized to the orchestra pit, and he succeeds in keeping the danger to a minimum for everyone else. Clearly the environment is chaotic, yet Batman is able to calmly deal with all issues that arise, including exploding grenades, flying batarangs, mace, and smoke everywhere!

Now, I will admit that it is currently impossible to get actual scientific information about changes in brain activity during a superhero's battle with multiple henchmen in a crowded theater. However, we can get a basic idea of focus and "no mind" and observe someone's brain when he or she imagines doing something. As you may remember, in Chapter 7 I mentioned that the part of the cortex called the supplementary motor area is active both when you actu-

ally do movements and when you think about doing them. Also recall the motor cortex, basal ganglia, and cerebellum discussed in
Chapter 7, in connection with stages of motor learning. Using a
modified form of functional magnetic resonance imaging (fMRI),
activity in the brain during skilled movement has been examined in
golf. The sport represents an interesting blend of fine motor skill and
gross muscular effort. Regardless of the task, expert athletes produce
smooth, effortless, and precise movements. They can also reproduce
the same movement pattern with little difficulty or variability.

John Milton and his colleagues at the University of Chicago
conducted brain imaging while high-skill (members of the LPGA)
and low-skill (novice) golfers imagined the preshot routine for a
one-hundred-yard approach shot. It turns out that more skilled golfers actually have less activity in the areas of the brain associated with
motor learning: the cerebellum and basal ganglia. Golf has some
clear similarities to martial arts but also some key differences. Like
martial arts or crime fighting, golf involves thinking on your feet
and dealing with unforeseen events but certainly doesn't have the
same risk of injury or death as Batman's nocturnal rambles!

If you examined these brain scans (shown in Figure 9.1), you
would be able to see that the supplementary motor cortex is active in
the golf pro. In contrast, the novice golfers tended to show activity in
many other parts of the brain, including those parts of the brain
more active during motor learning (cognitive level of skill learning)
and those related to emotion (the limbic system). In other words,
novices used more brain areas than are needed to simply perform
the golf shot. This means a greater chance of error and a greater possibility for interference and problems. Perhaps you remember that
we thought of the cortex as the CEO and the basal ganglia and cerebellum as its advisors. When these parts of the brain are active, as
was the case with the novice golfers, this means those "advisors" are
trying too hard to speak with the cortex and change the output for
movement. I would call this the difference between a "performance
mind" and a "practice mind."

Let's take a brief detour and look at how emotion affects motor
control. Emotion and the limbic system belong to very ancient
parts of our nervous systems. This part of the brain has very powerful effects on almost all other parts of the nervous system. Martial artists have long known about this, and Batman is certainly
aware of this. In "Daughter of the Demon" (Batman #232, 1971),

Expert
(Batman)

Novice
(Bruce)

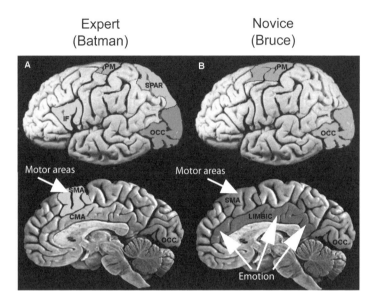

Figure 9.1. Brain imaging of expert (A) and not-so-expert (B) golfers shows less activity in the areas related to emotional (limbic) processing in the expert. Relative stages of Batman's training are indicated for comparison. Courtesy Ana Solodkin, Steve L. Small, and John Milton.

the nefarious R'as al Ghul is berating Batman for not showing enough emotion. In this story Robin and the bad guy's daughter Talia have both been kidnapped and whisked away somewhere. R'as has enlisted Batman's help to find his daughter. While they are developing a plan and trying to find Robin and Talia, Batman is shown reflecting on the situation in a very dispassionate way. He realizes how powerful and potentially dangerous it would be to let emotion carry him away. Batman finally replies and says "It won't do me any good to allow my emotions to gain control . . . for years I've trained myself to concentrate on the thing at hand." This is an excellent example of the "no mind" concept being extended to an overall detachment needed for cool decisions in combat and action planning.

The bottom line is that when it comes to brain activity during movement, less is often more. As in more efficient and more skilled.

You have probably noticed something like this but maybe just didn't think of it quite this way. Golf is again a good example, but it could be any activity that involves targets and skilled performance. You may have been doing really well but then out of nowhere made a bad play. Now all of a sudden you began to think about every aspect of your movements including the basic way to do each part of the skill. This put you right back into the cognitive or associative stages of motor learning (see Figure 7.5).

Recall that when we are learning motor skills, we move from the practice mind all the way to the automatic performance mind. We have all heard comments about golfers, tennis players, and other skilled athletes that they are "thinking too much about" what they are doing. When hitters are in a slump in baseball "overthinking things" is almost always invoked as an explanation of what has happened. It is interesting to reflect that this does not represent a hard-wired shift in how the brain operates. Instead we can move back and forth between practice and performance, but to be effective we must be able to regulate this shift.

Even the best and most highly skilled professional athletes, however, can be beaten by this interference. The example that I always think of is the 1996 British Open held at Carnoustie Golf Links in Angus, Scotland, and the way in which Jean van de Velde came apart on the final hole. After making a decision to use a driver off the eighteenth tee that produced a wayward shot, it was almost like his entire performance switched to "practice mind." Then every shot he tried to make went awry. Even the decisions about what shots to make seemed clouded by something not related to calm cool performance. This is an example of the "too much mind" we discussed above for *The Last Samurai*. In the case of golf there will be another shot, another tournament, another chance. In the case of Batman and his exploits and for real-life police officers, firefighters, and soldiers, who face real and present dangers and must perform at a high level under stress, it may be fatal to make a mistake.

Many years of training are needed to obtain the frame of mind of mushin no shin. Batman needed to practice movements and movement sequences until they could be performed unconsciously and arise almost spontaneously. This means that he needs to truly be in the automatic stage of motor learning that we talked about in Chapter 7. Remember that the state of no mind doesn't mean mindless! In fact, in trying to describe these mental states, we can look to what the famous Zen master Takuan Soho once wrote in his book *The Unfettered Mind*:

> The mind must always be in the state of "flowing," for when it stops anywhere that means the flow is interrupted and it is this interruption that is injurious to the well-being of the mind. In the case of the swordsman, it means death. When the swordsman stands against his opponent, he is not to think of the opponent, nor of himself, nor of his enemy's sword movements. He just stands there with his sword which, forgetful of all technique, is ready only to follow the dictates of the subconscious. The man has effaced himself as the wielder of the sword. When he strikes, it is not the man but the sword in the hand of the man's subconscious that strikes.

This mentality forms the heart of Batman's performance in combat and of his approach to combat and other activities.

Related to the concept of mushin is another martial arts "-shin" —*zanshin*. Zanshin basically means "remaining mind" and refers to the idea that awareness of danger or activity continues even after something has occurred. This is related to another concept called *gan*, which is an all-encompassing awareness of danger. In altercations, these concepts relate to maintaining awareness of the possible threat from an attacker at all times, even when he may appear to be subdued or to have given up.

Good examples of the absence of the zanshin mind can be found in almost any "teen slasher" horror movie ever made. Invariably in these movies the good guy defeats some evil human or monster and then moves on and leaves the scene for happier times. However, rarely does the good guy actually check to see if the bad guy is really unconscious or fully defeated after the fight seems to be over. Instead, almost always from a considerable distance away, he or she just has a look and assumes everything is fine. It is maddening watching this unfold. Sometimes another of the good guy cast will arrive on the scene, inquire about what happened to the villain, and then be told that everything is fine and that the bad guy is defeated. Then the good guy is suddenly caught unawares a few minutes later by the rejuvenated bad guy and more fighting ensues. This kind of thing does, admittedly, make for a dramatic finale to a movie. But allowing this to happen wouldn't be OK for Batman or other crimefighters, real or fictional.

Dorothy, We're Not in the Batcave Anymore

Batman is hardly ever active in what could be called a "controlled environment." Most of Batman's activities actually take place in what I would call an "out of control" environment. Total chaos—like that we saw at the opera earlier in the chapter—is often going on all around, and Batman is in the midst of it trying to defend himself, save the innocents, and take out the bad guys all without seriously injuring anyone. He can do all his training and practice in a regulated environment, but when he is called into action to battle the worst that Gotham City has to offer, he has to deal with whatever conditions are at hand. Batman is typically fighting in unstable environments that are similar to military, paramilitary, or police combat scenarios. This is where the concept of stress again makes an appearance. We have discussed stress in many different guises throughout the book. Now I want you to look at it in its most familiar form, one that you or I might look at and say "that situation is very stressful." For me, it would be most of Batman's battles!

What is known about the kind of stressful environment or situations we want to consider here? Features of high stress include sudden and unexpected events that demand immediate responses. These usually involve high time pressure, noise, heat, smoke, darkness, and other stressors. Also, and here is often the most important factor, a high-stress situation usually is one in which failure to perform properly will result in immediate and extreme negative consequences. Over top of all of this, a key feature of combat-related scenarios is that extreme threat is present. In military speak this means a "kill or be killed" level of stress. When all these are lumped together, even ordinary and routine procedures can be difficult to perform. Mistakes—often with dire consequences—can occur.

How all this stress can affect performance has been explored by Driskell and colleagues in military analysis of the tragic accidental shooting down of an Iranian passenger plane during the Iran-Iraq war. On July 3, 1988, the United States naval warship USS *Vincennes* was patrolling in the Persian Gulf. At mid-morning Iran Air Flight 655 took off with a flight plan that, after seven minutes of flying, put it directly over the USS *Vincennes*. The Iran passenger jet had left from an airport that had combined civilian and military activity. This plane was mistakenly identified as an Iranian F-14 fighter jet and was shot down by the *Vincennes*, killing all 290 passengers and crew.

It seems unfathomable that this could really have happened, doesn't it? Shouldn't it be a relatively easy task to identify aircraft appropriately and to take appropriate action (or not take action in this case)? Well, I think the answer would surely be "yes" if the environment in which all this occurred was calm, controlled, and predictable. However, we need to consider this situation more closely. We need to think about whether the Iranian plane could have appeared as a threat to the *Vincennes,* the actual time available to decide what to do, and whatever else may have been happening at the time the plane was identified.

As it turns out the USS *Vincennes* was not just sitting peacefully at rest in the Persian Gulf. Instead, this was during wartime, and the ship was constantly under threat from Iranian F-14s. In fact, fighter jets often took off from the same airport as the doomed Iran Air flight and during the month before this tragedy, ships of the U.S. Navy in the Persian Gulf had issued more than a hundred challenges to threatening aircraft. So, the jetliner could easily have been interpreted as a threat.

Time pressure was also high. There were only about three minutes between the time that the Iran Air flight first became a potential threat and the time it was shot down. So, not much time was available to ponder a course of action. Also, while all this was going on and the Iran Air flight was in the air, the *Vincennes* was engaged in a surface-to-surface battle with an Iranian naval ship. This meant that the USS *Vincennes* was maneuvering at high speed, firing its guns, all while being fired upon. The crew was therefore operating in an extreme, high-noise environment with changing lighting conditions on a ship pitching on the ocean surface.

So, what we are really discussing here is an emergency situation of extreme acute stress. Clearly, the conclusion that the Iran Air flight was an F-14 that was about to attack the USS *Vincennes* was not correct. The main point of discussing this example was to make clear just how much human performance and judgment degrade when in an extremely stressful environment.

We can transfer the general principles that emerged from the tragic naval incident to Batman's activities of fighting criminals. This means considering Batman's arousal level related to the level of stress. In psychology this has been described as the "inverted U" (shown in Figure 9.2), which depicts an optimal level of arousal due to stress that allows for the best performance. Remember no stress is bad. You need some stress to have enough arousal to perform. However, adding more stress to further increase arousal leads to a decrease in performance. So, Batman's performance will increase while his arousal level increases up to the top of the inverted U. Beyond this point, his performance will decrease. This has drastic implications for things like defeating criminals. Also, different activities have different places on the inverted U. The arousal level needed for maximum performance in golf is much lower than for maximum performance as an NFL running back. Also, different athletes respond differently to stress, and how they respond can change with training.

This idea of training can also be seen in the progression from Bruce to The Bat-Man to the finished Batman, shown in panel B of Figure 9.2. The beginner Bruce can only tolerate a very small stress level and a modest arousal to perform well. At the far right, the fully trained Batman has a better performance at much higher stress levels.

Part of the big problem of performance under conditions of extreme stress is related to something termed "perceptual narrowing." This term refers pretty much to what you probably guess—the more stressed you are, the less you will be able to pay attention. This phenomenon also occurs when we learn movement skills because we focus exclusively on certain elements. (Remember that when Bruce was first learning his kick in Chapter 7, he had to think about every step, but as Batman he no longer had to be aware of every aspect.) When things are narrowed this means that there simply isn't room for handling many different activities in the environment. With reference to the inverted U, when you are highly aroused—and beyond the maximum point—perceptual narrowing occurs while performance drops way off. This means that you have difficulty paying attention to and evaluating the importance of all the information in the environment. In this way you can miss some important things.

Have you ever wondered why a player in a team sport like basketball can miss an obvious pass that he or she should have been able to throw directly to a defender? Perceptual narrowing was occurring. This tends to happen when there are many players moving quickly and converging on the player who makes the mistake.

Baseball players and managers intuitively know this (but may not call it perceptual narrowing or stress) when they encourage their players to always run as hard as possible down to first base after a ball has been hit. Even if it looks like a routine out, if the third baseman thinks that there is a chance that the runner may actually make it

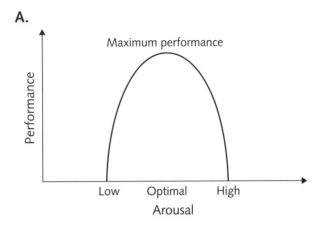

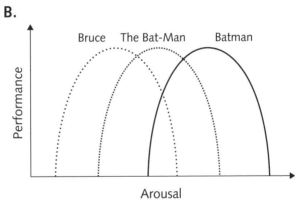

Figure 9.2. Inverted U relationship between arousal and performance for Batman. *A:* We can see that Batman's performance increases as his arousal level rises up to the maximum point shown at the top of the inverted U. Beyond this point, his performance will decrease. *B:* The progression from Bruce to The Bat-Man to the finished Batman. Beginner Bruce (*far left*) can tolerate only a small stress level and a modest arousal to perform well. In contrast, fully trained Batman (*far right*) has a better performance at much higher stress levels.

safely to first base, he may be distracted enough to not notice the ball take a slightly funny hop as he goes to pick it up. Then, because of the odd hop, the ball isn't exactly in his glove right where he expects it, and he doesn't grab it cleanly. All of a sudden his routine throw for the automatic out at first base goes too high, pulling the first baseman up and off the base, and the runner is safe. And it all happened because of the stress put on the third baseman by the actions of the runner.

When you are under stress, perceptual narrowing can reduce acuity in peripheral vision. That means you really cannot attend to other factors because you cannot actually perceive them at all! In fact this really forms a kind of selective attention, wherein we don't always pay attention to the right things.

There are also many examples in sports where the exact opposite occurs. Some players seem unflappable and impervious to pressure. They don't seem to succumb to this problem of perceptual narrowing. Two-time NBA MVP Steve Nash seems to be able to make passes to teammates who are just exactly where they ought to be to receive the pass, despite the fact that it should be almost impossible for him to see where they are. He seems almost to know where they will be and to able to see the whole court. One of my favorite athletes, former NHL player Wayne Gretzky, always appeared as if he could see all parts of the ice surface and knew not just where everyone was but where they would be at just the right moment to receive his passes. In these cases it is almost like the game slows down for the players.

Can a person train to do this, though? Many people can have the skill to do the physical performance needed but not everyone has the "grace under pressure" to perform calmly when needed. Let's consider what police and paramilitary forces use more and more these days to get at full-on live-fire situations in training. They use what is called "reality-based training." In very basic terms the main point of reality-based training is to incorporate training and responses in environments that can be very chaotic and that mimic the kind of stressors that a police officer might experience during a real encounter.

This is how we imagine Batman being trained and operating. His training, including the use of reality-based activity, would have allowed him to see the whole environment and would have made him largely immune to the stress of combat. Because of this, he can deal with all adversaries without problems and remain completely in control. The combat scenes in the movie *Batman Begins* are filmed with this idea very much at the fore. Another great example of this is found in a story called "Citizen Wayne," taken from the 1992 graphic novel *Blind Justice*. Here Bruce is undergoing some ninja-like training by Henri Ducard and is shown passing his test of defeating multiple attackers in an utterly chaotic environment. In the aftermath of his success, Ducard says to Bruce, "Excellent. Four attackers disabled, with no loss of life." So, not only was Batman able to skillfully work through and subdue four attackers in utter chaos, but he did so without killing any of them. This is a big part of becoming Batman. That is, being able to fight against those set upon trying to kill him while not dealing out mortal injury. And that brings us to the last part of this chapter. Is it really possible to become Batman and not use lethal force?

Can You Kayo without Killing?

We will finish this chapter by discussing the possibility of defeating as many enemies as does Batman without mortally injuring any of them. Batman is opposed to dealing out lethal force. This was recently illustrated in the film *Batman Begins* by a conversation between Bruce Wayne and Ducard, who tells Bruce that he has to demonstrate a commitment to justice and so Ducard brings in a prisoner to be executed by Bruce as part of his training. Bruce says "I'm no executioner." This statement is questioned by Ducard: "Your compassion is a weakness your enemies will not share." (You can see that this is a different version of Ducard from the one in *Blind Justice* above!) Bruce responds that this is "why it's so important. It separates us from them." Also, in the *No Man's Land* (1999) story arc, Batman states that "knowing how to kill doesn't mean you must kill."

This concept of not killing even in defense is preserved in a saying that sounds like it ought to be a legitimate martial arts saying directly from the Shaolin Temple. But it isn't. "Learn the ways to preserve rather than destroy; avoid rather than check; check rather than hurt; hurt rather than maim, maim rather than kill; for all life is precious, nor can any be replaced." This saying has been often used in martial arts stories and has been ascribed to Shaolin monks, but I have not been able to track down a reliable source. This phrase can be found on many Web sites and in many documents as either a Shaolin precept or creed. However, it seems to have no real historical roots in true Chinese Shaolin martial arts. Instead, this phrase can certainly be traced to the *Kung Fu* television series of the 1970s starring David Carradine. This phrase was spoken by Master Kan to a young Kwai Chang Caine in an episode from 1972. It was also later (or earlier depending upon how you reason the Star Wars timelines!) used by Yoda in the movie *Star Wars: Episode III: Revenge of the Sith*. There is no verifiable evidence that it was ever written by anyone in or related to the Shaolin Temple near Dengfeng in Henan Province, People's Republic of China. The quote does capture the essence of using nonlethal force that Batman adheres to and that many adherents of martial arts would identify with.

Despite the violence of his means, Batman deeply believes that life is precious. In "One Bullet Too Many" (Batman #217, 1969), Bruce Wayne, with Batman's masked countenance in the background, says that "All humanity is important to Batman—any life, no matter how insignificant in the public eye!" Clearly this concept forms the main philosophy guiding Batman's actions.

That is really an admirable approach. But here we are exploring if it is really possible to engage in nonlethal combat on a routine basis and emerge either with very little injury or without actually killing your opponent. Batman has a long history of nonlethal combat in which he incapacitates the bad guys without killing them.

In fact, Batman's use of lethal force was extremely rare. In his first appearance in "The Case of the Chemical Syndicate" (Detective Comics #27, 1939), Batman (actually then still "The Bat-Man") fights several criminals while on a rooftop. At one point he "grabs his second adversary in a deadly headlock . . . and with a might heave . . . sends the burly criminal flying through space." Although it is never definitively stated, we do see the burly criminal lying crumpled on a sidewalk, and it seems very clear that "The Bat-Man" has hurled him to his doom.

Despite this one exception, it is notable that Batman not only eschews deadly force but also weapons that carry with them almost certain lethal force—guns. Early on in the Batman history he occasionally used a gun. However, this was so rare as to easily stand out. In "Professor Hugo Strange and the Monsters" (Batman #1, 1940), Batman has another rare example of lethal force when shooting at a fleeing van, while he soars above it in an early version of the Batplane. Batman does say, while taking aim with the machine gun in the cockpit, "Much as I hate to take human life, I'm afraid this time it's necessary." His shots appear to indeed kill the van driver, causing the vechicle to crash into a tree, and thus freeing one of the monsters in the story's title.

He seems to have taken his current ethical stand soon after this. In "Victory for the Dynamic Duo" (Batman #4, 1941), Batman takes up a handgun that has been "dropped by a thug, takes careful aim—and fires." He says "Just want to wing him" and he does, simply shooting the culprit's hand. At this point in the story it is clear the editorial team wants to make a firm note of the Batman position on gunplay. At the bottom of one panel is written "Editor's note: The Batman never carries or kills with a gun!" As far as I have been able to find out, he did not use a gun again and only picked one up during the initial story of the *Batman Beyond* animated series (see Chapter 15), an event so traumatic that Batman chose to retire (temporarily!) after it. In fact it is clear in all subsequent Batman stories that he holds the firearm in the lowest regard. He often spouts lines such as this one from "The Cat" (Batman #1, 1940): "Crooks are yellow without their guns."

Batman's abhorrence of lethal force with empty hand fighting also is nicely captured in "Spirit of the Bat" (Batman #509, 1994). This was part of the "Batman Knightfall" story arc that I refer to extensively throughout this book. In "Spirit of the Bat" Bruce attempts to regain his edge after his defeat at the hands of Bane. He goes in search of Lady Shiva, his most respected martial arts opponent from over the years. Shiva is a formidable opponent, and Batman realizes she can help him regain his former capacity. However, her help comes at a price, which includes trying to set Batman up so that he must kill (he doesn't). As part of this training Shiva shows a special technique called the "leopard blow." She says, "Its mastery causes death with a single strike." Batman's response is "Then it is a lesson, Lady Shiva . . . which is best not taught."

I bring all this up to provide a context for how Batman operates. Also, though, it highlights a main element of the Batman ethos: nothing about training to become or being Batman is easy. The easy way to dispatch thugs, criminals, and pathological supervillains would be to use firearms or at least some form of bladed projectile weapon. However, with the rare exception—the batarang being the most obvious and frequently used—Batman engages in close-quarter unarmed combat with most of his foes. It is also relevant that despite Batman's considerable experience and skill with all manner of martial arts weaponry, he has only infrequently used a bladed weapon.

Figure 9.3. Advancing skill and ethics in martial arts. The way the good guy, dressed totally in white, deals with the threat and attack of the bad guy, wearing some black, shows how ethics in combat change with skill. At the lowest skill level, the easiest response is of the novice is to deal lethal force in response to lethal force. With intermediate skills, the good guy has a weapon but defeats the attacker by disarming him without injuring him. At the culmination of training as an expert, the good guy defeats and then disarms the bad guy without using any weapons at all. Courtesy Westbrook and Ratti.

This is in keeping with his overall objective of nonlethal combat and can be seen in an extreme degree in the philosophy of the martial art of aikido. An example of this is shown graphically in Figure 9.3. To make it easy, this figure is put together just like a Western movie. The good guy is dressed totally in white, whereas the bad guy is wearing black (either a shirt or pants). The way the good guy deals with the threat and attack of the bad guy shows how ethics in combat change with skill. At the lowest skill level, the easiest response is to deal lethal force in response to lethal force. In the intermediate phase, the good guy has a weapon and defeats the attacker and disarms him but without actually injuring him. By the culmination of training, the good guy now defeats and then is able to also disarm the bad guy all without using any weapons at all. The message is meant to be that the ultimate objective of training should be to defeat an attacker or aggressor without causing him harm. This is a pretty tall order, though, in real life-and-death interactions with attackers bent on killing you.

Is it feasible to fight as often as Batman fights and emerge most of the time as the victor without using lethal force? It probably goes without saying that the level of skill needed to do this is extremely high. Many martial traditions may at least have this as an objective of training, however difficult it is to achieve. Batman's approach to criminals also reflects what is known as a "use of force hierarchy" or "use of force options" in modern police services. These terms describe the idea that a police officer ratchets up the use of force depending upon the scenario.

While the details differ from jurisdiction to jurisdiction and country to country, a general hierarchy is like that shown for Batman's use-of-force options in Figure 9.4. This figure is to be read from bottom to top, with the lowest step being Batman's mere physical presence frightening away the criminal and the topmost step, shown with a big X, representing lethal force. We now know that Batman will never get there. The point is that if step 1 works, if just "showing his face" (or really his mask) is all Batman needs to do, then great. There is no need to go farther. This often does the trick for Batman, actually.

A fantastic example of this is found in the Batman "Tears of Blood" (Batman #529, 1996). In this story, Nightwing, Robin, Huntress, and others have been caught and penned in by an out-of-control mob. They are barely holding their own until Batman arrives. As soon as the mob recognizes his silhouette, the crowd begins to thin out and move on. Then all Batman says is "Disperse—now" and that is that. As written at the bottom left of the panel "Major intimidation and not a knuckle dusted."

However, if needed, Batman will take the next step by trying to reason with criminals and then will engage them in hand-to-hand fighting, use knockout gas, or use weapons if they will not yield.

Part and parcel with being able to make a use-of-force continuum work is that there must be extreme motivation for the criminals to give in. What else can Batman do to help give himself the best advantage when he does fight his enemies? Clearly, he isn't going to

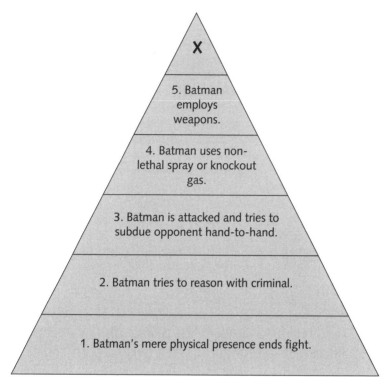

Figure 9.4. Batman's use-of-force hierarchy, reading from *bottom* to *top*, indicates escalating force. At the pinnacle of the pyramid is a big X, which represents lethal force.

grab a gun to help even the odds. What else can he do? First of all Batman ensures that his foes are nowhere near their best on those performance-arousal curves we discussed earlier.

Now, what I am about to say next may seem simplistic, but it is an essential point. A really good way to ensure that the criminals Batman must fight are in no shape to fight is to scare them silly! This is actually the major reason for the coloration and look of the batsuit. Bruce Wayne has reflected numerous times that "criminals are a superstitious and cowardly lot," and he designed the batsuit to scare them. Thinking back to the "fight or flight" stress response we discussed in

Chapter 3, Batman wants the "flight" response in his enemies. As shown in many of the reworkings of Batman's origin story, a bat was chosen because so many people are afraid of bats. In "Broken City" (Batman #620–625, 2003–2004), Batman says "I wear a mask. And that mask, it's not to hide who I am, but to create what I am."

Batman rarely skips levels on the use-of-force hierarchy and only uses the force needed to subdue the opponent. However, despite his best intentions this is a very dangerous approach to take. Any small error means that Batman could be killed or injured. In theory the use of incapacitating nerve strikes, chokes, locks, and other blunt impact techniques should subdue most assailants. However, when opponents are in extreme rages or have taken psychotropic drugs, many of the more subtle techniques will be ineffective, leading rapidly up the use-of-force hierarchy. Similarly, real police officers are at risk when they attempt to take down a suspect. They must make a quick judgment of danger and use appropriate force. For example, on this hierarchy the use of tear gas, while uncomfortable, is nonlethal and is a preferred increment before the use of weapons that carry with them the increased possibility of serious injury or death. The bottom line is that it is not very simple to be an effective crimefighter while simultaneously trying to keep the well-being of your attacker at the front of your mind. Batman in the comic books and movies does an admirable job. But the reality is that this would be next to impossible to implement in real combat situations engaged in every day.

In the Batman stories, though, we must recall that Batman is the ultimate martial artist. He has the highest training and is a natural and gifted fighter. He also has the mental fortitude and the psychological capacity to take on all comers and present himself in the best and most formidable light. A byproduct of all this training is Batman's inherent self-confidence and well-founded faith in his abilities.

In closing this chapter I want to leave you with a quote from "Public Enemies" (Superman/Batman #1–6, 2003–2004). In this panel Superman and Batman are fighting against a huge gang of President Lex Luthor's henchmen. In my view this panel is the best illustration of the warrior attitude that Batman brings with him—and still manages to balance with the ethics of combat we just discussed. He and Superman are surrounded and outnumbered. Just before they leap into action, Superman comments that Batman "always thinks we can take them." To which Batman says "Yes, I do." And into battle they go and on to a safe victory.

Now we know that Batman does all he can to keep from injuring others. Let's look at what happens when—and you know it has to happen sometime!—Batman gets injured himself.

PART IV

BATMAN IN ACTION

Knight moves with Batman when he acts as the Caped Crusader

CHAPTER 10

Batman Bashes and and Is Bashed by Bad Boys (and Girls)

WHAT CAN HE BREAK WITHOUT GETTING BROKEN?

Batman was not a super-hero, nor, of course, am I. He wasn't bitten by a radioactive spider. He had no superpowers . . . He earned every bit of what he had, fired by an iron resolve.
—*Batman Illustrated* by Neal Adams

Batman is capable of some pretty cool stuff. He can punch, kick, and throw with wild abandon and just generally sport around like nobody's business. There are, of course, limits to what we human beings can actually do. These limits have to do with how our bodies work when we try to produce movement. Batman clearly pushes all these limits and is a really powerful fighter. In "Death Flies the Haunted Sky!" (Detective Comics #442, 1974), a panel shows that the villain Batman is fighting is practically incapacitated from what Batman describes as "just a tap." In the panel he says that "a real hit would have hurt," and in so doing echoes his fighting code of ethics we discussed in the last chapter.

But how hard could Batman punch and kick, anyway? How many bad guys could he hit in one second? How is it possible for a person to break concrete blocks with his bare hands? In this chapter we look at how much Batman would be able to do as a mere mortal and also at whether all the fighting he undergoes would have an impact on his mortality (or on his health and well-being, at least!).

To consider these questions we are going to do a sort of superficial biomechanical analysis of kicking, striking, throwing, and joint locking. As we discussed in Chapter 8, most martial arts systems have differing proportions of these components. In our examples here we are going to use karate, wing chun, and boxing to stand in for kicking and striking; judo for throwing; and aikido for those most related to joint locking.

Do you remember muscle forces from Chapter 4? To bring you back up to speed, (1) a message from the brain (2) causes contractile proteins in our muscles to produce force that then (3) acts on the bones of our skeletons and (4) produces movement. This series of actions is a form of Sir Isaac Newton's first law of motion: "An object at rest will remain at rest unless acted upon by an external and unbalanced force. An object in motion will remain in motion unless acted upon by an external and unbalanced force." Now we are going to put these forces to use in combat.

Going with the Flow . . . of Energy

Let's begin with concepts related to kicking and punching, as these actions would be done in a martial art such as karate. First let's look at how explosive power can be generated by people of relatively small stature. Think about Bruce Lee and the powerful punches and kicks he could produce. Movements like punches and kicks are considered ballistic actions. By ballistic here I don't mean going crazy but rather something that goes in a trajectory—something that once in motion remains in motion in a given direction (just like in Newton's law above).

Any time movements that are essentially ballistic are performed, the concept of summation (or adding) of forces comes into play. This concept applies equally well to the punch of Bruce Lee or Batman as it does to the fastball of your favorite pitcher. Think of the body as a set of linked parts or segments. We could start just with the arm and think of the upper arm (the part from shoulder to elbow), the fore-arm (from elbow to wrist), and the hand (from wrist to knuckles or fingers) as each being separate segments. Of course, we really do need to consider more than this, but I will get to that in a moment. We have muscles acting on or across each segment to bring the upper arm forward, extend the forearm, and turn the wrist. Summation of forces refers to the adding each of the forces produced by muscles for each segment. Typically the timing of muscle activity is in what is called a proximal (closer) to distal (farther away) pattern. In this case, that would be from shoulder to hand. This usually means that the strongest muscle groups—typically those closest to the body core—contract first followed by the weaker, distal muscles. Soon we look at some numbers to give a better idea of how forces are added. I know you can't wait for a little (and I promise a little!) math.

Before coming back to Batman, I want to think of a more common example. Think about the mechanics—restricted just to the arm for now—of pitching a baseball or throwing a football. Once the arm is brought back in preparation for throwing, the basic motion involves rotating the shoulder, then bringing the upper arm forward. After this process is started you see that you are extending your elbow during the motion—but not at the beginning of the motion. Last, the motion of the wrist is added on to the motions at the shoulder and elbow. Then the football or baseball is released to move toward the target. The principle of summation of forces is really no different from the relative motion examples used in high school physics classes. You know the one where someone throws a ball at 50 mph while stationary on the ground. Next that same person throws the ball at 50 mph but this time while standing on the flatbed of a big truck that is traveling in the same direction at 50 mph. How fast is the ball traveling relative to the ground in the second case (neglecting air resistance, of course!)? Now we have an ordinary Joe who can pitch a baseball at 100 mph.

I said earlier that we needed to consider the motions of the body in addition to that of the arm. Using the example of baseball pitching again, this means that we have to pay attention to the fact that the trunk rotates and the player pushes with his legs. Actually, good pitchers throw the ball with their entire body, not just with one arm. Batman's punches are no different. When he punches he uses his whole body, including the segments of his trunk and legs, added all together with his arm motions to hit the target. If he steps forward to punch, he is also adding together now the energy from his forward step onto that of his punching arm. All of this adds the motion of each segment together such that peak velocities are all added up for each segment. This means that Batman's punch will hit the target with as high a velocity as possible.

Why is velocity so important? Well, what Batman is trying to develop in his kicking foot or punching hand—and also what a pitcher is trying to achieve with a baseball—is maximum kinetic energy, or energy of motion (recall our discussion in Chapter 6). Kinetic energy is defined as $\frac{1}{2}m \times V^2$, where m is the mass of the object (hand, foot, baseball, etc.) and V is the velocity at which the object is moving. (See, I promised you some math!) To hit the target with the largest impact forces possible, the highest kinetic energy is needed.

In the example of a punch, Batman is really having a collision between his fist and the chest or face of Joker, Killer Croc, or Bane. In such a collision, the time of impact is very important. This brings us to a term from physics, *impulse*, which is defined as force × time. A small force applied over a long time can be the same impulse as a high force applied over a short time. Thus, this same impulse from both scenarios can create the same change in momentum of the object to which the force is being applied.

However, in the case of crime fighting, speed is often essential. So, Batman needs to move quickly with high forces to change the direction of his foes' attacks as well as plant some debilitating blows of his own. Here we are talking about derivations from Sir Isaac Newton's second law of motion: "The rate of change of momentum of a body is proportional to the resultant force acting on the body and is in the same direction." This law applies to the forces acting within Batman's body, as his muscles work together to produce movement. It also concerns forces Batman's whole body applies to the evildoers who are the target of Batman's controlling forces.

Now let's talk about a term you may be more familiar with: "collision." When you collide with another car, damaging yours, it is generally an accident. When Batman punches the Penguin or his henchmen, it is a deliberate collision. Luckily for Batman, the human body is nowhere near as rigid as a car! Remember our pitcher? His arm moves in segments, and the force of his pitch was the sum of the force of the segments. This provides much needed flexibility and reduces damage to ourselves when we collide with an object. However, at impact the muscles remain tense to provide rigidity to the fist so that maximum transfer of force and energy from Batman's hand into the target occurs. As part of this, Batman also tries to strike through the target somewhat so that impact moves into the physical space occupied by Killer Croc or the Joker. Also, the targets themselves have some flexibility in the softness of their flesh and muscles and in the fact that they will move back on reflex when someone comes forward to punch them! Too bad the criminals are not made of wood or concrete! We'll learn more about what happens when you collide with these substances later.

Something else to keep in mind regarding striking and kicking is in martial arts it is preferred to strike small targets using small parts of the body. This action increases the pressure of the attack because pressure is equal to the applied force divided by the surface area over which that force is applied (in a mathematical formula: pressure = force × area). Think of high-heeled shoes. Imagine someone putting a running shoe on one foot and a stiletto high-heeled shoe on the other. With which foot would you rather be stepped on? Obviously, the stiletto heel will hurt much more. But the force of gravity pulling down the mass of the woman in both cases is the same. The surface areas are different, though, and so are the pressures.

Good examples for fighting are knife hand and sword hand strikes (we will revisit the knife hand in the next chapter). The tips of the fingers are the striking surface with the knife hand and represent a very small surface area. In this way, maximum force is imparted to the target over a small area. Other examples include using the side edge of the foot instead of the sole of the foot for side kicks, the ball of the foot instead of the instep for front kicks, and the area of the first two knuckles only and not all four knuckles when punching.

Boards Don't Fight Back

With all this in mind let's return to some of the questions I led off this chapter with. How powerful are martial arts blows? In karate a good way to get a handle on this is to look at the practice of what is called *tameshiwari*, or test breaking. This practice follows on from the much older practice in Japanese swordsmanship known as *tameshigiri*, or test cutting. Tameshiwari refers to the test breaking of materials like wood and concrete to gauge the skill and preparation of the strikes applied. There are four things to consider in this analysis: the force generated, the peak velocity of the body part used, the energy generated by the blow, and the deformation of the material that is struck.

First off, it has been calculated that an expert in karate—and this would be similar for any of the striking arts—can generate a striking force greater than 3,000 N (in which N stands for newtons, a measurement of force used in the metric system), or approximately 675 pounds. Is that a large force? Well, to break materials of simple structure like wood requires a force of 670 N (about 150 pounds), while concrete needs 3,100 N (almost 700 pounds). To break bone such as that in the jaw requires a force of only 1,100 N (about 250 pounds).

However, in many altercations a broken jaw isn't the biggest worry; it is getting a concussion (which we will look at more in Chapter 13). Forces in the range of approximately 800 N (about 180 pounds) applied for only eight milliseconds are enough to produce head accelerations of 80 g that can yield a knockout blow. Here the *g* measures the effects of acceleration; it is roughly equivalent to 10 meters (32 feet) per second squared. As with your car, acceleration here means something is going at an increasingly faster speed. To put the number 80 g in perspective, roller coasters usually have a maximum of 3 to 4 g for a few seconds. Fatal car accidents can have a measure of 80 g.

In addition to the magnitude of the force, the velocity of the hand that must be reached to break wood is about 6 meters (about 20 feet) per second, while that for concrete is 10.6 meters (about 35 feet) per second. Remember that to calculate velocity you need two things: how far something is going and how fast its speed is changing. This is determined by dividing change in distance by change in time. The thresholds of hand (or foot) velocities needed to break wood and concrete are shown in Figure 10.1. The plots shown there are for hand techniques, and it is easy to see that wood can certainly be broken with a lower velocity strike than can concrete.

Learning to break a single pine board of one-inch thickness with something like a hammer fist strike is pretty easy. Almost anyone can do it with a little practice. Referring to my training terms here, even "Bruce" could do it! However, to break numerous pine boards all stacked together or to break concrete requires much more skill. Back when I was a teenager I used to do breaking as part of demonstrations. The most I ever did was six unfinished pine boards (no spacers!) with a sword hand strike.

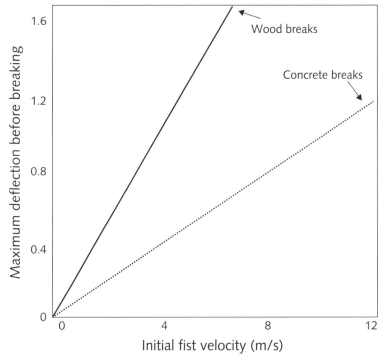

Figure 10.1. Fist velocity and the deflection (in millimeters for concrete and centimeters for wood) needed to break two objects. Modified from Wilk et al. (1982).

A lot of what we know scientifically about the physics of martial arts techniques has come from studies conducted by Michael Feld, Ronald McNair, and Stephen Wilk. The name of McNair may be familiar to you for a tragic reason. McNair was not only a gifted martial artist (fifth-degree black belt holder) and MIT-trained physicist, but he was also a NASA mission specialist on board the ill-fated space shuttle *Challenger* when it exploded on January 28, 1986. McNair had an interest in physics applied to martial arts and was involved in taking measurements of hand and foot velocities from experts in empty hand fighting. I have extracted some of their data into Table 10.1 to give you an idea about the peak velocities of Batman's hands and feet when striking and kicking.

To give another reference, these kinds of impacts have been likened to the force you would receive from Batman if he hit you with a wooden club weighing about 6 kilograms (13 pounds), lightly padded, and swung at about 20 mph. Keep in mind that Babe Ruth, the "Sultan of Swat," used a bat that weighed 1.5 kilograms (3.5 pounds) early on in his career but later used a one-kilogram (2.5-pound) bat. The bat that Barry Bonds used in 2007 to hit his record-setting 756th home run was 85 centimeters (34 inches) long and weighted about .9 kilogram (2 pounds). It is worth noting that elite baseball players can swing the bat with peak speeds of about 90 mph. An equivalent baseball bat impact for Batman's kick or punch would need a Barry Bonds style bat swung at about 45 mph. Of course, hitting with a maple bat and hitting with a closed fist do not produce identical impacts. However, this at least gives you a ballpark—sorry, pun intended—idea as to how hard those empty hand hits would be.

So the forces and velocities generated by experts such as Batman are well able to break such seemingly hard objects as wood, concrete, and bone. Now let's look at why Batman's hand doesn't break while he is dealing all these blows. It stands to reason that if the forces generated in a hand strike are large enough to break bone and concrete they should also break the hand, too, shouldn't they? Well, it isn't quite that simple because of the way the force is applied and the geometry of the part of the body that is used. For example, because the fist is really a collection of bones held together with muscle, tendon,

TABLE 10.1. Maximum velocity of different martial arts techniques in meters per second

Body part	Technique	Maximum velocity (m/s)
Hand	Front punch	10
	Downward hammerfist	14
	Downward sword hand (a.k.a. "karate chop")	14
Foot	Front kick	14
	Back kick	12
	Side kick	14

and connective tissue, it compresses when it hits something instead of breaking. Your bones can actually withstand impact forces much higher than "harder" materials. Remember in Chapter 5 we learned that your bones are basically stretchy material (collagen) embedded with hard minerals. Because of the overall structure of the fist, it can actually withstand forces of up to 25,000 N (more than half a ton) without breaking! It has also been estimated that the foot can withstand two thousand times more force than can a concrete block.

Let's look at how this discussion of force translates into fighting strategies. In Western fighting such as boxing the intention is to impart a large momentum to the entire body mass of the opponent. Boxers both generate and receive repeated blows with high forces. A central strategy is to chip away at the opponent by applying punches to the body and slowly wearing the opponent down. This contrasts with the typical objective of most Eastern martial arts traditions in which a quick and expeditious finish to any altercation is the focus. Many of the empty hand traditions actually operate around principles that are similar to those from the weapons traditions, particularly those of cutting bladed weapons. In Japanese swordsmanship there is a concept called *ikken hissatsu*. This battlefield term means to kill with a single cut of the sword. It has become associated also with empty hand fighting. In modern application this doesn't actually mean killing. It refers to decisive and successful action taken in a confrontation that ends the fight as quickly as possible. This doesn't argue against the effectiveness of Western empty hand fighting, but it does speak to the difference in tactics and overall approach to be found when contrasted to Eastern martial arts.

Consider another sport in which the athlete is always on the giving—or receiving—end of blows: boxing. How do the padded gloves of the "sweet science" of boxing affect the severity of blows during a boxing match? The gloves reduce the peak impact forces of the blows yet also increase the time over which the forces are applied, resulting in an increase in the impulse (which we learned earlier in the chapter is equal to force multiplied by time). Smaller peak forces lead to reduced damage to hard tissues like bone and cartilage. However, an equivalent or greater impulse can lead to very large accelerations to body segments such as the head, which can be quite damaging to the boxer.

Despite the use of gloves and helmets in sport boxing, the risk of knockouts does not seem to be lessened. This is so even when increasing the padding in the gloves (220 to 280 grams, or eight to ten ounces, for example). The peak forces generated by professional boxers can be greater than 4,000 N (900 pounds). This level of force could induce an acceleration greater than 50 gs on devices mimicking the human head. This easily exceeds any threshold for a knockout.

In real fighting, however, a one punch knockout is very unlikely. This is the case for Batman as well. He talks about this in a story called "The Blockbuster Breaks Loose!" (Detective Comics #349, 1966). In this story Batman fights a huge mountain man—you guessed it, he's the Blockbuster—bent on his destruction. In one series of exchanges Batman manages to knock out the powerful Blockbuster with one sword hand strike (or "karate chop"). He is then shown saying "A one-punch kayo! Robin won't believe this!" It is very interesting to note that in a few panels prior to this one-strike knockout, Batman's hand was hardened by an unknown "calcium compound." So, this probably had a lot to do with how he was able to dispatch his opponent with one blow!

How Many Minions?

Just for fun I am going to answer some questions rather than posing them for a change! First, the answer to the question what is the quickest punching motion Batman can make is as low as 140 milliseconds. If Batman struck his blows in this range he would be able to punch Bane seven times in one second. If instead of how many *times* he can punch one bad guy in one second, we asked how many *bad guys* he can punch in one second, then the answer is three. This assumes the bad guys aren't dummies and don't line up to fight Batman but encircle him instead! But what if the punches and kicks—medium range techniques as shown in Figure 9.4—aren't enough and Batman finds himself in hand-to-hand range? Let's see what happens with throwing and judo next.

Throwing Down the Batgauntlet

When we consider throwing and falling, we are really talking about balance and posture and about how to uproot, unbalance, and destabilize someone so that they can be thrown. The term "throwing" really describes just placing an opponent in an unstable posture where his balance is "broken" and then letting him fall to the ground. Of course, more "oomph" is added to the fall by active throwing from a position of strength. The founder of judo, Jigoro Kano (1860–1938), took his training in jujutsu and the principle of *ju*. The term *ju* can mean suppleness, gentleness, or even "easy," but this term has to do with using the strength of an attacker against himself. That is, instead of opposing the force of an attacker, you redirect and use that force to add to his.

Remember earlier in the chapter when we looked at the pitcher and how each of the segments of his throw adds up and contributes to the total force of his throw? Now we are imagining each person in a fight as one segment and that we add up their forces to make a combined force. Let's say, for example, Batman has a maximum force of ten, and he is fighting Batgirl who can only generate a maximum force of five. (These numbers are just for illustration because their forces would be way higher than this!) There is no way for Batgirl to defeat Batman using force on force in this case because Batman's force is double hers. However, if Batgirl uses her force in the same direction as Batman, her force of five is added to the ten of Batman. This gives a total of fifteen. Now, Batman cannot withstand this blended attack since he can only resist with ten. In this way a weaker opponent can defeat a stronger one.

I have fallen victim to this over the years. I am a fairly solid 1.9-meter (6'2"), 94.5-kilogram (210-pound) man. Many times, visiting Japanese masters—who were much, much smaller than I am—have come to Canada to give clinics. Often I would be selected to help with a demonstration of some particular technique. Frequently, those demonstrations involved small pulls and pushes on my body. These were followed quite quickly by a look at the ceiling of the training hall! I am thankful I knew how to fall without injuring myself. In those cases my own attacking forces were used against me. That was OK, though. I got to learn how to do the techniques as well as how effective they could be firsthand.

Another key component in determining force—and one that beginners such as Bruce often overlook—is the force of gravity. This force is always acting straight down from the body or body segment. It is a constant that can be used by the skillful expert to easily unseat and unbalance an opponent. When trying to throw an opponent using the principles in judo or other throwing arts, you are always pushing and pulling in various combinations on the opponent. This will turn the person and push the center of mass outside his or her base of support. Once the center of mass is positioned outside the base of support, the person will begin to fall. If he or she cannot recover balance (by stepping, for example) a fall to the ground will probably occur. If you add a little extra push or pull to this, a fall is certain.

Unless you actively practice martial arts or other activities like gymnastics, you don't really spend much time each day thinking about your center of mass. The center of mass, also called the center of gravity, refers to the central point on an object or body through which the force of gravity acts. If you were a big sphere of a material with constant density, your center of mass would be right in the very middle. However, since you aren't a sphere and you don't have constant density (your bones, muscle, and connective tissue all have different densities; think back to Chapter 1 when we talked about body composition), your center of mass isn't as easy to locate.

Having said that, we can consider your center of mass to be roughly near your belly button in height above the ground and approximately in the middle of your abdomen. When you are standing we can imagine a line of force because of gravity acting straight down at this point.

To get a feeling for the idea of stability and base of support related to the position of the center of mass, you can do your own simple test. If you just stand up and assume a posture where you feel stable, your center of mass is within a base of support defined by where your feet are. If you are standing with your feet slightly apart and on the same line, your center of mass is right between your feet. That fact that you aren't falling over (and aren't holding on to anything for support) means that your center of mass is within your base of support. Now, start to lean forward slightly. As you continue to lean forward at some point you will feel yourself go off balance and will try to correct for this by stepping forward. It is at that precise moment where you felt the need to step forward that your center of mass strayed outside your base of support. In throwing someone you are trying to manipulate that exact scenario in order to tumble them to the ground.

As with other aspects of the human body we have examined in this book, you might be surprised to know that you are creating and storing energy when you stand still. Can you recall our discussion of potential and kinetic energy? We discussed a rock pushed to the top of a hill. The movement uphill was kinetic; when the rock reached the top of the hill, it was storing potential energy and just needed a little tap to roll down the hill rapidly. This concept of energy can also be seen in the first law of thermodynamics: energy is neither created nor destroyed.

So when you are standing still you are storing energy. This potential energy is calculated as the mass of the object times the height of the object above the ground times the acceleration due to gravity. The force of gravity has the potential to do work on this object, in this case a person, and the act of falling is the conversion of the energy from potential to kinetic energy.

By the way, you make use of these principles every day even if you aren't a martial artist or a gymnast. The "simple" act of walking really involves continually pushing your center of mass outside your base of support and then catching up to your falling body with a subsequent step. Think about the—probably infrequent—times when you have fallen while walking. Usually something happens to one of your feet that causes a trip or prevents a forward step, thus keeping you out of your center of mass and off balance.

Well, throwing in martial arts just means basically doing those things on purpose instead of having them occur accidentally. Kind of accidentally on purpose, you might say! Figure 10.2 shows an example of this taken from "The Batman vs. The Cat-woman!" (Batman #3, 1940). In the first panel, the bad guy can be seen trying to plunge a knife downward into the Dark Knight. However, Batman grabs the wrist of the attacker and then, without stopping the downward projection of the blade, swiftly turns his body and pulls the arm farther downward. This extra pull is the concept of adding forces together we talked about already. The next panel shows how the attacking fiend is now thrown off balance and crashes to the floor. The figure also shows a cartoon schematic of judo's *seoi-nage* (hand throw). It is easy to see when looking at these drawings that Batman really was applying basic judo principles in his early encounters.

They All Fall Down

Batman seems to get thrown almost as much as he throws Gotham City's worst. Let's look at why he doesn't get seriously injured from the falls. One way we can think about it is to examine what happens to professional sports entertainment performers such as those in

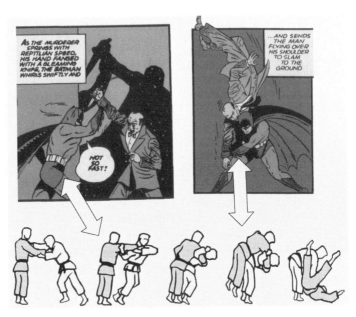

Figure 10.2. Batman does judo (*top*). The bad guy can be seen trying to plunge a knife downward into the Dark Knight. However, Batman grabs the wrist of the attacker and then, without stopping the downward projection of the blade, swiftly turns his body and pulls the arm farther downward. You can compare this move with the cartoon schematic (*bottom*) of judo's *seoi-nage* (hand throw). The arrows show the main points of overlap between Batman's move and a real judo throw. Top panel from "The Batman vs. The Cat-Woman" (Batman #3, 1940); bottom panel modified from Imamura et al. (2006).

WWE to keep them from injuring themselves when falling. Sure, the throwing and scenarios leading up to throwing in the wrestling bouts may seem to be and probably are contrived. However, the performers are actually thrown through the air and actually land on the canvas. How is it they (mostly) emerge unscathed?

The basic concept is actually rather simple and relates again to the concept of transfer of energy from potential to kinetic. Recall that before being thrown, the opponent is standing and has a certain value of potential energy. When he is thrown, the energy will be transformed into kinetic energy. If that energy isn't used up or dissipated, it can cause injury. So we will have to discover a way that the wrestlers and Batman dissipate energy when they throw or are being thrown. Bear with me, I promise we will!

Think of the way racing cars in NASCAR or Formula 1 racing seem to almost disintegrate—except for the cage protecting the drivers—in an accident. This is so the huge energies involved in any crash can be dissipated or taken up and dispersed into breaking up the vehicle and not breaking up the driver. Well, break-falling in martial arts (yes, this does mean how to break your fall!) is quite similar in principle.

Two main classes of techniques protect your body during a break-falling movement. One—the roll—is for use in those times when your body is projected outward (you go sideways) and the other—the break-fall—is for those times in which your body is projected downward. Breaking the fall is really about spreading the energy of the throw and the ground contact forces over as large a surface area and as large a time as possible. So our wrestlers will land as slowly and as spread out as possible. They wouldn't want to land quickly on one foot or hand!

The forces of these throws are actually pretty large. If Batman is thrown over Catwoman's shoulder, he would find the ground hitting him with a force of more than 5,000 N (more than a thousand pounds)! And that is the calculation if Catwoman just drops Batman from her shoulder and doesn't actually throw him down. Breaking up this force involves having as much of the body as possible in contact with the ground. It also involves actually striking the ground on purpose with the arms and legs. There are therefore two actions occurring. One is to try to generate a large impulse (recall that impulse = force × time over which the force is applied) the other is to reduce the pressure (remember that pressure equals force divided by the area of applied force). To accomplish these things a judo expert like Batman will "roll with the forces" and strike the ground deliberately. This striking the ground creates an opposite reaction force to that experienced in the fall and helps to reduce the overall magnitude of any force involved when the whole body contacts the ground.

This can be seen many times in Batman comics. My favorite example is found in "Paint a Picture of Peril" (Detective Comics #397, 1970). As we read at the top of the panel "Batman's intensive judo training serves him well! He wills his body to limpness and, at exactly the proper instant, twists to land on his shoulders and forearms." He is then seen to perform a kind of back break-fall. Hitting the ground with his hands and forearms is what helps break the fall. It is clear that Batman knows how to throw and fall and to strike with great power. A well-trained fighter like Batman really can bash as well as be bashed. We'll talk more about the cumulative effects of getting bashed in Chapter 13. Before leaving this chapter, though, we should address the question: Where should Batman bash?

Where Should the Bat Bite?

Batman can clearly strike with great power and is skilled at applying joint locks and throws. (For those of you new to martial arts, I will explain the art of joint locking later in the chapter.) But where exactly, should his attacks be aimed? Is it OK to just hit anywhere or are certain places better than others? Clearly knocking his opponents unconscious would be great. However, that is really hard to do, and directing blows to the head carries with it the high potential for mortal injury, which we know from Chapter 9 that Batman wants to avoid.

Choosing where to strike comes down to attacking weak points in the body, of which there are actually quite a few. Some are pretty obvious, some less so. I want to discuss two kinds of attacks on weak points, striking weak points and using weak points in the skeleton for joint locks. We can categorize the weak points in a variety of ways. By the way, some of the things we're going to briefly talk about here have gone by names like pressure points, vital points, or even the fear-inducing "death touch" in some overly hyped martial arts traditions. However, I prefer weak points because all of these things are literally parts of the body that are weak and exposed to attack. If I asked you to name weak points that would make good targets on the body, my bet is you would have groin at the top of the list. This might be followed by the throat and the solar plexus (that part of the chest just below the breast plate. You may know the last of these as the little bit you are *not* supposed to push on during CPR). Those are obvious ones for sure. You might not have thought of the armpit, the shin, the top of the foot, the inside of the arm, the outside of the thigh, or the small of the back. However, these are all weak points.

Weak points are places that cannot be made strong (so groin, throat, bridge of the nose), places where nerves run very shallow under the skin, or parts of the body that only move in certain ways.

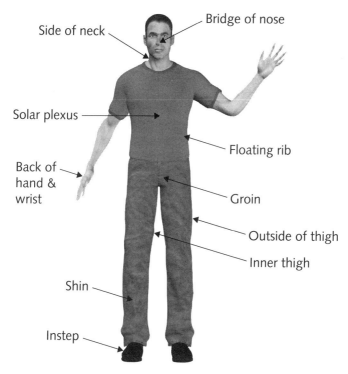

Figure 10.3. Some weak points of the human body.

Figure 10.3 shows a simple diagram of the human body with some superficial weak points marked out. This kind of diagram can be found in many martial arts books and can be much more detailed than this one. These weak points and ways of attacking them are included in many martial arts systems. In Chinese arts they are often called *chin'na*, and in karate they are often referred to as *tuite* or *kyusho*. These terms refer to the general idea of kneading, striking, and impacting these weak areas.

When considering nerves as weak points, all you have to think about is your "funny bone." We have all smacked our elbows into something and had that sharp jarring pain plus tingling in our arms. Well, you don't have a special receptor in the elbow just for smacking on things and then informing you that you just smacked your elbow! Depending upon where you smack your elbow, you are activating the nerve fibers from the ulnar and median nerves that bring information to and from the skin and muscles of the forearm and hand. Well, attacks on weak points in the body where other nerves come close to the skin make use of this same basic idea. The reason they are so effective is that they are being attacked with great force and high pressure (as we discussed above), and the connections in the spinal cord that are activated evoke powerful reflexes that help destabilize an attacker.

Think of the top of your foot. Have you ever accidentally dropped a hard object (maybe a jam jar or something) onto the top of your bare foot? If you have, you may recall that you pulled your foot away from the jar after it hit your foot. Well, what would happen if you were standing on that foot when that happened? Now imagine that you are at least allowed to have a sock and shoe on but instead of a jam jar it is Batman's hard heel? You would fall down, of course. Batman has to exploit these weak points to be an effective fighter. And he does do this in many of his encounters. A clear example of this is found in the Batman Broken City story arc. Batman is relating one of his dreams (or nightmares really, since they center on the night his parents were killed) how he would disarm an opponent. He is certainly making good use of exploiting weak points in a similar ways to those in most fighting traditions when he says, "I know exactly the right bundle of nerves I need to squeeze to make him drop the gun."

Now let's turn to weak points in relation to joint locking. There are many different joint locking techniques that can be used on the arms, legs, head, and whole body. However, they all adhere to a very simple set of principles. These are to take the slack out of the arm (or leg, or . . .) and make the joints bend in directions or ranges they don't normally go.

So, imagine a "simple" wrist lock. If you want to lock to the wrist, that is, focus the discomfort on that part of the body, you have to be aware that the hand is the handle but that the arm is pretty much a big bungee cord. You can twist the handle but all the energy in the twisting is going to be taken up all the way along the hand up to the shoulder. So, the hard, forearm, arm, shoulder, and posture of the attacker all have to be manipulated by Batman to effectively cause discomfort in the wrist that will force the Joker to drop his gun. Now that the slack in the arm is taken up, Batman twists the wrist in directions that it doesn't normally go. Your wrist is a bit tricky in how it moves. You can bend it up and down, side to side, and turn it over. So, that means all of these directions have to be taken into account in joint locking.

Gently try this on yourself. Place your right hand so that it is palm down. Now take your left hand and grasp your right then bend the right hand down as far as it will go. If you keep pushing, it starts to hurt, right? But your wrist can also twist. So, keep some gentle light pressure to keep the bend, but now twist your wrist and then lightly push on an angle. What you should notice is that this hurts a lot more! What you have done is remove the slack (this is actually reducing the degrees of freedom, but let's keep it simple) from the wrist. You have now activated nociceptors, or pain signals, that we look at more closely in the next chapter when we discuss steps Batman takes to minimize pain and injury from battling crime.

So actions like joint locking help give Batman victory! That is pretty much all there is to it. Of course, applying a joint lock on a hostile opponent like Bane is maybe not quite as simple as that!

CHAPTER 11

Hardening the Batbody

CAN STICKS AND STONES
BREAK HIS BONES?

The suit had power . . . I could barely move
in that suit. To this day, one hip has not
been right because I practiced when I first
kicked that guy on the roof, and it was very
difficult to get my foot up that high. It was
like fifty thousand rubber bands holding you
down.
—Michael Keaton, quoted in *Batman: The*
Complete History by Les Daniels

If you are going to make your living engaging in mortal combat
with evildoers and ne'er-do-wells and you refuse to give yourself the
offensive equalizer of something like a gun, you might want to
beef up your defenses. Well, in all truth, Batman is the ridiculously
wealthy Bruce Wayne. He doesn't actually make his living doing
that. However, it is a pretty obsessive hobby at best. What advantages
can Batman try to give himself for his moonlighting adventures? I'll
discuss two main ones in this chapter. One is to harden his body by
training, and the second is to harden his body by using a special
suit—the batsuit.

There is a process that exists in many old martial arts traditions, particularly those coming from China and Okinawa. It involves training and conditioning body parts to be strong and resilient. It has been called "body hardening" and "body conditioning" and has been used for the hands, feet, shins, forearms, and even the forehead! Severe training in these methods can condition the body to the point that you can do extreme things like break baseball bats in half with your shin or smash concrete blocks with your head.

Now, would Batman do this kind of training, or not? Is it a good idea to do this training in the first place? While it does hurt to do this training, we also want to know if it is harmful. We learned in Chapter 5 that bones respond to exercise stress, and in Chapter 10 that bones are strong enough that hands and feet can be used to break boards and concrete. Is a special method for training bones needed and, if so, how would it work?

The Method of Body Hardening

So, I'll be completely honest here: the basic principle is very, very simple and quite obvious. It really amounts to continually banging the body part that is to be conditioned against a hard or coarse object like a wooden post. There are many advanced aspects to this, of course. Just as with any kind of physical training (such as we discussed in Part II) the approach is related to gradual progression of the stresses that are applied to the body. This allows for gradual adaptation to the stresses.

Many difficult forms of this have been described for different martial arts and often been closely related to Shaolin martial arts. For example, David Chow and Richard Spangler detail the process of "iron fist kung" where the hand must be repeatedly bashed into small pebbles, then rocks of increasing mass until punches are against 45-kilogram (100-pound) stones. The images in Figure 11.1 are from their book describing ancient and esoteric Chinese martial arts training called "hard chi kung." On the left side of Figure 11.1 this method is shown for conditioning the head, and the image on the right illustrates a technique called "iron broom kung," with a person conditioning his foot by hitting it against a tree. The main point is that the body part (head or leg in these examples) is repeatedly struck against other hard objects in an effort to "harden" and condition them.

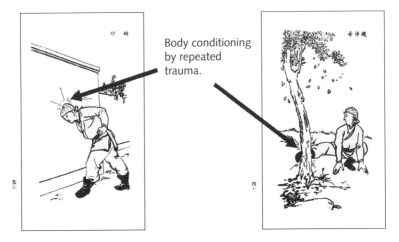

Figure 11.1. Traditional body conditioning exercises in Chinese martial arts. *Left,* conditioning the head; *right,* a technique called "iron broom kung," or conditioning the foot by hitting it against a tree. Modified from Chow & Spangler (1982).

We can see Batman going through a parallel form of training in the Frank Miller Batman: Year One story arc in "Who I Am and How I Came to Be" (Batman #404, 1986; shown in Figure 11.2). At the top of the panel, Bruce Wayne is shown driving his hand—fingertips first—through a stack of bricks. This kind of strike is called a "knife hand" in many martial arts traditions (although often the hand is vertical). In the middle and bottom panels, Bruce is kicking a tree in a manner very similar to that shown for the iron chi kung training in Figure 11.1. Assuming Batman did enough training with proper technique, you now know from Chapter 10 (have a peek at Table 10.1) that he would be able to move his hands and feet fast enough to generate the kinetic energy needed to break bricks and wood. However, breaking things with your fingertips is actually very difficult. Also, breaking a wooden board is not the same thing as kicking a tree in half! Looking back at Figure 10.1 tells us that the object you are hitting has to bend a fair bit before it will break. I don't think the tree here will really break in this way! Despite that, Batman is shown training in ways that could be forms of body hardening.

A modern-age example comes from the experiences of the writer Mark Salzman, who in the early 1980s traveled from the United States to China to learn martial arts. His experiences were subsequently described in his excellent book *Iron & Silk*. Relevant to the subject at hand here was his meeting the Chinese martial arts master Pan Qingfu. Pan practiced a harsh form of hand training—only on one hand—that gave rise to an enormous and tough callus in his knuckles. In fact, his nickname, according to Salzman, was "Iron Fist." Pan developed his calloused hand by performing punches against a 22.5-kilogram (50-pound) iron plate that was nailed to a concrete wall. He was reported to hit the plate between one thousand and ten thousand times each day.

The three components to this whole method are changing bone density, hardening the skin, and changing the perception of pain. The conditioning of the bone underlying the skin fits right into the framework we talked about back in Chapter 5. So, subjecting the body part to repeated impacts may affect the bones in the fingers (called phalanges) or the long bones of the shin and forearm. Because

Figure 11.2. Batman's extreme body conditioning and training. From "Chapter One: Who I Am and How I Came to Be" (Batman #404, 1986).

we already talked about bone density back in Chapter 5, I am not going to go over that again. Instead we will focus on the skin and pain perception.

Only Skin Deep?

Conditioning the skin is probably the easiest to think about. This part of body conditioning is essentially forming a callus on purpose. A callus is the dermatological name for a part of the skin that has become thickened and hardened as a result of repeated pressure or contact. A runner can develop a callus on her foot due to the repeated pressure and to friction's occurring inside the shoe during running. So, to induce a similar kind of adaptation in the skin of other body parts, such as the hand, a special method is needed. That is because repeated stresses such as those happening during running are not common on the hand (or head).

This kind of thing can happen even in common practices like playing a guitar. Guitar playing will stimulate the growth of a callus on the fingers used to manipulate the strings against the frets. If guitarists don't play for a long time, their calluses will shrink and pressing down the frets will be painful.

Even if hand conditioning is not a major objective of the training, some forms of this persist in many martial arts in the form of what are called "knuckle push-ups." These are just like ordinary push-ups except they are performed on the first two knuckles with the hand and forearm aligned as in a punch. Another important part of the special training methods is to keep the callus from becoming especially hardened. If it is hard and dry it is also brittle and may easily rip. So, a supple callus is in order! Various tinctures and herbal ointments have been used in different traditions to help speed callus formation, reduce healing time, and keep the callus from drying out.

Calluses develop via a process known as hyperkeratosis. Pressure or friction of the skin due to compressive or shearing stresses leads to overstimulation of the keratinocytes in the outer skin layer—the epidermis. Keratinocytes make up about 90% of the cells found in the epidermis and come from stem cells in the skin. Producing more cells is a normal response to protect the skin and is the desired outcome of the body conditioning. This is commonly used also in the martial art of wing chun.

Repeated impact that creates calluses may "deaden" the sensitivity in areas you are trying to build up. There are receptors in your skin that tell about touch, pressure, and tissue damage. Well, those receptors in the hand or foot that repeatedly feel the impact of hard objects may no longer respond to touch or other inputs in the same way. However, getting accustomed to hitting a hard immovable object may easily prepare someone for striking a soft movable target like a person!

But when Batman fights even a soft movable target—and even if he emerges unharmed—he will be hurt and feel pain. Body conditioning trains a person to deal with the pain of fighting in practice so it can be ignored during real combat. The great martial arts historians Robert Smith and Donn Draeger in their fantastic book *Comprehensive Asian Fighting Arts* wrote that a martial artist "needs to be stung frequently and hurt occasionally. For without this he cannot learn to respond coolly."

No Pain, No Gain?

Now let's look at what pain is. Then we will be in a position to assess how easy it will be for Batman to deal with. Well, the next thing I am about to tell you may seem surprising, but an important thing to understand about your body is that there are no such things as pain receptors. That's right—you don't have any receptors to detect pain or to make you feel pain. But, you do feel pain from time to time, and obviously Batman certainly has many a pain-filled night while out patrolling the streets and heights of Gotham City.

Instead of actual pain receptors, what we have is nociceptors—literally receptors for detecting tissue damage. Actually, if all that nociceptors did was detect tissue damage, they would be kind of useless, because the damage would already be done! The real job of your nociceptors is to go off at the onset of damage to our tissues. These receptors are in the skin, joints, muscle, internal organs, and so on. They become activated by stimuli that, if continued, could lead to damage. Think of the skin on your hand. If you absentmindedly place your hand near a hot burner, it seems to really hurt while you yank your hand away. Yet, often there is no damage at all to your skin. No blister forms and after only a few minutes you feel fine again. The nociceptors were activated by (in this case thermal) stimuli, and you perceived this as pain. This is mostly to get your attention!

Whether we perceive these sensations as painful or not has to do with what goes on in the brain and spinal cord. This is why different people can respond so differently to the same stimulus like hot sand at the beach. This is also why it is possible for some people to have a "high pain tolerance" or "threshold." The sensors in our skin that tell us about tissue damage don't have a different threshold. But the way the information from those receptors is processed can be very different. I think it is fair to say that Batman, while having the same receptors as you and I, has a much higher threshold for pain. In fact, you can completely override the automatic and reflexive responses that would normally be activated by the nociceptive input. Flashing back to the hot burner example, you could, through sheer force of will, keep your hand near that burner if you really focused your attention on doing so. You would still have an initial reflex flinch—those nociceptors activate powerful reflexes—to pull your hand away. You could, though, force yourself to keep your hand there. I am not advocating this of course, but merely using it as a very striking example of how so-called painful events can be handled.

Why all this is possible has to do with how the sensation of nociception or pain is processed. Pioneering work in this area was conducted by Patrick Wall and Ronald Melzack in the 1960s. Their research led to the discovery of endorphins and enkephalins, which are the internal morphine-like painkillers of the body. Also, you have likely made use of certain pain-management techniques without paying any attention whatsoever to the underlying neurophysiology. You have probably taken advantage of the gate control theory of pain, which is what Wall and Melzack called the way that we experience pain.

This theory can best be explained by a few examples. If you have ever rubbed a body part after you have hurt it—maybe you banged your elbow or hand on something—you have actually been activating messaging in your spinal cord that made the pain feel less or weaker. This is also similar to what children do it they hurt something—they shake it. All that shaking and rubbing yields feedback from receptors in the body part (in this example, the arm or hand) that in turn inform the nervous system about movement. In the spinal cord, this feedback interferes with transmission of the feedback from the nociceptors. The nociceptive signal does arrive at the spinal cord; it is just that it is basically blocked from fully making its way up to the brain where it would then be perceived as pain—the gate is closed.

The gate control theory of pain is also the basis for a commonly used form of treatment in physiotherapy: transcutaneous electric nerve stimulation. This treatment typically produces pain relief by means of electrical stimulation or vibration treatment over the skin of an injured body part. Commands coming down from the brain strongly affect how information is relayed in these paths. This is how you are able to sometimes ignore or pay little attention to things that you might think of as "painful."

Another kind of body conditioning related to deliberately activating the nociceptors in the skin and joints is often performed by students in Japanese traditions like judo, jujutsu, and aikido or in applications of the Chinese martial art tradition of chin'na. These are all martial arts involving of joint locking and manipulation.

If you watch aikido practitioners throwing each other, the most striking thing is that the person being thrown appears to fly through the air when a joint lock is used. You might think this is an overly theatrical response to a mere twist of the wrist. Of course, the simplest response would be to just let the person rip the ligaments holding the wrist together. However, jumping into the air and flipping over is often the best way to get out of the pain of the lock. Repeatedly practicing simplified versions of the joint locking exercises is a kind of body conditioning in which the ability to tolerate the painful lock is practiced.

When Batman throws someone using these types of joint locks he is triggering a response based upon the pain inflicted by the lock. This has been very well described by martial arts writer Dave Lowry. He wrote that "with time and practice, your reaction to these kinds of joint locks will become much less immediate. You will begin to see that pain, especially when you know it is coming, is something over which you have some control. You can learn to compartmentalize it and accept it without allowing it to absorb your entire attention." The point is that the onset of the pain—signaled by the nociceptors—occurs before tissue damage but will still give the response needed in the fighting application. Batman is clearly well trained in this. In the story called "No Rest for the Wicked" (Batman #497, 1993), Batman talks about how he needs to "isolate the pain. Lock it away. Put it in a tiny box in a corner of my mind." This allows him to carry on with his work.

The way Batman can exploit this in his opponents is well illustrated. A good example is the "The Lazarus Pit" (Batman #243, 1972).

In this comic, Batman is shown fighting empty handed against a very powerful villain who is armed with a knife. Batman uses his superior skills to maneuver the bad guy into an arm bar pin and still gives him the option to give up without being hurt at all! Batman says "I have years of practice in judo—either the knife goes . . . or your arm does." Even if the bad guy doesn't give up, the absolute worst thing that will happen is a broken arm. It seems very gracious behavior on the part of Batman, if you ask me, but is in keeping with Batman's approach to fighting that we talked about in Chapter 9. Batman causes the bad guy to drop his weapon by invoking this nociceptive response but doesn't actually break the man's arm or harm him. This does make a nice illustration of the issue we are discussing but causes more work for Batman! In later pages of that same story, the bad guy just grabs another weapon (actually the same knife again), and Batman is forced to disarm him once more.

You can also imagine examples from sports that you may have played or watched where something happens to one athlete—maybe a collision or a twisted limb—that causes him to spill to the ground and roll around in pain. After a few minutes of treatment on the sidelines the athlete is sometimes able to carry on as if nothing happened. It is almost like he wasn't hurt at all. Well, hurt has occurred—imminent tissue damage and pain was sensed—but harm didn't happen. There was no actual damage, just the warning of damage about to occur. Your receptors work really well in this regard since they tell you about possible damage usually before it is too late to avoid actual injury. Martial artists exploit this to evoke the response needed during fighting.

Is All This Really Good for You?

Despite everything we have discussed above, we still haven't really met head on the questions of whether this kind of training is good for your body and if Batman would do it. Taking the last part first, Batman clearly would do this kind of training because it would provide an additional edge for him. But he wouldn't likely have the time to devote to the harsher versions of this type of training. He doesn't really need to have the extreme body conditioning because he has a fantastic batsuit. We'll talk more about that in a few pages. So, that part is simple.

Answering whether this is OK physiologically, that is, does it hurt you, is not as simple. However, the scientific data are really very poor in answering this, so the best I can say is that it probably doesn't have that many serious "side effects."

To look at how this type of training would affect a real-life person as opposed to a cartoon crimefighter, let's turn to the man who trained in what was actually described as "the savage technique"! The person in question was the famous karate man Mas Oyama, who founded the Japanese karate style of Kyokushinkai ("society of the ultimate truth"). This is a very "hard" martial arts style that includes full contact fighting as an integral part of the curriculum. Mas Oyama performed savage hand conditioning that involved repeatedly punching hard objects with the fist until the skin broke and the tendons were exposed. In this type of training eventually a very firm callus forms that is anchored on the tendon. Clearly calling this the savage technique isn't hyperbole! Oyama conditioned many body parts including multiple surfaces of the hands and feet (described in two of his earlier books *What Is Karate?* and *This Is Karate*). In *This Is Karate* Oyama describes his early training of punching telephone poles until the wires shook in the air and made a humming noise. He also describes using only his bare hands and feet to fight and kill a bull. I think it is clear that the form of hand and body conditioning performed by Oyama is very harsh.

Oyama was involved in an x-ray study in the late 1960s that included only "six so-called serious hand conditioners." No really obvious degenerative changes in the bones or joints of the hand were noted in the x-rays. However, it is really very difficult to know for sure the long-term consequence of this training. Also, the more sophisticated imaging techniques available today would be helpful in shedding more light on this. It is worth mentioning, though, that the authors do mention that "some decrease in manual dexterity will result from prolonged hand-conditioning."

I used to perform this training with the knife hand strike. The knife hand is the one using the fingertips that is shown at the top panel of Figure 11.2. Recall that this panel taken from "Who I Am and How I Came to Be" (Batman #404, 1986) outlines some elements of Bruce Wayne's training that are quite like the body hardening methods that we are discussing here. I used to practice striking against a lightly padded hard wooden target using the knife hand. I would hit the target only 50 to 100 times each day with each hand, not the thousands that true devotees use. Certainly my knife hand technique was strengthened by doing this. However, I lost a great deal of sensitivity in my fingertips. I realized that being able to type effectively was more directly related to my actual day job than was being able to have tough hands to do knife hand strikes, and so I stopped after some years. Clearly since I have been able to write this book, I have recovered fine! However, the tips of my index, middle, and ring fingers (the ones actually making contact during the striking training) on both hands still have much less sensitivity than my little fingers (which didn't actually hit anything).

This idea is also echoed in a story told of one of the early masters of Goju ryu karate. Yagi Meitatsu described how when he was young he participated in forearm conditioning (*kote kitai*). "Every day we'd do this and our arms were always bruised with no time to heal. After practice we'd go and buy ice in a bucket to drink. This kind of training made a strong body, but when I'd go to school my hands would shake so much I had trouble holding a pencil." A common training method in Okinawan and Japanese karate is to hit a hard, lightly padded object called a *makiwara* (which is the name of kind of object I hit). The point is to develop such power in the strike that hard objects can be crushed. Also, you can quickly see if the arm and hand alignment is strong and coordinated enough to resist buckling on impact.

A remnant of this practice of body conditioning can be seen in the common practice in many martial arts of using knuckle push-ups, which we discussed earlier in the chapter. The idea is to get used to proper hand alignment for punching, to deal with contact on the fist, and to work on wrist and forearm strength. A related practice is that of a particular challenge called "knuckle hopping," which is part of the yearly World Eskimo-Indian Olympics. In knuckle hopping, participants get into a prone position supporting themselves on their knuckles and toes in a kind push-up-like formation. At this point, the resemblance to push-ups ends and the relationship to body conditioning begins. That is because the next step is to move across the floor by hopping on the fists! So, the fists are repeatedly hit against a hardwood floor. The world record for this event, held by Rodney Worl, is almost 57.6 meters (192 feet). As you might clearly have guessed, callused knuckles are the most minor of outcomes from this form of training. Split skin and bleeding are indeed very common. It is really quite similar to the "savage" technique of hand conditioning mentioned above.

Beefing Up the Buff Body

OK, so far we have talked about some ways to condition and harden the body. Probably body toughening is the best term. But Batman doesn't usually engage in combat with the inmates of Arkham Asylum dressed simply in his boxers (or briefs) and nothing else. He has done some body hardening, but he also gets some help from using a special suit. I refer of course to the iconic batsuit.

There really is no doubt about it. Bruce Wayne uses his fortune to benefit his alter ego Batman's toy collection. The batsuit is one of the coolest of those toys. In this sense I mean "cool" as in hip, awesome, and fantastic—not cool as in temperature, which you'll read about in a few moments. That suit can do all sorts of stuff and seems to have an almost inexhaustible capacity for hiding things and for taking a real walloping. In all seriousness, I, personally, would like to have one of those suits. I admit that I am not sure what I would do with a batsuit. I would definitely stand out a bit too much wearing it around the university during lectures or in my lab. It would also look out of place for teaching martial arts. It would be fantastic once a year at Halloween, though!

Putting on a batsuit every day isn't a decision a person would make lightly. First, it is what scientists would call an "exoskeleton." (I apologize for inadvertent negative flashbacks to high school biology and grasshopper dissections that this word may have conjured up. I am hopeful the positive associations won out.) So, wearing a second skeleton would be much more of an effort than sporting a suit and tie for the office or throwing on old clothes to clean out the garage. It is really a suit of armor. Yes, the armor is light and flexible, but it is still armor. This creates some real challenges for Batman when he moves. This issue was well-captured by the quote from Michael Keaton included at the beginning of this chapter. That Hollywood batsuit was clearly not that light or easy to maneuver in. However, we will assume that the "real" batsuit that the real-fictional Batman wears is the best it can be. Despite that, it is still out of the ordinary range of human experience to wear that kind of gear. Unless you spend a lot of time in a HazMat suit, or working as a mascot for a sports team, or perhaps testing out some new combat suit from the army, you just aren't used to being inside something like the batsuit. That is the best descriptor, by the way. Being inside the batsuit, rather than wearing the batsuit.

From the time you were a little kid, your body has adapted to staying fairly well calibrated for how big you are and how your body moves. When you put an armored suit on top of everything, you throw off this fine calibration and you are just asking for problems. Just consider it from a movement control perspective. For example, recall from Chapter 7 that you have sensors in your arms and legs that tell you about movement. Well, wearing any kind of suit means adding on an additional layer that doesn't have any sensors in it. This reduces the kind of feedback you might get from moving your body.

Some people actually have to deal with wearing an exoskeleton. There is a very large emerging field related to robotics that has to do with interfaces between humans and external devices that support the body. These exoskeletons—a kind of wearable robot—have important applications for helping to restore and recover movement when it is lost after injury or damage to the nervous system, such as happens after a stroke or a spinal cord injury. These exoskeletons aren't nearly as grandiose as a full body suit like Batman's batsuit, though. In contrast to the tools mentioned above, the batsuit is a "passive" device; it doesn't have motors to assist with movement such as is being explored for use in rehabilitation.

Astronauts also use a kind of exoskeleton. The bulky suits they wear create many of the same issues as wearing the batsuit—controlling movement and regulating temperature. However, a recent innovation is being worked on by Dava Newman, who is a professor of aeronautics and astronautics at MIT. She is incorporating spandex and nylon into a new space suit design called the "BioSuit." Although it is still some years (probably about ten) away from actual use, it was designed for protection with mobility and will weigh much less than the current 45-kilogram (100-pound) suits worn now.

Batman uses a powered robotic exoskeleton in Frank Miller's graphic novel *The Dark Knight Returns* (1986). In this story arc, Batman has been retired from crime fighting for some years. However, he makes a comeback when he is older. He is a sort of enemy of the state, however, and Superman is called upon to rein him in. To fight Superman, Batman designs and constructs an exoskeleton, and there is a climactic battle between the two. "The Dark Knight Falls" is the specific story in which this occurs. Having an exoskeleton powerful enough to attempt to fight Superman needs a lot of power. In fact, it is plugged right into a light standard! However, this isn't the kind of suit that we typically think of when we hear "batsuit."

Let's be more realistic as to the composition and function of the batsuit. The best details on this come from Scott Beatty's *The Ultimate Guide to the Dark Knight*. The batsuit encompasses both the body suit and the cowl that covers Batman's head. The powered exoskeleton that Batman built to fight Superman had to both protect Batman and provide more "oomph" for his attacks. In contrast, the standard batsuit is really mostly for protection. Two things it protects Batman from are bullets (remember the criminals Batman fights don't share his disdain of the gun) and heat.

The batsuit isn't a 100% preshrunk cotton garment. It isn't a 50-50 polyblend either. It is instead composed of Kevlar and reinforced Nomex, which are both "aramids" (a contraction of "aromatic polyamide"). These are strong synthetic fibers that are resistant to fire. Nomex has the highest fire resistance and was first discovered in DuPont labs in 1961. It is used in the hoods of firefighters and the facial cowls of NASCAR drivers. The very strong fiber Kevlar was created in the DuPont labs in 1965 and is five times stronger than steel, when compared on a weight-to-weight basis. However, unlike steel, Kevlar is light and flexible and can be knitted or "spun" into fabric ropes or sheets to be used in a variety of applications, for example, body armor of police, the military, or Batman. Batman's cowl has Kevlar-reinforced inserts for when he has to head butt someone or takes a blow there.

As an aside, you might think of Kevlar and bulletproof vests. Something to keep in mind though is that bulletproof vests aren't really bulletproof. They don't really deflect bullets but rather absorb and deform the bullets by spreading the force of impact over a large body area. This makes sense if you think back to the concepts of impulse and break-falling we talked about in Chapter 10. These vests usually protect the wearer from the piercing injury of the bullet itself. However, all that force still has to be absorbed and can often lead to dramatic bruising or broken ribs. In "Reasons" (Batman #604, 2005), Batman takes a few direct shots from a handgun. He says "Kevlar protects me but my ribs are cracking." Bulletproof vests may be made from materials such as Kevlar but are often reinforced with steel or titanium.

Now let's look at what it must feel like to prowl around in a batsuit.

Is the Batsuit a Batoven?

At this stage I want to talk about how uncomfortable it would really make you feel to wear something like the batsuit. To be effective it has to be close fitting and follow your body movements. No matter how "breathable" the fabric may be, it is still another layer on Batman's body. So, what I want to consider is how that suit would affect body temperature. Scientists call this thermoregulation, or the ability to adjust your body temperature within a normal range. Kind of like a room temperature setting for your internal organs!

Recall in the beginning of the book we discussed homeostasis. But our system of regulation was certainly not designed for a person wearing a batsuit! So, putting one on and then doing maximal exercise might be expected to cause a few problems. The kind of problems the Batman would experience in the batsuit are similar to what happens to athletes like speed skaters who wear aerodynamic "rubber" suits or to firefighters who wear heavy and very hot protective gear.

Two main concerns for Batman to contend with are the possibility of the suit's interfering with breathing and its overheating. Restrictions to the movement of your chest wall can affect exercise performance. If you have ever had to wear, even briefly, a life jacket that was too small, you know how uncomfortable this can be. This is actually very much like what happens in morbidly obese people where the body fat begins to interfere with elastic movement of the rib cage. We'll assume the batsuit is very well designed—and tailored to fit—and doesn't affect breathing that much.

Temperature, though, is a very significant issue. Let's talk about what it means to be a homeotherm, from two Greek words meaning "same" and "heat." That is what you, I, and Batman (and bats too) are. This means we regulate our internal body temperatures within a very narrow range. Typically this is between about 35.5 and 37.7°C, or 95.9 and 99.9°F. If we were a vehicle motor we would call that the operating range. It is tricky to keep our internal temperature within that band. We are constantly producing heat through metabolism and as a byproduct of muscle contraction. We are also receiving heat from the environment in terms of radiant heat (think of the sun or a hot fire) and conductive energy (think of sitting on hot sand). At the same time we lose heat as radiant, conductive, convective, or evaporative heat loss. These sources of heat loss or heat gain in the body from the environment are nicely summarized in Figure 11.3.

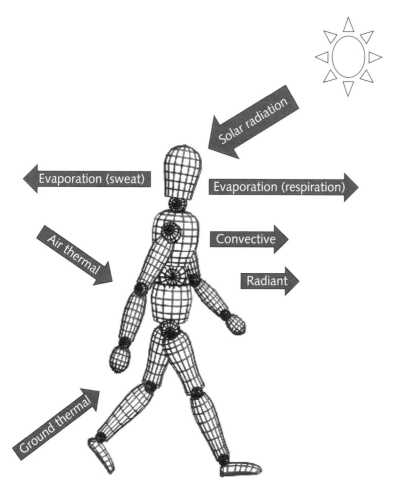

Figure 11.3. Loss and gain of heat during exercise.

The really cool thing—no pun intended—about our bodies is that we can operate over a very wide range of external temperatures and still keep our internal temperature inside that "operating range." Our bodies can regulate between about 10 and 55°C, or 50 and 131°F. Receptors in the arms and legs and in the body core help inform the central nervous system (actually the hypothalamus) about temperature. Then we either try to gain or lose heat. We can quickly do so by bringing more blood to the skin to help cool off or by reducing blood flow if we want to keep ourselves warm. This is why your fingertips are cold when you are cold. You are unconsciously reducing blood flow to the skin to keep your internal organs warmer. The goose bumps we get when we are cold are an attempt to reduce the area of our skin to again help preserve heat. This is also why you shiver—to generate heat as a byproduct of muscle contraction.

The opposite happens when we are hot. We sweat to help cool us by evaporation of water off the skin. In fact you can actually lose as much as 1.4 liters (50 ounces) of fluid per hour with heavy sweating in the heat (at about 43°C or 110°F). This is summarized in Figure 11.4. This figure shows how much water loss can occur at different temperatures (shown along the bottom) and at different intensity levels of exercise. A quick glance at the top right-hand corner, which is for the highest temperature and moderate activity, shows significant water loss. It is important to realize that this water loss is what helps cool the body and keep it in the operating range. A lot of this is in the form of evaporative (think sweat) heat loss. This gives you a good idea what kind of potential temperature-regulation problem Batman might have to contend with when he is out fighting crime.

However, there are a couple other considerations that make Batman's potential difficulties here less of a worry. Right off the bat (OK, sorry about that pun; I have been waiting to use that line for the whole book so far and couldn't wait any longer), Batman is almost always out at night when the temperature is much lower. In fact, he is likely well below the minimum shown on Figure 11.4. Also, according to Batman expert Scott Beatty, Batman's newest suit includes an internal cooling (and I guess heating when needed) system.

A final consideration for Batman and overheating is that we need to assume that he has become acclimatized to the hot and humid environment that the batsuit could be. I say could because even if it has a cooling system, it could fail! The concept of acclimatization is one in which there is a gradual (and homeostatic) shift in things like sweating rate that occurs when we humans get used to different climates. If you have ever traveled from a cold and maybe dry place to a hot humid place for a vacation you underwent an acclimatization just like this. Let's say you went from Chicago in February to the Cook Islands in the South Pacific. You probably sweated like crazy for the first number of days. Then you got used to it and adjusted to the temperatures after about a week. This wasn't just you thinking it was

Moderate activity (e.g., fighting the Riddler)

~0.4 qt (L)   ~0.75 qt (L)   ~1.0 qt (L)

Light activity (e.g., driving the Batmobile)

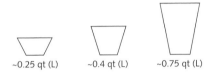

~0.25 qt (L)   ~0.4 qt (L)   ~0.75 qt (L)

Rest (e.g., waiting outside the Batcave)

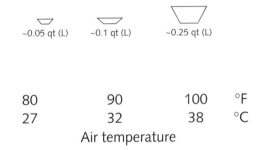

~0.05 qt (L)   ~0.1 qt (L)   ~0.25 qt (L)

| 80 | 90 | 100 | °F |
| 27 | 32 | 38 | °C |

Air temperature

Figure 11.4. Fluid loss during exercise at different temperatures. Data from McArdle et al. (2005).

better; your body really had changed the way it handled the new heat stress in the climate you found in the Cook Islands. Then, when you went back home again, you probably felt much colder than you normally would in a Chicago winter. After about a week, though, you would have adjusted again to the new climate.

Sports teams try to make use of this by traveling to hot environments to train and get ready for competition well in advance of the competition itself. Batman would need to train in the full gear often to maintain adaptations in light of the cold climate of Gotham City. As he wears his batsuit each and every day, we will assume he is well acclimated to it.

I mentioned earlier that a major consideration for body temperature regulation for Batman is that he is usually out at night when it is cooler. Well, it is exactly that nocturnal aspect of Batman's life that we turn to next.

CHAPTER 12

Gotham by Twilight

WORKING THE KNIGHT SHIFT

> Sleep is at best a necessary evil. Bruce Wayne sleeps, and one less crime is thwarted, one less innocent life is saved.
> —From "The Sleep of Reason" (Detective Comics #598, 1989)

It is clear from the quote above that despite his monetary wealth and resources, sleep and rest are not luxuries that Bruce Wayne indulges in. Instead, he takes a rather Spartan and frugal approach to sleep. This might not be such a problem if Batman and Bruce Wayne didn't have such an odd existence. Obviously that is actually a bit of an understatement! What I mean to say is that Batman lives a large portion of his life at night.

Typically, we human beings operate as diurnal animals. That means we are active during daytime and rest at night. This, by the way, is a common feature of many mammals, birds, and insects and can be contrasted with nocturnal animals such as the bat, sea turtle, or owl. I guess instead of saying that Batman has an odd lifestyle, we might be charitable and call him a "night owl." He is named Batman after all! In any event, working the nocturnal beat of the Batman can be considered an extreme form of shift work. He punches the clock when others get ready for bed, hangs out all night dealing with the criminals of Gotham City and all over the four corners of the world, and then hits the sack early in the morning. He does it day after day, year after year.

In this chapter, we will look at the cumulative effect of this type of lifestyle. One of the advantages we have as warm-blooded mammals is the ability to function at night despite the cooler air and decreased temperature, but does the "batshift" push this too far? To explore these issues we are going to take a journey and look at jet lag and shift work and have a little chat about sleep itself.

It's as Different as Night and Day

Our bodies work according to prescribed rhythms—called circadian rhythms from the Latin words for "about a day"—across a period of about 24.5 hours. For example, your body temperature fluctuates in a very consistent pattern throughout the day, rising and falling between about 36.5 and 37.5°C (or 97.5 and 99.5°F). Remember that these numbers are within the carefully regulated operating range we touched on in the last chapter. Our sleeping and waking cycle is the most obvious example of a circadian rhythm. This cycle is regulated by the pineal gland and a cluster of nerve cells called the suprachiasmatic nuclei, which are located in the base of the brain in the hypothalamus. These nuclei are the home of the body "clock" that sets circadian rhythms.

American biochemist Julius Axelrod made key contributions to our understanding of the role of the pineal gland and of the hormone melatonin, which it secretes, in our sleep-wake cycles. In addition to this work Dr. Axelrod shared the 1970 Nobel Prize for Physiology or Medicine for his studies on adrenaline and noradrenaline.

The suprachiasmatic nuclei change their activity in response to the level of the hormone melatonin in the blood, which is in turn affected by the amount of light that the eyes receive. Melatonin is thought of as a "dark hormone," because the more light there is, the lower the release of melatonin. This hormone is involved in circadian rhythms whether we are talking about Batman, actual bats, or algae clumped together in a batlike form.

The main function of the body clock is to ensure standard cyclical regulation of hormonal levels in multiple systems in the body. In

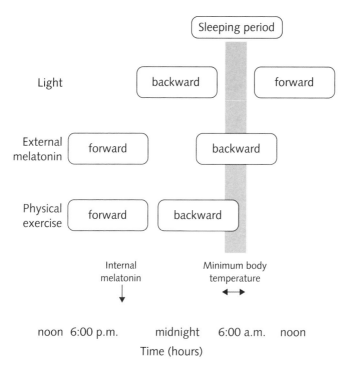

Figure 12.1. The body clock is affected by exercise, levels of light, and melatonin concentration. The normal release of melatonin from the pineal gland is triggered by decreased or dim light levels at night (internal melatonin). The highlighted section at right shows minimum body temperature, which is the anchor of the circadian cycle. Modified from Waterhouse et al. (2007).

humans, the body clock is also affected by information about physical activity and overall level of stress or excitement. The key point is that the internal clock is synchronized with the external world by cues taken from light levels and physical movement related to activity and exercise. This makes sense if you consider that low light levels at night would naturally coincide with low levels of physical movement. In contrast, the opposite would be expected during the day. The relation between light, additional melatonin taken from outside the body (in a pill for example), and exercise and the body clock is shown in Figure 12.1.

An important reference point is the rise and fall of body temperature mentioned before. The circadian rhythm is anchored to the minimum core temperature observed during the day, which typically occurs some hours before waking. Bright light shifts the body clock backward when it is provided before the time of minimum core temperature and forward when given after the time of minimum core temperature. That is, light makes you less sleepy in both cases. Exercising early in the evening moves the clock forward, but exercising at night, during what would be the early part of normal sleep, shifts the clock backward. So, light and exercise can push the body clock in different directions based on when they are enhanced relative to the normal sleeping cycle, particular in relation to the normal light-related release of melatonin and body temperature minimum. These points essentially anchor the beginning and late phases of sleep.

Every day there is adjustment of the internal body clock to the external environment. These adjustments are mostly from light-related cues called "zeitgebers" (meaning "time givers" in German). When we are living and working in a standard relationship to the daily light levels in our region, the body clock stays nicely synchronized and our mood and energy levels fluctuate in a consistent cyclical pattern. While you probably haven't strongly considered the link to rising body temperature, you have certainly noticed that your mental performance likely improves in the hours after you wake up. This isn't just because you have had your morning coffee, by the way! This trend generally continues on into the early evening. After that point, deterioration in mental productivity occurs.

Unless Batman has a way to reset and reanchor his body clock (which we will explicitly discuss in a few pages), this effectively means that he will be called on to do his best—and most dangerous—work when physiologically he is on the falling edge of performance! Many aspects of physical activity, including peak muscle forces, anaerobic power output, and motivation to perform or sustain activity, rise and fall on circadian rhythms. Even something as simple as spinal reflexes changes according to circadian rhythms. Shown in Figure 12.2 are reflexes (similar to the stretch reflex discussed back in Chapter 7) taken every four hours across a 12-hour period from 8:00 a.m. to 8 p.m. The important point is that the size of the reflex increases steadily from early morning until early evening.

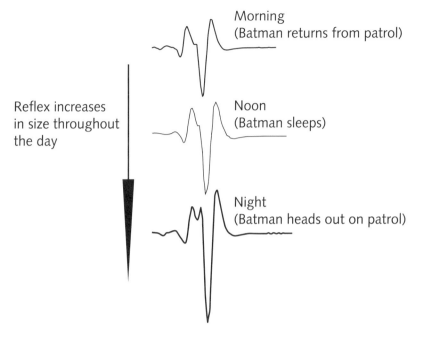

Morning
(Batman returns from patrol)

Reflex increases
in size throughout
the day

Noon
(Batman sleeps)

Night
(Batman heads out on patrol)

Figure 12.2. Change in nervous system excitability in the spinal cord over the course of a day. Relative time points for Batman's daily activities are shown for comparison. The black arrow indicates the progression of time during a single day. Modified from Lagerquist et al. (2006).

The levels of many hormones in the blood also follow a daily pattern. Cortisol levels in blood plasma are lowest just after noon and reach their peak just around late evening. These rhythms are partially synchronized to our daily routine. But at the base level our rhythms across the day—circadian rhythms—are tied to the level of light we are exposed to during the day and at night.

If you look at Figure 12.3, you will see the levels of melatonin (A), body temperature (B), subjective alertness (C), and task performance (D) across a 24-hour period. Also shown is the level of triacylglycerol (E), which is used as a marker for metabolism. In this figure the dashed vertical line indicates the time of minimum

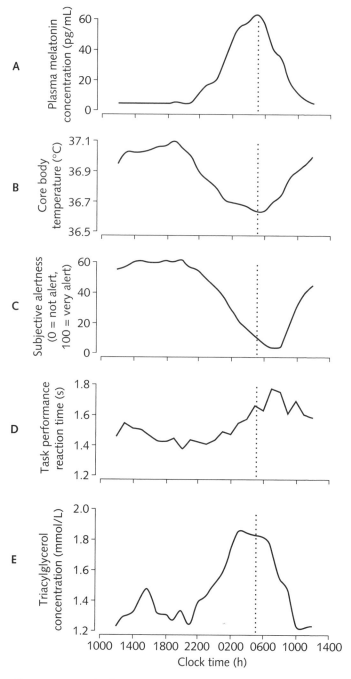

Figure 12.3. Levels of melatonin (A), body temperature (B), subjective alertness (C), and task performance (D) across a 24-hour period. Also shown is the level of triacylglycerol (E), which is used as a marker for metabolism. The dashed vertical line indicates the time of minimum core body temperature (see Figure 12.1). Courtesy Rajaratnam and Arendt (2001).

core body temperature that we discussed up above. The key thing to notice is the close parallel of these levels as they change across the day.

When the Bat Hitches a Ride on a Jet Plane

There is evidence that working night shifts can throw off our diurnal patterns of metabolism and cognition and may be unhealthy. What are the effects Batman should be concerned with for working his night shifts? For that matter, we can easily imagine similar factors at play for firefighters, police officers, or ambulance workers. However, before exploring the extremes of shift work, which involve an attempt at chronic and long-term change in circadian rhythms, I want to begin first with shorter term and brief changes in rhythm that just about everyone of us—shift workers or not—have experienced at one time or another. What I am referring to are the effects of seasonal changes in light levels and the effects of air travel and what is known as "jet lag."

Jet lag is really a minor, temporary version of the bigger issues that arise with chronic night shift work. The basic concept to carry forward from our discussions above is that we have a certain set point in our circadian rhythms and our sleep-wake cycles. These points are not set in stone, so to speak, but are subject to seasonal variations. These changes across the seasons vary depending on where we live. They are gradual and minor at latitudes near the equator and extreme near the poles. In Anchorage, Alaska, for example, the longest day of the year in 2007 was June 21, when sunrise was at 3:30 a.m. and sunset at 10:42 p.m. This extreme "light" day can be contrasted with the winter solstice of December 21, 2007, when sunrise was at 10:14 a.m. and sunset at 3:41 p.m. Then contrast both of these with Quito, Ecuador, where the sunrise and sunset times for the summer solstice were 6:12 a.m. and 6:19 p.m. and for the winter solstice 6:08 a.m. and 6:16 p.m. Across the seasons, then, the ambient light levels fluctuate from a daily range of about 20 hours in the summer to about four and a half hours in the winter in Anchorage and pretty much evenly 12 hours for Quito.

However, even if we live at a latitude like that of Anchorage where there are extreme differences in the actual hours of daylight between summer and winter, we don't move in one 24-hour period from summer light levels to winter ones. Instead, the changes across the seasons are typically very gradual. Because of that, our set point can slowly adjust—mostly—to these differences. Despite that, it can still be very difficult, and there can be considerable differences in an individual's ability to adapt to the seasonal differences in the extreme north and south. As mentioned above, a key regulator of sleep and waking cycles is melatonin. There seem to be two points of melatonin secretions across a normal day, and the off and on signal of the secretions help trigger the sleeping and waking cycles. The melatonin cycles themselves are triggered by levels of ambient light. This is why there can be such large differences in set points across the seasons.

However, very large and abrupt changes happen when we travel from one part of the world to a completely different part with a radically different time zone within a single day. This is now quite common because of ease of worldwide travel via airplane. This change in our physical location means our set point is no longer in line with the actual ambient light levels in our new time zone. We may experience dramatic effects in blood pressure, body temperature, and hormone release. Over time, though, we do adapt to the different time zone. Then we get to repeat the process when we return home!

A Serious Example

Let's pause here to consider an interesting example of where jet lag can have very widespread and significant impact in important activities related to physical activity. This is going to be a serious pause for a very important issue so please pay attention. I am speaking, of course, about Monday Night Football and the National Football League. If you think carefully about all our discussions about circadian rhythms and in consideration of your own experience being the owner of your own human body with varied alertness and energy across a day (and you can look at Figure 12.3 for the physiology behind this), you might begin to wonder what would be the effect on your overall performance of switching time zones to the same local time in different parts of the country. An excellent example of this is professional sports events and in particular those staged in North America where regular daily travel across three or more time zones occurs to play football, basketball, hockey, or baseball. Given all of this, it might be supposed that competing at certain times of the day might offer an advantage for some teams traveling out of their time zone.

This was precisely what Roger Smith and colleagues at Stanford University wondered with regard to NFL teams playing on Monday Night Football. They examined the outcomes of 25 years' worth of Monday Night Football games when teams based on the West Coast played teams based in the East. This gave them 63 games to consider. This is an interesting comparison because these Monday night games are always played at 9:00 eastern time, regardless of where the game will be held and from where the teams are actually traveling. Smith and colleagues thought that West Coast teams should have an advantage since the actual game time would always be earlier in circadian body clock time. Hold on, you might say at this point, this whole idea would only work if you had some way to control for the fact that different teams from the East and West are always playing and those different teams are going to be of different skill and caliber. That is going to mess up any comparison related to circadian issues, which should be smaller anyway. However, these scientists where actually quite clever and turned to other experts to give information about who should have done better or won each game. The other experts are, of course, the ones who set the Las Vegas point spread.

The results of the analysis showed that West Coast teams won more often and by more points per game than did East Coast teams. In fact the winning percentage for West Coast teams on Monday Night Football was 63.5% compared with only 36.5% for East Coast teams!

You might wonder if maybe the East Coast teams just didn't play well under the pressure of Monday Night Football. After all, there would be more viewers actually in the East watching the games. Maybe that entered into the players' heads during the game and affected performance somehow. However, when those East Coast teams with the 36.5% winning percentage played other East Coast teams, they won 65.2% of the time. The scientists suggest that this is an example of getting increased performance by not adjusting the circadian clock to the new time zone and therefore gaining a performance benefit. This can be considered in the context of a "one off" event but probably doesn't have much carry forward to ongoing performance as the Dark Knight.

A lot of work has gone into attempts to develop schedules to minimize the effects of jet lag. These are largely based on using the

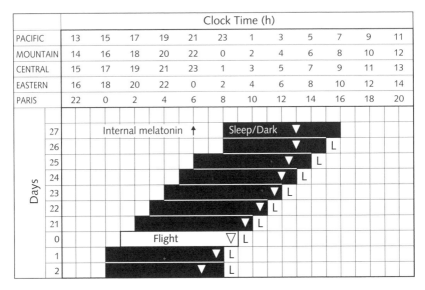

Figure 12.4. Schedule for in altering circadian rhythms before a flight to reduce jet lag in travel from North America to Europe. The four main North American time zones and one for Europe (Paris) are shown at top. The sleep schedules at bottom are from seven days before the flight (Day −7) to two days after the flight. Internal melatonin secretions triggered by dim light levels are shown by the arrow. The minimum body temperature is indicated by the open triangles. Ls mean the administration of intermittent bright light for two to three hours each morning. Adopted from Eastman et al. (2005).

key contributors of the circadian rhythm—light and associated melatonin levels. From these, elaborate schedules involving progressively shifting the ambient light levels in advance of the flight have been suggested. For example, Charmane Eastman of Rush University Medical Center in Chicago has come up with an idea (shown in Figure 12.4) that involves using bright light to help shift the circadian rhythms before a flight.

The schedule shown in the figure is for travel from North America to Europe. Here the top time axis shows the four main North American time zones and one time zone for Europe (Paris). The sleep schedules are shown from seven days before the flight (Day −7) to two days after the flight, moving the body clock forward by one hour per day. That means that the time for awakening is advanced one hour per day as well.

If Batman were flying from Gotham City (eastern time zone) instead of from Los Angeles, fewer days in the schedule would be needed. Anyway, using this example from Los Angeles, Batman / Bruce Wayne would arrive in Paris already adjusted to the new time zone. It is possible, then, to deliberately modify the body clock as long as the important timing cues—zeitgebers like bright light exposure— are used.

However, jet lag, for most people, is a rare thing. Now let's look at how much our—or Batman's—body clock set points can be altered long term for activities such as shift work.

Working the Batshift

Some of the considerations we already described for travel and jet lag also apply for shift work. Probably it is best to consider jet lag as an intermittent and temporary change to the body clock set point. Regular shift work can be ongoing and permanent—always working the same night shift—or ongoing and rotational, as with police officers whose shifts rotate around through days and nights.

Whether permanent or rotational, when we start thinking about night shift work, we have moved into the territory of a permanent (while we work that job at least) change in a set point. However, the set point changes are still heavily dominated by light levels. Because of that, we are usually working against the body for the circadian rhythms to be synchronized to the light levels. A big problem for night shift work is that it is unlikely that the internal body clock is permanently shifted to the requirements for the work environment. This is opposite to the situation with jet lag, then, but central to what Batman does (and notably emergency personnel such as firefighters, police officers, and ambulance workers do) on a daily basis.

There are some documented hazards associated with chronic night shift work. Eating meals at unusual times relative to the internal circadian rhythms can increase the risk for cardiovascular disease, hasten the onset of diabetes mellitus, and lead to ulcers. Also, since Batman is sleeping mostly during the heart of the day, he is not out in the sun. Being out in the sun is where we get loads of vitamin D, which is essential for bone metabolism. By the way, vitamin D doesn't directly make your bones stronger. What it does is dramatically increase the absorption of dietary calcium (by between about 30 and 80%). So, it is very important for bone health. Vitamin D3 is produced in your skin by the pigment melanin (not melatonin, although the words are similar) when the skin is exposed to ultraviolet light. So sporting around at night (when ultraviolet light levels are virtually nonexistent) or while wearing a batsuit means that Batman gets very little vitamin D from sunlight exposure. Batman needs to drink lots of fortified milk or use a tanning bed!

Batman is forced to do his patrols and deal with the crazy criminal element of Gotham when his body is physiologically ready for sleep. Then he has to come home late (early in the morning) and try to sleep when his body is trying to get ready to be awake. Because of that, any sleep that Batman will get after his night shift is likely to be about two hours shorter than what he would get if he were sleeping at night. This also highlights another problem. Batman and most other shift workers go to sleep after their night shift, not before. If you think for a moment you will see that this is the reversal of a normal daytime schedule where you wake up and go to work.

We already talked about why having a misaligned body clock was a problem for mental alertness and physiological function when we were thinking about jet lag. What can be done to help out in the case of shift work? As with jet lag, the dominant factor seems to be levels of ambient light. The solution, then, is actually quite simple but is very difficult to implement. Basically, keeping well adapted to the new requirements of a nocturnal work schedule means trying to maintain a new light-dark cycle. That means reducing light levels when they should be low but are actually naturally high (during the day) and increasing light levels when they need to high but are actually low (at night).

This all seems simple enough. However, the body clock is extremely sensitive to light and any inappropriate bright light exposure can derail the best attempts to shift the body clock to a nighttime phase. It is a bit like checking on how a cake is baking or bread is rising. The very act of checking it can make it fall! Well, letting in even a little light at the wrong time can do the same thing for circadian rhythms. Things that have been tried include having a night shift work environment as bright as possible (to increase light in the new "day") and wearing very dark glasses to go home after the shift and heavily shrouded curtains in the room where daytime sleep will occur (to reduce the light exposure in the new "night"). However, the necessary sunglasses can actually be so dark that they are dangerous to use while driving!

This wouldn't be that much of a problem for Batman, since he does have a chauffeur and butler in Alfred, and who can just go to bed when he returns from patrol. However, this is a real and significant issue for the example night workers of emergency personnel. Also, because these workers often do other things (like take kids to school) when they get off the night shift they wind up with all that additional ambient light at the wrong time for their body clocks and are therefore constantly reshifting their body clocks. For Batman there are a couple of problems with this. He is out in the dark swinging around Gotham City. He cannot really do his job while using a giant high-intensity light! It is worth noting that the permanent mismatch between biological body clock and environmental zeitgebers virtually guarantees that Batman never adapts fully to his night shifts. He will be tired almost all the time.

There may also be an interesting link between sleep deprivation and sleep regulation and metabolism (think back to Chapter 6). While we are awake we have the expression of certain genes that affect and modify the activity of our mitochondria and the movement of glucose around the body. Genes for key regulatory enzymes that can affect the levels of hormones and neurotransmitters in the brain are changed depending on the how long we are awake and when we are awake. So, in many ways sleep deprivation is a kind of stress or challenge to homeostasis and metabolism.

Let us turn now to chronic sleep loss. Recall that we found out previously that night shift workers may sleep during days on average two hours less than they would if they were allowed nighttime sleep. Well, that kind of situation means that over the long term a night shift worker like Batman is going to be incurring a chronic sleep loss and sleep "debt." Some really interesting information on this issue has come from ultra-endurance races and military operations.

What is sleep debt? There is obviously a huge range for actual hours of sleep needed per night for different people, but the typical range is between about 5 and 10 hours. Athletes often sleep more than regular Joes and Janes. However, you can read in a panel from the "The Sleep of Reason" (Detective Comics #598, 1989) that Batman "barely sleeps." Recall the quote at the beginning of this chapter about Bruce Wayne and sleep. In "The Sleep of Reason" it is stated that "with sufficient practice, the body can be trained—the muscles relaxed, the heartbeat slowed—so that one hour's sleep does the work of eight."

Well, this is certainly a time when the Batman universe is not at all realistic! Batman and Bruce Wayne do need to sleep. And there isn't a kind of sleep efficiency training that could allow one hour to do the work of eight. I think I hear you asking why not. So, why not? Why is sleep even necessary in the first place?

In That Sleep . . . What Dreams May Come

I paraphrase the Bard a bit with that heading, but while questioning and raising the specter of nightmares during sleep one thing Shakespeare did not question was that sleep was necessary. However, an issue we haven't even discussed is why we need to sleep. I will cut straight to the chase here and admit that sleep itself remains quite poorly understood in science. To borrow and paraphrase from a Winston Churchill radio broadcast in October of 1939, I think sleep can be considered as "a riddle, wrapped in a mystery, inside an enigma." What is the additional advantage of sleep over and above just getting rest? Many animals don't seem to need sleep. One thing is very clear, though: even if we don't understand exactly why we need sleep, we die if we don't get it. In fact, many features of sustained sleep deprivation have a great deal in common with the stress syndrome we originally discussed with regard to Hans Seyle back in Chapter 1.

Before answering the trickier question of why we need sleep, let's explore something a bit simpler by first asking, on a basic physiological level just how much sleep do we really need? One quick way to get a superficial answer to this is to think about what happens to us when we don't have sleep at all or when we aren't getting anywhere near enough sleep. As we found out a few pages back, our inherent circadian rhythms lead to daily fluctuations in many different systems that in turn cause changes in alertness, reaction time, and so on.

Let's continue our discussion of how essential sleep is by looking at what happens when people are sleep deprived. This kind of thing has been studied in laboratory and real-life situations. Incredibly, people can perform one hundred hours—I will do the math and tell you that is more than four days—of nonstop moderate intensity exercise if food energy is provided. However, despite being able to keep doing exercise, things like reaction time are really impaired. Indeed, "impaired" is the absolutely correct word to use for performance when sleep is withheld, because it links to the idea of alcohol impairment. Have a look at Figure 12.5 to see what I mean. As we all know, performance capacity drops as alcohol concentration in the blood is increased. On the top of the figure in panel A this predicted drop in performance with increased blood alcohol concentration is shown. Immediately below that in panel B performance over time of wakefulness (literally how long you have been awake) is shown. It is pretty clear that no major problems or decrements are seen until around 16 or 17 hours of wakefulness. Within a very normal range of waking, then, performance is maintained pretty well. However, once we reach 24 hours of wakefulness, severe decrements are seen.

If you match up the valley between 24 and 27 hours with the blood alcohol concentration in panel A, you will see that staying up for a full day can lead to performance impairments equivalent to about 0.08% blood alcohol concentration. Stated another way, it would be as if Bruce Wayne took five drinks and then attempted to drive the Batmobile! In fact sleep-related accidents in motor vehicles tend to cluster between the hours of 2:00 and 6:00 a.m., when drivers may either be up late or just getting up. In either case, these times are quite near the lowest ebb of performance and occur near the minimum body temperature.

In another real-world example, military personnel can often operate in conditions of sleep deprivation for several days. In those cases, significant issues arise after 36 hours of no sleep. These include extreme fatigue and problems with accuracy during rifle shooting. In most cases there is a relation between the performance and the circadian rise and fall of hormones such as adrenaline and noradrenaline. Clearly, complete sleep deprivation creates many problems. It isn't very representative of the normal work environment for most people, though, including Batman.

Let's now look at what scientists believe may be the reasons that we need sleep. Most physiological adaptations have what is known as "survival value." That is, they provide or provided some form of evolutionary advantage and therefore were traits passed on to following generations. Some see sleep as one of those items that provided benefits at one point in evolution as a way to understand its role. Arguments related to the "need for sleep" have very often been based on several themes. The most compelling is that animals involved in

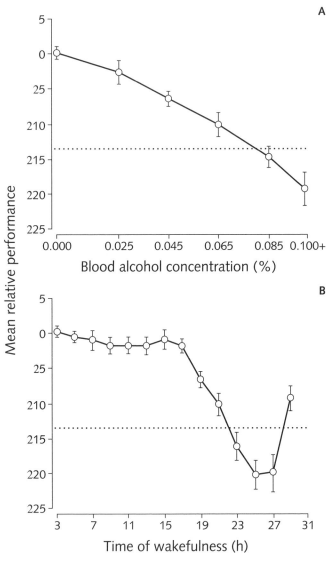

Figure 12.5. Similar effects of blood alcohol (*A*) and extreme wakefulness (*B*) on performance. Courtesy Rajaratnam and Arendt (2001).

long-term sleep deprivation experiments die. This is likely due to a process very similar to Seyle's original stress and the last (and failing) stage of the generalized adaptation syndrome. A related argument involves the kind of observations we discussed above, where cognitive and motor performances are decreased even in short-term sleep deprivation.

Note that there is a difference between sleep and rest. We often appear to be resting while we sleep but we can also rest without sleeping. What is the difference? Rest is really a period of low metabolic activity and can be seen in all animals, both warm- and cold-blooded. The term "sleep" is often used only for mammals and birds. Birds, which do sleep, can go for excessively long periods without sleep during long migrations and during times of incubation and hatching. A good example of this, because it conjures up one of Batman's key foes, is that of the king penguin. During the incubation and posthatching period, the king penguin may be called on to defend his territory thousands of times per day! Clearly, very little sleep can occur with such demands. Yet the king penguin survives and flourishes.

So, why does Batman need sleep? We just don't know for sure right now. All we can say is he does and that he is also chronically sleep deprived. However, he muddles along as best as he can just like most of us!

Now we've seen how Batman has protected himself with training and his batsuit and how he attempts to subsist with little sleep. Let's turn our attention to what happens to Batman when he is not in peak performance and even gets injured.

PART V

A MIXED BATBAG

Pondering possible pitfalls along the path to bathood

CHAPTER 13
Injury and Recovery

HOW MUCH BANGING
UNTIL THE BATBACK
GOES BONK?

Years of rigorous athletic training have en-
abled the Batman not only to resist but to
recover from the brutal beating that would
have mortally injured most men!
—"Professor Strange's Fear Dust" (Detective
   Comics #46, 1940)

Have you ever had a back strain that seemed to be brought on by
the mildest thing? If not, you probably have heard somebody say,
"I threw my back out just lifting up the milk at breakfast time." Even
professional athletes experience such injuries. When we subsequently
read that a powerful man playing a rough sport like ice hockey or
football hurt himself getting out of his car, we may have difficulty
imagining that such a trivial-seeming event could lead to injury. But
it can and does happen regularly. Every time we do anything we subject our muscles, bones, and other tissues to stress and strain.

Our biological tissues are just like many other materials, and
over time they can weaken. Think of the old-style metal coat hangers. When I was a kid we were constantly using coat hangers to make
all kinds of things—including awesome marshmallow-toasting

forks! To do so usually meant unfolding the coat hanger and then breaking it in half. Except we didn't break it with a wire cutter or any tool. Instead we bent the hanger back and forth over and over again until it heated up and then snapped in two. What we were doing is a bit like the way your tissues are repeatedly put through their paces by all your activities. However, your body is constantly rebuilding itself, unlike the stress and strain of that coat hanger or the head of your golf club when you take much too large of a divot.

Despite the ongoing repairs, small little things can really be the proverbial "last straw that broke the camel's back." So, Batman is constantly straining his body at the best of times and constantly getting really pummeled at the worst of times. What can his (or your) body take before injury occurs and how long does it take to recover from those injuries? For somebody as busy as Batman, there may be some injuries from which he never recovers fully. In "The Autobiography of Bruce Wayne" (The Brave and the Bold #197, 1983), Batman's body really shows wear and tear. He has loads of scar tissue, as noted by Catwoman (who was cooperating with him in this story), who stares at his back and says, "It's just . . . all this . . . scar tissue on your back . . ." In Batman's own words "Oh, that. Occupational hazard. Fifteen years of fighting will do that to a person."

Batman's back is not the only part of him to get injured. Batman also takes a lot of blows to his head and pretty much anywhere else we can imagine. While trying to imagine the sort of occupational injuries that Batman might experience, let's start with examples of other activities that could be considered similar to the main physical demands Batman faces on the job.

Occupational Dangers of the Dark Knight

To give an overview of what we could expect, I will describe injuries in two categories—one for brain and one for body—as concussions and strains. In talking about these categories we'll focus on bumps to the head (concussion) and things like whiplash injuries (for strains). Batman really does find himself in very rough and physical encounters on seemingly a daily basis. It probably goes without saying that fighting Killer Croc (crazed maniac with unique "armor-like" skin disease), Blockbuster (crazed gigantic mountain man) and Bane (crazed humungous adrenaline junky experimental soldier) are not safe activities. The most dangerous foe that Batman has ever faced must be Bane. My stating this is largely due to the grievous injuries that Bane was able to inflict on Batman. In his "Rogues Gallery" Scott Beatty describes Bane as 2 meters (6'8") tall and weighing 140 kilograms (350 pounds) with no known "real name" and with a listed occupation of "professional criminal." Bane was born into a military prison and underwent experiments involving brain injections of a special "venom" that was supposed to create unstoppable super soldiers.

Bane first appeared in January 1993 in *Batman: Vengeance of Bane #1*. In a series of stories played out in a story arc called Knightfall, Bane beats Batman and actually "breaks his back" in a titanic battle. The seriousness of this injury in this story is captured by Robin when he says, "But it's never been this bad. He could be paralyzed. He could die." Batman is left to recover and has to relearn how to walk while various successors are tried out for him. Eventually, Batman recovers and defeats Bane. However, not before Bane earns infamous distinction as the most physically formidable foe Batman has ever faced. We will return to this story later in this chapter.

I want us to think about two examples of real-life (and extreme) activities that encompass much of what Batman might experience in his fights but which don't involve the extreme injuries of Bane. We will come back to Bane in a bit, though, so just hold on. These other examples will provide real-life benchmarks for what would be entailed in the Dark Knight's crime-fighting activities. For just simply getting bashed around, let's use NFL football in general and running backs in particular. For the grueling experience of fighting, I'll use "ultimate fighting," also known as "mixed martial arts."

What kinds of injuries are typically sustained when your job has the demands of a football playing, mixed martial artist? Let's look first at mixed martial arts. In several recent surveys of over a 10-year period, about 27% of matches were stopped because of head impact, 16% because of "musculoskeletal stress," 13% because of neck choke, and 12% due to miscellaneous trauma. So, more than two-thirds of the time significant trauma was experienced. Overall, the injury rate for these competitions is about 29%. This is higher than that seen for boxing, which is around 17%. Even in controlled semirealistic fighting, injuries are a serious concern. For Batman, it would be even more of an issue as there are no rules on the rooftops of Gotham City.

What happens in football? In gridiron football lower-extremity injuries are the most common, although concussion is a major concern, particularly for quarterbacks and running backs. So, let's begin with concussion and follow that up with skeletal injuries and muscle strains.

What Happens When the Batbrain Gets Bumped?

In football, a running back has to fight through and across the line of scrimmage and try to gain as many yards as possible. While he is doing all that, opposing players are running flat out right at him with the sole intent of slamming into him and forcing him to the ground. Oh, yes, in theory the opposing players are also supposed to be trying to get the ball. Mostly that seems kind of secondary to a thunderous tackle. It is a pretty rough job. As quoted in a 2007 *Sports Illustrated* article, former New York Giants running back Tiki Barber describes the experience: "Lie down on the floor 30 times and then get up. It's hard. Now imagine getting knocked down 30 times and getting up. Every day." If we change "every day" to "every night" we would have a good description of what happens to Batman.

The question that is relevant to us is whether that is really such a horrible thing to happen to somebody—does getting knocked down repeatedly really cause some bad things to occur? The answer is mostly "yes," and mostly it has to do with what happens when someone is actually hit by someone (or something) else. When this occurs, large forces are experienced, and these result in large accelerations of the body of the person being hit. (Recall that we learned about acceleration and force in Chapter 10.) This is a very big problem if the part of the body getting hit—or subsequently hitting something—is the head.

Despite the many knocks on the head Batman takes regularly, he hardly ever seems to suffer from symptoms of concussion and is rarely even shown as being susceptible to concussion. One of the closest admissions that getting slugged all the time might not be so great can be found in "This One'll Kill You Batman" (Batman #260, 1975). In this story Batman suffers the effects of both getting hit—again—and drinking some coffee with a sedative in it. He remarks (as Bruce Wayne) to Alfred that despite needing "a computer to count the skull knocks I've taken . . . I've never experienced symptoms like these!" Later, when revisiting of the story of Man-Bat in "Wings" (Legends of the Dark Knight #5, 1998), Alfred comes right out and says, "You received a severe concussion in that fall with those idiotic birdwings." Despite the fact that Batman corrects Alfred in using "batwings," this is still one of the rare times where there is an admission of the possibility of concussion. Putting aside for a minute how unbelievable it is that Batman could take all the falls and the direct blows to the head that he does and yet rarely experience a concussion, let's continue to look at what concussion really means.

We've all heard the term "concussion" so often that the real meaning is probably pretty much lost on most of us. The Merriam-Webster dictionary defines concussion as "a jarring injury of the brain resulting in disturbance of cerebral function." What does that really mean, though? What is a jarring injury and does something as mild sounding as "disturbance" really have any significance? If we heard on the six o'clock news that a weather "disturbance" could be expected I doubt we'd get up in arms about it. However, a disturbance of cerebral function does sound a bit more ominous. Let's look at what that could really be.

If we delve somewhat deeper and beyond the rather superficial dictionary definition of concussion, we might find something such as prepared by Kimberly Harmon, which reads that concussion, the "most common form of head injury in athletics," is "a transient disturbance of neurologic function caused by trauma." Concussion symptoms include dizziness, headache, and impairment of vision, balance, and the ability to concentrate. Amnesia for events that happened after the traumatic head injury and outright loss of consciousness may occur. It is the latter that made diagnoses and response to concussion so difficult for so long in sports. It seemed for the longest time that, if a player wasn't knocked unconscious, he didn't have anything to worry about. Batman is just the opposite and routinely finds himself knocked unconscious and being groggily revived by Robin, Alfred, or someone else but still doesn't have a concussion!

Concussion—and postconcussion syndrome, which we will discuss later—is considered a "diffuse" injury. This means that there isn't any localized specific injury site but rather a very large and global injury. Imagine what happens when you are playing a DVD or a CD and then the player is jostled. Typically, there is a "skip" followed by a delay, then the movie or song resumes where it left off (or close to there). Concussion is a bit like this in that the jolt to the player can be considered to be the blow to the body (or head) that leads to the acceleration that causes the brief change in neural function. Most symptoms of minor concussion resolve after two to three days, but effects can linger longer.

A better analogy than DVDs or CDs is actually an old-style record player. When the record player gets bumped, it skips just like the CD player. However, it doesn't resume exactly where it left off (kind of like the amnesia effect) and, in contrast to the digital CD with its laser that doesn't really harm the CD itself, bumps to the record player that cause the needle to skip and jump actually do scratch the record. If you substitute "brain cells" for "record" you will begin to appreciate why concussion might be a concern after all and why repeated concussion could be a real problem.

This brings up the question of what exactly is happening to the neurons and Batman's brain when he is hit. What is concussion at the cellular level? We can think of a concussion as inducing a harsh chemical imbalance in the neurons of the brain after impact. This is really a challenge to homeostasis (yes, it is back again!) in the metabolism of the neurons in the brain. Rapid accelerations induce these changes. Although the neurons in your brain aren't meant to respond to impact, they can be affected by physical trauma.

Think of your eye. You have photoreceptors that respond to the photons of light hitting your retina. However, if you have ever been hit in the eye, even lightly, you probably saw a flash of light or sparks. You activated your photoreceptors mechanically in that case. Kind of like the example above of the skipping CD. The CD player wasn't designed to respond to mechanical input; however, it does produce a response of sorts by resetting itself. Well, neurons are after all just cells, and all cells are squishy and have numerous pores in them. Through the pores (called channels) ions move in and out of the cell to maintain function. Physical trauma can therefore make cells do things they don't normally do by changing the way the ions move.

An important thing about all cells is that the watery material on the inside is maintained with a different concentration than the watery material in which the cells live. A membrane—really like the skin of the cell—keeps a concentration of some ions on the inside of the cell different from those on the outside of the cell. Some key ions are potassium (which you find in bananas and some other foods) and sodium (which we find in too many foods!). Well, when the head is subjected to concussive forces, the main outcome is that potassium ions are ejected from neurons. This disrupts the function of the neurons and affects communication between neurons in the brain. Sodium ions are also affected, as are neurotransmitters that are used to excite neurons.

This leads to a synchronous activation in the brain. While your cortical neurons are always active, they are not usually active all at the same time. However, blunt mechanical trauma causes many neurons to synchronize and discharge all at once, kind of like a seizure. As such the neurons are "stunned" and slowly wake up again over time (and some don't wake up at all). The normal concentrations of sodium and potassium ions are restored in several hours but other ions like calcium may take several days to return to a normal level.

Another negative consequence of the neurons' discharging all at once is that they need a lot of extra energy in the form of glucose and oxygen to keep on doing their work. The problem is that the energy supply isn't there because the demand was artificial. So, the normal "warm up" of blood flow and oxygen delivery was absent. Also, the presence of all that calcium actually reduces and interferes with the ability to provide blood and oxygen to the neurons that demand it.

This cascade leads to an energy crisis—kind of malevolent neuronal oxygen debt—that causes the neurons to fail (shown in Figure 13.1). The increase in energy demand coupled with reduced blood flow and reduced metabolism is the energy crisis. Some neurons may die but many will take several days to recover from this massive shift of ions. The memory problems and mental confusion seen during this time after concussion occur because of what has happened at the cellular level. Returning to normal concentrations of neurotransmitters can sometimes take up to two weeks. Note that the main areas affected by repetitive mild head trauma are the hippocampus as well as the frontal lobes. As we learned earlier in Chapter 7 on motor learning, these areas are very important for memory formation and storage.

With repeated concussion we enter the territory of secondary impact syndrome and postconcussion syndrome. The best-case scenario for Batman is that the blow he suffers doesn't injure him unduly (remember what we learned in Chapter 11 about the cushioning provided by the batcowl) and that he has time to recover after he is concussed before suffering another one. It is quite dangerous when

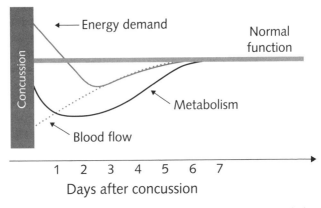

Figure 13.1. Effects of concussion on energy demand, metabolism, and blood flow over time.

someone hasn't fully recovered from the initial concussion and then suffers another blow to the head. In this scenario, even a very minor impact to the head can trigger a change in the regulation of blood supply to the brain. This is called "secondary impact syndrome" and can lead to swelling and blood pooling and is very often fatal.

A less severe outcome of multiple concussions occurs when there has been good recovery after each concussion but impacts are repeated. This is clinically defined as "postconcussion syndrome," but anecdotally it is called "punch drunk" syndrome. It is called this—not surprisingly since scientists and physicians are often very literal—because this syndrome is often present in boxers (who do absorb many blows to the head). The issue here is that, while the person—including Batman—does recover and may seem "symptom-free" between concussions, the nervous system doesn't really truly return to the preconcussion state. Damage has occurred but is kind of "covered up" so that when more injuries occur, there is less and less ability to make repairs.

It is kind of like patching the knees on your jeans when you were a kid. The patch covered the hole but if you kept getting more and more holes and applying more and more patches, eventually there was nothing left to attach the patches to. You had no choice at that point but to go and get some new jeans. This is a pretty easy fix. Getting a new brain is much more problematic.

Even though most people don't routinely ram their heads into something hard and suffer no ill effects, some other animals do just that. The woodpecker is a good example. So are goats and rams. They all routinely smash their heads together or against another hard object. Yet we don't see mounds of mountain goats lying concussed everywhere when we go to the zoo. Nor do we find our path through the forest blocked by red-crested woodpeckers strewn about. These animals can tolerate acceleration forces that can be up to a hundred times greater than what you or I could tolerate.

Probably the most dominant feature of the woodpecker is the straight beak that it uses to pound away forcefully on tree trunks. It has been calculated that velocity of the beak at impact may be as high as 7 meters (23 feet) per second. The negative acceleration that occurs can be as large as 10,000 m/s^2, or a thousand times the force of gravity! As a frame of reference, to experience an equivalent negative acceleration, Batman would have to be able to run into a brick wall at about 315 mph without suffering a concussion. Of course, his grievous musculoskeletal injuries would be a bit of a problem.

The question, though, is why is that so? The short answer is that the long answer is not really clear. However, it seems likely to have a lot to do with the nature of the acceleration experienced. It turns out that the woodpecker mostly experiences linear (straight line) acceleration and very little angular acceleration. Minimizing the angular acceleration of the head is a major job of helmets worn in sports like football and is incorporated into the cowl of the batsuit.

Protecting the Batbrain

Clearly, Batman's line of work means he is likely at risk for not just single concussive events separated by months or years, but more often he will have multiple repeated "exposures" to concussion. So, what can be done to moderate the effects of being hit in the head? Well, wearing a helmet would be a great idea since it would help reduce the accelerations that Batman's head experiences.

There have been many attempts to cushion blows to the head in sports like football and boxing by using padding in helmets and gloves. The batsuit includes a padded and protective helmet as part of the cowl. In combat sports that use heavy contact there is a real need to protect the head and prevent broken noses and other injuries.

In my own karate training we used to practice a full-contact form of fighting that made use of robust sparring gear called *bogu*. This included headgear that was similar to a modified kendo helmet, which was easily strong enough to withstand the hardest punch or kick that could be delivered. It was a sturdy helmet with a big metal grid on the front. So, of course, we hit each other pretty hard.

I remember vividly one of the first times my brother and I tried out the bogu gear for our sparring back in the mid-1980s. We had been training with this gear for only a very short time when I launched a punch that hit my brother and knocked him unconscious. He was only briefly concussed, but the main point is that he had no facial abrasions or broken bones. By the way, there is no direct relation between my knocking out my brother in this instance and the fact that he had broken my nose a few years earlier. Honest.

However, getting knocked out is more of a significant concern, because our bones heal much better than do our brains. Since that time the bogu helmets have undergone many design changes. This can be related to what has happened over the centuries with boxing. Boxing and boxing-related injuries have been around since the sport began. Back in ancient Roman times, boxers would often use hand wraps with spiky protrusions that caused more bloody injuries and eventually led to a ban on boxing. Fast forward to the seventeenth and eighteenth centuries when boxing was a very popular sports activity in the United Kingdom. However, it could be quite brutal with almost anything—including biting—allowed.

In an effort to make the sport less injurious and more palatable, the Broughton rules in 1743, the London Prize Ring rules in 1839, and finally the Marquis of Queensbury rules in 1867 were introduced. These rules all limited the techniques that could be used, how fighters should behave, and how matches would be conducted. So, biting was right out at that point! In particular, in attempts to make the sport safer, the Queensbury Rules called for the use of boxing gloves, ten-second knockout times, and three-minute rounds.

However, none of these measures actually eliminated the impact that boxing has on the nervous system. So, what kinds of design changes are needed and what considerations need to be addressed to make activities with lots of head contact safe? The best place to explore this is in the design and redesign of football helmets such as used in the NFL. Let's spend a moment to look inside the origin and development of helmets and explore briefly concussion-related issues in football. Football is clearly a high impact sport where body contact is guaranteed. Over the history of this sport, injuries have been fairly common. In the period from 1869 to 1905, 159 serious injuries—including 18 fatalities—occurred during football games. Despite these serious injuries, helmets weren't used in an American football game until 1893 in the Army-Navy game played at Annapolis, Maryland. Navy won 6-4, by the way. Helmet use was not enforced until 1939 in the NCAA and 1940 in the NFL. When helmets were first introduced, they were basically lightly padded leather skull-caps. Examining the period from 1945 to 1999, there were almost five hundred deaths as a result of injury in football. More than two-thirds of the deaths were because of brain injury with the remainder due to spinal cord injury or bleeding in the brain. These rates have dropped off in recent years as a result of prohibition on leading with contact from the head and face during blocking and tackling. However, the problems of concussion remain.

The use of single and double bars on the face mask didn't come along until the 1950s. Since that time helmets have undergone dramatic transformation. They now incorporate light injection-molded inserts and are used along with neck bracing to help shield the spinal column from damage. In many ways the newer helmets are similar to what Batman has in his cowl. The cowl is padded and acts like a helmet and also incorporates some form of neck protection. A good helmet or batcowl acts to change the impulse (recall from Chapter 10 that impulse = force × time over which it is applied) so that lower peak forces are experienced by the head inside.

Despite that, concussion is still a serious issue in professional football. It was reported in 2000 that almost 50% of players in the Canadian Football League had suffered at least one concussion. Considering secondary impact syndrome (repeated concussions and brain damage), those CFL players who had already had a concussion were about six times as likely to lose consciousness with subsequent concussions than were players who hadn't had one before. So, obviously further refinements to helmets might be in order!

Strains and Sprains

It is now time to have a look at the more routine injuries that Batman experiences: his normal bumps, strains, and sprains. These are the more painful injuries, but they aren't usually as potentially debilitating as concussion.

We have all hurt ourselves doing some activity and said we "strained" or "sprained" something. Probably you have heard the phrase "repetitive strain injury." These kinds of injuries can be understood by using the concept of "microfailure," which means that small loads repeated many times can also yield injuries. The tissues that are being strained—particularly those with poor blood supplies like tendons, ligaments, and cartilage—are not able to fully repair themselves between subsequent events. This is a bit like the repeated concussion concept above except it is with other tissue. Commonly it turns up in the context of workplace-related injuries and might be included in the serious sounding carpal tunnel syndrome. The basic concept is that a consistent and repeated low-level load can lead to injury in the same way that a very large load can lead to injury with only a few (maybe even one) loading events (shown in Figure 13.2). High loads with low repetitions are shown at the top left while low loads with high repetitions are shown at the bottom right. The point to note is that injury can happen anywhere on that continuum.

Fighting techniques can also produce repetitive strain injuries. Even in my own martial arts training—which, obviously, is much less intense than that of Batman—repetitive strain injuries are a major concern. I cannot train day to day with full intensity on the same weapon, for example. Instead I have to rotate through different techniques, patterns, and forms and alternate empty hand training and weapons training.

Let's look more closely at what a strain is. To understand what happens to our muscles, tendons, bones, and ligaments when we have an injury means first thinking about what these tissues are made of and what happens to them when we subject them to force. Now we have entered the arena of tissue biomechanics. This field shares many features with materials science and materials engineering. Keep in mind that biological tissues like muscle and bone have mechanical properties that help explain some of the weird things that seem to happen to us when we are injured. Remember that in mechanical terms "stress" refers to the forces applied to a material, whereas "strain" refers to the change in length or size of the tissue to which the force is applied. So, it is fair to say that repeated stresses lead to strains. If you were to measure the relationship between stress and strain of something like the long bone of your upper leg

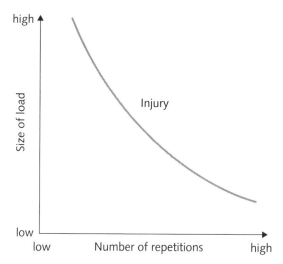

Figure 13.2. The number of repetitions and the size of loads leading to injury. High loads with low repetitions are shown at the top left and low loads with high repetitions are shown at the bottom right. Injury can result from many repetitions with a small load as well as from few repetitions with a large load.

(your femur), you would find that at some high stresses the strain is too high and the bone would break (failure or rupture in mechanical terms). This is where you would have an obvious injury such as a broken leg. You could really make it sound better by calling it a severe strain, but it is still very painful.

Whiplash Injuries and Sore Muscles

I hope you haven't been in a car accident and experienced an injury known as "whiplash." However, you have almost certainly done a new activity that led to sore muscles the following day (and for a few days after that). There are some similarities between what is going on in the two scenarios, and the similarities have to do with how our muscles work.

We can think of our muscles doing three general kinds of contractions. When you pick up an object (like this book) and flex your elbow to bring it closer to your face, you are doing a "shortening" contraction—so called because the muscle fibers in your arm muscles are physically shortening. In contrast, when you lower the object (or book) back down to the table or wherever, you are doing a "lengthening" contraction. Last, when you are just holding the book in front of you and not moving it up or down, you are doing an "isometric" (literally no change in length) contraction. When your muscles are performing lengthening contractions they can be "over-stretched" by whatever you are doing. A good example is walking down a hill or down stairs. When you have gone on a mountain hike or even one in a very hilly area you probably found your leg muscles (particularly the ones on the front of your thigh, your quadriceps, or the front of your shin, your ankle flexors) to be very sore the next day. That's because those muscles were doing lots of lengthening contractions on the way back down the trail from the mountain.

That sort of pain can also occur when you do some new exercise or movements that you haven't done before (or recently). You aren't adapted to them yet (or again), and you are causing a little muscle damage when you move around. This is called delayed onset muscles soreness and typically reaches a peak in discomfort after one to two days and is gone after three days. Whiplash injury is much like what happened to your leg muscles when you came down that hilly trail. Rather than your leg muscles, in a whiplash the neck muscle is stretched and lengthened when the head is snapped forward.

There is a common misconception that having sore muscles the day after a new or more intense activity is due to the buildup of lactic acid. The soreness is due, instead, to the small microtraumas experienced by your muscles and resolves in a few days, leading to an increased adaptation to the exercise you did. Then when you do that exercise again, it doesn't hurt so much. Lactic acid is a metabolic byproduct during muscle contraction, but it breaks down immediately into hydrogen ion and lactate. The hydrogen ion concentration interferes with ongoing contractions (leading to muscle fatigue), while the lactate is shuttled off to be used as an energy source in other muscles—your heart muscle actually uses up a lot of it!

Recovery?

Everyone, including costumed crimefighters, experiences injury. Now let's examine whether Batman recovers more rapidly from his injuries because of his training as was suggested by the quote at the beginning of this chapter. It might be supposed that, since Batman is in such great shape, he should be able to recover faster from his injuries. But this is not likely the case. In fact, Batman may be perpetually on the border of overtraining. Before going on a bit more, I should mention that a small amount of evidence indicates that exercise generally might lower cortisol levels and could help increase healing rates. However, in the state of overtraining, which refers to the situation that can occur when the volume of training is too high, there cannot be any meaningful adaptation to training.

Think back to our discussion of the GAS (generalized adaptation syndrome) in Chapter 3. We talked about how an organism—from bats to Batman—will respond to a given stress in a way that minimizes the effect of that stress. This occurs to minimize any changes in homeostatic balance. However, if the stress is too large, there will be a steady decline in performance. This is what athletes experience when they say they are "burnt out" leading up to major events like the Olympics. I hope they feel burnt out after their events and not before! However, poor timing of training can sometimes result in being in a state of overtraining prior to an event.

This was shown for Batman in "Knightfall: Part 1: The Broken Bat" (Batman #497, 1993). Bane, Batman's steroid-laced nemesis, has set Batman up for overtraining by releasing all the criminals from Gotham's Arkham Asylum. Batman must battle most of the escaped inmates and gets so fatigued that when Bane eventually fights him, Batman is fairly easily defeated. Robin, Alfred, and Nightwing deal with the aftermath of Batman's injuries sustained during the fight with Bane. These include a broken back, probably in the lower back (lumbar region), which has left Bruce temporarily paralyzed. As it turned out, his lower limb paralysis was temporary, and he made a good recovery after much rehabilitation.

I don't know about you, but I am kind of suspicious that Batman can have temporary paralysis and then get better! After all, aren't spinal cord injuries supposed to be relatively permanent? Yes, they are, despite some excellent work in different animal experiments pointing the way to treatments that might eventually lead to spinal cord repair. However, with strong traumatic injury that doesn't actually lead to physical tearing or crushing of the spinal cord, it is possible to have a more temporary paralysis followed by recovery. This is a bit like a spinal cord concussion, actually, in that the function of the neurons and nerves in the spinal cord are disrupted temporarily but slowly recover.

The types of injuries Batman likely sustained would have ranged from the cellular level to the spinal cord itself. Those cellular powerhouses the mitochondria would have experienced interruption of their metabolic function. Remember that mitochondria produce energy used by the cells (and hence by the person!). So disrupting their function could have a dramatic weakening effect. Spinal shock can result, which can mean lower blood pressure and temporary reduction of spinal cord function. Spinal cord injury commonly involves stretching or compression of the cord due to movement or direct damage to the vertebrae. So, to counteract this, a doctor would surgically decompress the spinal cord.

By the way, in several alternate versions of Alfred's history—or backstory—he has attended medical school, so we assume that he is competent, qualified, and knowledgeable to treat Bruce's back injuries. I don't recall ever reading any story where he did a specialization in neurology or neurosurgery, however! Alfred is shown helping treat Batman and indicates to Robin that he needs a certain drug called "decadron" to help with the repair.

This part of the story bears a resemblance to medical fact. Scientists attempting to repair the spinal cord after traumatic injury have used various "cocktails" of different drugs. A major issue of concern is reducing the swelling and inflammation in the spinal cord that occur within minutes of the initial injury and build up rapidly in the hours after. This inflammation can lead to significant additional damage to the spinal cord unrelated to the first injury. Catabolic steroids work well to control inflammation. Remember that catabolic means to break down. These steroids literally break down tissue and so reduce inflammation. Think back to Chapter 3 when we talked about cortisol and steroid creams for itchy skin. Because of this catabolic property, various attempts have been made to use such steroids in the initial treatment of spinal cord injury.

I think this is what the comic's writers were referring to with decadron. The generic name of this steroid is dexamethasone, and it is now commonly used to reduce inflammation typically found with rheumatoid arthritis. Back in the 1960s and 1970s many steroids were evaluated for this use, two of them being dexamethasone and methylprednisolone (MP). Despite mixed results, MP remains a commonly used drug intervention for treatment of spinal cord injury and is typically administered as soon as possible after the injury (there may be key window extending only to six to eight hours) and for 24 to 48 hours postinjury. So, it is quite accurate for Alfred to seek such treatment for Batman.

Having now looked at steroid use for something you probably didn't anticipate, let's continue a bit further with our talk of steroids in a performance context. Let's address the question: Would Batman have taken steroids as part of his training to build up his strength and reduce his likelihood of injury?

Does Batman Take Steroids?

Steroids are covered a lot in the media, particularly when the Olympic Games are on or when Major League Baseball enters spring training. Unfortunately, baseball's home run leader, Barry Bonds, and one of its top all-time pitchers, Roger Clemens, have both been the focus of continuing controversy stemming from allegations that they used steroids and other banned substances. Other potential Hall of Famers are also under investigation. In this context, steroids seem like they have a well-deserved bad rap.

However, steroids actually are necessary for your body to function. We have seen that in Chapter 3 and elsewhere in the book. But, what the media is covering and what I am going to talk about here are anabolic steroids that are not produced by your body to help it function; they come from a jar or a syringe. They can do some good in the short run, but it comes at a price. This price can include a heavy toll on much of your body, including many of your internal organs.

If Batman needs an edge, is it worth it for him to take steroids? What would he become if he did take steroids? Steroids did play a key role in that Batman: Venom story arc from 1993 that I keep referring to. The "venom" used by the infamous Bane is a steroid derivative that gives great strength and superhuman muscle adaptation. It also makes you crazy, though, as Batman found out. At the very beginning of this story arc Batman fails in his attempt to save a kidnapped girl. To save her from drowning, he has to lift and move a huge boulder, but he is just not strong enough and the girl dies. Batman trains even harder as a result of this failure and eventually seriously injures himself. Then he goes in search of something to make him stronger and falls prey to a scientist who wants to set him up with a dependency on his supersteroid, which is also the formulation for the venom that Bane uses. The evil scientist eventually tells Batman that he can have all the strength he desires without any work by saying, "One capsule will replace all that sweaty grunting and groaning you must do to keep in shape."

Is that realistic? Well, anabolic steroids are basically a stimulant for muscle growth. Recall that anabolic means building up. However, the muscles still need the stress stimulus to get stronger, which comes from doing actual training. And going back to our fictional batworld for a moment, also notice that the one who gave the drug to Batman is an evil scientist, who neglected to mention the small side effect that involves going insane and becoming a complete slave to this drug.

To understand how anabolic steroids work, let's focus on testosterone. It is the primary male hormone and is manufactured in the testes as well as in the ovaries of females and in small amounts in the adrenal gland of both sexes. This hormone regulates many functions across the life span, notably during embryogenesis and puberty. In the adult male, testosterone is responsible for regulating protein metabolism, sexual and cognitive function, and bone remodeling. The proper name for anabolic steroids is actually anabolic-androgenic steroids (AASs). That is because it is impossible to separate completely the muscle-building role from the role in promoting secondary sexual characteristics, such as body hair and genitalia. Perhaps surprisingly, the term "primary sexual characteristic" refers to whether a person has ovaries or testes and not to other features that distinguish the sexes.

Although testosterone was first discovered as a specific chemical in the body in 1935, the history of its use for enhancing performance dates back to Charles-Édouard Brown-Séquard (1817–1894) in 1889. He self-injected testicular extract from nonhuman animals and found that doing so resulted in some form of antiaging and increased vitality. In 1896 a colleague of Brown-Séquard also self-administered testicular extract and examined the effect on finger strength (which increased). The practice of using steroids to enhance athletic performance really hit its stride behind the "iron curtain" in the 1960s and 1970s when many female East German athletes were thought to have taken AAS.

The two main commonly observed outcomes of AAS use are the increase in muscle mass and strength and the effects on the brain giving rise to euphoria and aggression. AAS works to increase strength in three (more threes!) general ways. First, these steroids help improve the use of ingested nitrogen and protein, which leads to more muscle building. This occurs largely through messenger RNA activity. Remember in Chapter 2 we learned that this is the part of the cell involved with protein construction.

Second, recall from Chapter 3 the whole balancing act that the endocrine system uses to maintain homeostasis. Increased anabolic activity would normally be balanced by catabolic activity, but when AASs are used, this balance is disrupted. So, catabolic activity is blocked and more protein buildup occurs.

Last, the use of AAS produces a euphoric "high," increased aggression, and lessened fatigue. These can all serve to allow for more vigorous and more frequent training that will then maximize muscle building.

Of course, all this comes at a cost. Chronic use of AAS in extremely high dosage—such as typically found in those using them for the anabolic benefit—can lead to liver damage, elevated cholesterol levels, high blood pressure, decreased ability to regulate blood glucose, extreme mood swings, psychosis, and extreme aggression. In addition to these major health problems, cosmetic changes such as breast atrophy in women and breast enlargement in men, changes in body hair, and acne can all result. Dependency and withdrawal issues are also significant problems. Batman fans may be interested to know in *Batman: Venom* Batman noticed these problems and worked himself off the venom.

Another way to increase AAS levels is to increase the metabolic substances that can be converted or metabolized to the desired hormone (such as testosterone). One example you may be familiar with because it was much in the media recently is androstenedione. This legal supplement was the one that the Major League Baseball player Mark McGwire admitted to taking during his then home-run-record-setting season in 1998. Milder forms of steroids such as androstenedione can lead to increases in testosterone level, but these are small. For example, at most about 15% of the dose of androstenedione is converted to testosterone, and this would likely have a negligible performance benefit.

I must mention that AASs do have huge potential to help people with certain health problems. Examples include counteracting muscle wasting in patients with HIV or in those with unusual hormone profiles. There is also potential benefit in aging that we will discuss in Chapter 15.

Now we will have a little diversion from all this talk about becoming Batman and ponder the age-old question: Who would win in a batbattle of the sexes?

CHAPTER 14
Battle of the Bats

COULD BATGIRL BEAT BATMAN?

She may well be the best fighter alive, master of at least a dozen forms and weapons.
—Batman reflecting on Lady Shiva in "Spirit of the Bat" (Batman #509, 1994)

Congratulations. Even I have never beaten Shiva hand-to-hand.
—Batman to the new Batgirl after she defeats Lady Shiva in *Bruce Wayne: Fugitive,* Volume 1

In the world of comic books and comic book movie adaptations, the battle of the sexes can be very literal. In the DC Comics universe, there are many femmes fatales who fight with and against Batman. Most notably these include the good, in the form of Batgirl and Batwoman, the bad, in the guise of Lady Shiva, and the sometimes good and sometimes bad and overall we don't really know, embodied in Catwoman. The earliest to be introduced was Catwoman, first seen as "The Cat" (Batman #1, 1940). She was later elevated to "The Cat-Woman" in Batman #4 (1940). The first Batgirl (Barbara Gordon, Chief Gordon's daughter) appeared in Detective Comics #359 (1967). Lady Shiva appeared in January 1976, and the second Batgirl (Cassandra Cain) was introduced relatively recently in Batman #567 (1999). Just to be complete, I should also mention that there was another Batgirl (and a Batwoman) in the 1960s as well. However, she only made a few appearances and wasn't a major batplayer in the comics.

Are there reasons to suppose that either Batman or Batgirl might have an advantage over the other? I will outline what would happen if they actually did do battle a bit later. First let's start by addressing the main issue of whether men and women are different when it comes to exercise capacity and responses to training.

Many studies have examined any possible gender effects on performance in sports and athletics. Track events have been particularly well studied. In Figure 14.1, running velocity in meters per minute is shown across a historical timescale for the world records in the 100 meter, 400 meter, and marathon events. The triangle and circle shown at the right of each panel indicate the running velocity predicted by Samuel Cheuvront and colleagues for men and women in 2028.

A couple of other factors must be mentioned when looking at male-female performance differences. First of all, women weren't always allowed to compete in the same events as men, and therefore no data existed before the 1950s for the 100 meter and before the mid-1980s for the marathon. The difference between men and women was called the "gender gap," and it was said to be narrowing rapidly in all these events as soon as women first began competing. Second, there has now been a plateauing of the gender gap such that it is now fairly consistently at about 10%. That is, in timed track events men run about 10% faster and thus have finishing times that are about 10% lower than those of women.

Why does this difference exist? For muscle, there is no clear evidence for any real difference in how men and women respond to strength training. When discussed as relative changes, the percentage increases in things like muscle cross-sectional area are quite similar between men and women. However, it is important to note that the maximum size of individual muscle fibers in men is about twice that of women. Also, when studies have been done on highly trained men and women—for example, world weight-lifting champions—contractile tissue in muscle takes up to about 30% less of the body mass in females than in males.

In Chapter 4, I said that maximum strength for weight lifting is roughly equal to the height (in meters) squared, multiplied by a constant. For purposes of estimating weight that they can lift, I have tabulated the heights and weights of the Batman and his four female

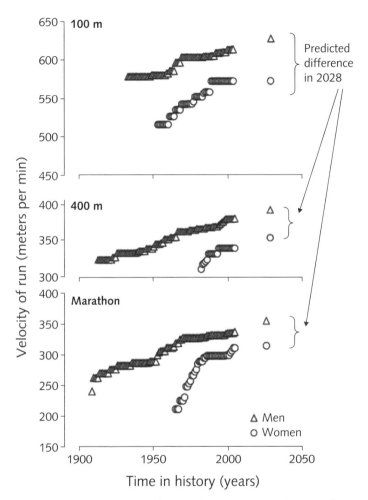

Figure 14.1. Performance differences between men and women for world record times in running velocity in meters per minute. Shown across a historical timescale for world records in the 100 meter, 400 meter, and marathon events. The triangle and circle shown at the right of each panel indicate the running velocity predicted by Samuel Cheuvront and colleagues for men and women in 2028.

friends and foes and how much they should be able to lift (shown in Table 14.1). In this rough estimate you will see that Batman is about 30% stronger than the four women.

When it comes to absolute performances, such as the most that could be lifted, the fastest running speeds, and so on, there will always remain a gender difference. However, in activities where skill and strategy are key components, such as fighting, a much more equal playing field is created. The use of weapons adds to the equalization. Let's consider, then, an "Ultimate Battle of the Bats" in which Batman fights Batgirl. By the way, in this discussion I refer to most recent Batgirl, Cassandra Cain. The reason for this is that she has a legitimate training pedigree. This is shown very clearly in the graphic novel *Batgirl: Kicking Assassins* (2005). Here Batgirl, who was trained from childhood to be a martial artist par excellence, is shown going through her typical morning routine, which involves copious amounts of martial arts practice. She is shown as on par with Batman in the various books and is clearly a fantastic fighter. The quotation at the beginning of this chapter highlights that. The "old" Batgirl was no slouch, either. However, she was kind of airlifted into the Batman comics as a result of the producers' wanting to add a female character to the 1960s TV series *Batman*. Later on she is given an update in the excellent graphic novel *Batgirl: Year One* by Scott Beatty and Chuck Dixon.

TABLE 14.1. Comparison of Batman and female characters from Batman comics

Character	Height	Weight	Maximum amount lifted
Batman	6'2' (1.88 m)	210 lb (95.3 kg)	496.3 lb (223.2 kg)
New Batgirl	5'5' (1.65 m)	110 lb (49.9 kg)	281.3 lb (126.5 kg)
Old Batgirl	5'11' (1.80 m)	126 lb (57.2 kg)	306.9 lb (137.7 kg)
Lady Shiva	5'8' (1.73 m)	115 lb (52.2 kg)	295.0 lb (132.8 kg)
Catwoman	5'7' (1.70 m)	125 lb (56.7 kg)	289.9 lb (130.5 kg)

Before going farther, let's return to the quote at the beginning of this chapter. Batman's comment that Batgirl could defeat Lady Shiva but Batman could not does not actually mean Batgirl could beat Batman. This may be confusing, but a key issue here is the size of opponent and size of vulnerable areas. Think of baseball as an example. It is much more difficult for a pitcher to throw strikes to a very small batter than it is to a very large batter. The absolute vertical size of the strike zone is much larger in the large batter because the definition of the strike zone—roughly between a batter's shoulders and his knees—changes with each batter. This means that the room for variability and error when throwing to the smaller batter is also much smaller and thus more difficult. If the strike zone were instead an absolute size, say between 0.6 and 1 meter (2 to 3.5 feet) off the plate, then this argument wouldn't apply. Well, replace strike zone with vulnerable area in fighting and you have the same idea.

The four areas to discuss for a fight between Batgirl and Batman are use of weapons, striking and kicking, throwing, and grappling. Right away it should be obvious that the use of weaponry is the great equalizer in fighting or combat. This is so even in the case of the weaponry that Batman and Batgirl would use. That is, projectiles such as batarangs or impact weapons such as a staff or cudgel. An aspect that may not be so obvious is that unlike making hands or feet (or elbows, knees, etc.) into weapons, actual handheld weapons have their own mechanical properties. That is, with the example of the staff, they are made of wood (or some other material) and are much harder than your fist could ever be. Think back to Chapter 10 and the example of the one-punch knockout Batman produced against Blockbuster when Batman's hand was temporarily "calcified." Accordingly, we are "even Steven" with weapons. There is no real advantage for either Batman or Batgirl when weapons are used.

For striking and kicking, I can vouch from practical experience that fighting smaller opponents is much more difficult than larger opponents or those of about the same size. When I used to fight competitively I always preferred fighting someone my size. Certainly I had a larger reach than the smaller opponents I competed against, but I always seemed to be fighting down toward smaller targets and was susceptible to quick counterattacks.

A major component of Batgirl's strategy when fighting Batman would be based on that—but in reverse of course. She would then probably do mostly counterattacking. That means waiting for Batman to close the distance between them with his attacks and then attacking after parrying his attack or simply as he closed in. It is often foolhardy to initiate attacks against opponents with significantly larger reaches if they are equal to or of higher skill level than yourself. However, for them to attack the smaller fighter they must close the distance and do half the work for the other.

While real fighting and tournament competitions are not the same thing, they do share some common elements of strategy and distancing. In fact, in one of the very first point scoring tournaments I ever fought in, I lost to a much smaller female opponent. She very carefully used my own attacks to close the distance and thereby negated my reach advantage. I would chase her all around the ring with her withdrawing, withdrawing, withdrawing and then counterattacking at times when my attack slowed. It was a very instructive experience!

You might suggest that since Batgirl is smaller and of lower absolute strength and power than Batman, her ability to hit his larger targets would be largely ineffective. To a certain extent there is some validity to that. Certainly Batman's punch has more destructive power than does Batgirl's. However, not by that much. This is for two main reasons. Batgirl's limbs are smaller and can be moved slightly faster. Kinetic energy is equal to mass times velocity squared, if you remember from Chapter 10. Therefore she will need slightly less energy in her strikes because her limbs are lighter. In Chapter 10 we also learned that pressure is greater in smaller areas. Batgirl is striking with hands and feet that are of smaller area, and therefore the pressure is higher in her strikes. Although Batman's attacks may not as easily hit the vital points on Batgirl's body, she still will absorb a lot of "body blows," which will be very fatiguing and tiring. Unfortunately for Batgirl, even though she makes up for her smaller size with her technical competence, on balance the scales are either even here or tipped slightly toward Batman.

When we are talking about throwing, the same issue as above for striking and kicking comes up—the scaling issue. Batman is taller than Batgirl and therefore has a higher center of mass. This means it is easier for him to be thrown, all things being equal, than if he were shorter and of similar size to Batgirl. As we discussed in Chapter 10 (that was sure a useful chapter!), throwing is all about making somebody unstable and off balance and then toppling them over. Well, the higher the center of mass of an object—including a human body—the easier it is to topple over. Assuming again equal technical ability, we will give the slight nod to Batgirl here.

Lastly, we come to grappling and wrestling. In this context technique is still of paramount importance. However, we have been assuming all along that Batgirl and Batman have equal technical competence. For "close quarters" fighting on the ground such as wrestling and grappling, absolute strength is much more important than in any of the other areas of fighting. Because Batman has higher absolute strength, he has a clear advantage over Batgirl in grappling and ground fighting. The only real way for Batgirl to minimize Batman's advantage is to make use of the distancing we talked about earlier and try to avoid closing the distance that makes grappling a likely outcome. She needs to ensure that Batman stays upright and fighting with her to have a chance. The caveat is if the fight between Batman and Batgirl became one of ground fighting, in which case strength becomes much more of a significant factor. In that case the odds weigh heavily in Batman's favor.

In the Batgirl comic "Tough Love" (Batgirl #50, 2004), Batgirl fought Batman. A small skirmish started between the two when Batman asked Batgirl to "stand down" from further fighting. Then, an evil mad scientist sprayed them with "soul," a drug that causes manic behavior. The fight escalated and covered most of Gotham City and an entire comic. Batgirl did very well in the encounter and really held her own. We find out later that Batman was in possession of himself enough that he used the encounter as a cathartic training exercise for Batgirl. That is, he held back his own attacks but only slightly.

Taken overall I give the nod to Batman over Batgirl—but only just. If they fought in the "Ultimate Battle of the Bats" as a best of seven World Series, I would bet on Batman to defeat Batgirl four fights to two. Batgirl's two wins would be by knockout!

But just wait, I hear you asking now: "Why don't more of Batman's fights with Catwoman end in draws"? This brings us back to the caveat used all along in the discussion above. Catwoman does not have the same technical competence that Batman or Batgirl have. Therefore, while she does exploit the use of weapons including her long cat of nine tails, she does not have the same technical ability in other areas of fighting. Too often, she violates the old adage of using weapons. That is, we must learn to use them but not depend on them. So, when she loses her whip, she often loses the fight. The fact that she does so well clearly shows how important weapons can be as equalizers.

Overall and taken on balance, in Batman's world just as in our own world, women can perform just as well as men when skill and relative performance are the main criteria for success. When absolute physical performances—like the longest running distance, shortest time, largest weight to be lifted, and so on—are the main criteria, the balance shifts toward Batman.

We have seen in previous chapters the effects of training and fighting on Batman and have now seen how he would fare against the toughest male and female opponents. Now let's see how the Caped Crusader stacks up against an opponent we all must face one day—Father Time.

CHAPTER 15

The Aging Avenger

COULD THE CAPED CRUSADER
BECOME THE CAPED CODGER?

An older head can't be put on younger
shoulders.
—Adam West as Batman from the ABC TV
series *Batman*

My main interest is Batman himself . . .
Bruce Wayne and the other heroes in Batman are human beings. I think that is what
separates Batman the most from the other
DC Comics heroes. I guess you could say
that I admire Superman, but I'd want to be
Batman if I could.
—From an interview with Kia Asamiya, author
of *Batman: Child of Dreams* (2003)

In this chapter we are going to explore what it would be like to be
Batman as he ages and gets older. Batman after becoming Batman,
as it were. We'll look at how long Bruce Wayne could continue to
work as Batman. As such, the title of this chapter must really be
taken kind of tongue in cheek. We are not going to explore Batman

at age 100! Rather, the point is to discuss how well a person can really offset the effects of aging and how well someone like Batman can really prepare for getting older. To do that I will talk about the cumulative effects of Batman's repeated combative activities and examine how an aging Batman would fare over time.

An important first principle in discussing aging is that Batman has always been an aging Batman. Right now, while I write and while you read, we are both aging. Biological aging is a steady, continual process that starts after life has begun. The more accurate term that covers what I am trying to get at is "senescence," which shares the same Latin root as the word "senile." The term indicates a decline in function that occurs after a certain age. For us humans, this age is about 30 and beyond. What we want to address is the concept of how becoming an aging—senescing—Batman would affect his continued ability to be Batman. To evaluate this, we revisit Bruce's imaginary twin brother Bob some years into the future. We won't go too far, just until the twins are 50 years old—or maybe that should be 50 years young?

There are going to be some surprises for you in this chapter. For example, Batman is at increased risk for osteoporosis as a result of his nocturnal lifestyle. All of the bonks to the head he has taken seemingly without consequence increase his chances of dementia, such as occurs with Alzheimer's disease.

It is worth noting that this issue has been explored in several stories of the DC Comics panoply of Batman comic and graphic novels. A particularly good example can be found in the graphic novel *The Dark Knight Returns* (1986) by Frank Miller. In this story, Batman has been retired for ten years. However, when things in Gotham City get totally out of hand, Batman comes out of retirement at age 55 to bring order to the city. His functional capacity has diminished with age—Batman remarks while climbing up a building that he is "old enough to need my legs to climb a rope"—but he is revitalized by the experience.

This idea of a retired Batman was the explicit focus of the animated television series *Batman Beyond,* which ran from 1999 to 2001 and took place in the future—2039 actually. Batman has gradually been slowing down and has modified the batsuit and other devices to compensate for his declining physical prowess. These modifications include a powered exoskeleton and interfaces to activate his muscles, wings, and rocket thrusters in the boots. However, despite all these technical enhancements, Batman suffers a heart attack one evening while trying to subdue some bad guys. To save himself he picks up a gun from one of the thugs and threatens them with it. This brings him great shame since it violates his code on firearms. This shame forces him into retirement.

Now let's see what the physiological effects of aging would be on Batman. Let's look at what happens to your body when you age. I hinted above that aging is really not a process that has a sudden onset or offset point. You don't just all of sudden start experiencing "aging" on, say your 28th, 39th, or 53rd birthday. Instead, all animals, including *Homo sapiens,* begin to age as soon as we begin to live. However, I think what most of us think of when we hear the word "aging" is a decline of our physical capacity.

We will soon get into some specifics, but first we need a bit of grounding in what our cells do as we age, because aging and maturation are closely related to the basic operation of our cells. In Batman's body, the total number of cells is kept pretty steady by ongoing cell division (mitosis) matched with cell death. This is needed to maintain—get ready for this because this will surely shock you—homeostasis. Unregulated cell growth or death would be completely inconsistent with homeostasis. When this balance between cell division and cell death is altered, negative outcomes such as tumor growth can occur.

The basic idea about how long cells could live was originally described by Leonard Hayflick in the 1960s. Through his extensive work at the University of Pennsylvania and the Wistar Institute in Philadelphia, Hayflick made some observations that were the opposite of the prevailing paradigms. He showed that animal cells have a limited capacity to reproduce. Instead of having the ability to replicate indefinitely, a limit of about 50 times was observed, which has subsequently become known as "the Hayflick limit." These experiments showed that there were separate cell "lines" of what are called "immortal" and "mortal" cells. This work has not only been crucial for improving the understanding of how aging works, but it has also been extremely useful for laying the groundwork for modern cancer research.

What does aging really mean for cells? Senescence as applied to cells means the loss of the ability to divide. Some suggestions have been that normal cellular processes lead to accumulated damage. In particular damage to the DNA occurs, and the cells fail to flourish or actually die via self-destruction. This is termed "apoptosis" and is a form of programmed "deliberate" cell death. This has often been likened to cellular suicide, which does get across the general idea quite effectively. However, apoptosis is actually very useful and a bit too much of a negative impression is created by using a term like "suicide." That is because the programmed cell death is meant as a form of generalized cleanup that benefits the rest of the cells in the organism. I guess it would be fair to say that your cells are quite selfless in their behavior and are real team players.

All these changes to our cells are just one facet of aging. When we put changes to each of Batman's cells together to see the effect on the man as a whole, we see that aging is the ongoing decline in the ability to respond to stress. Homeostasis slowly becomes more difficult to maintain, and overall function gradually declines. Of course, the ultimate result of this process is death.

The life span of any organism is therefore the sum total of all the processes occurring in all cells in the organism. Different animals have different rates and have different maximum life spans. However, the general pattern of aging is similar across species as shown in the shape of the different curves for worms, mice, and humans in Figure 15.1. These "viability curves" essentially tell about the survival and mortality within each species over time. A human is considered elderly at 85 or 90 years of "real time," while a mouse is elderly at the age of three years. These different life spans occur due to differences in genetic components that affect physiological processes, including the efficiency of DNA repairs.

Occupational hazards and chronic exposure to an unsafe workplace are real concerns for Bruce Wayne as he continues being Batman and continues to age. These are in addition to the concerns he must have over getting injured (and which we discussed in Chapter 13). There are really three (here we go again with the threes . . . I know, I know) main themes we will touch on here. I want to address the declines in cognitive and motor performance that Batman will experience while he gets older. The third theme, though, is to explore the possible protective role that Batman's—get ready for the understatement to follow—fairly "active lifestyle" might have on reducing the impact of normal aging on cognitive and motor impairments. To make a lot of these points we are also

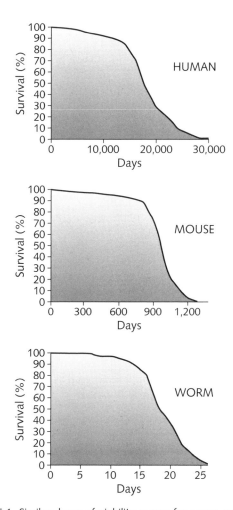

Figure 15.1. Similar shape of viability curves for worm, mouse, and human. Modified from Kaeberlein et al. (2001).

going to revisit our old—pun intended, sorry—friend Bob Wayne, Bruce's twin. This will be important since that is the only way we can really hope to understand how much of the changes in Batman's cognitive ability and motor performance are due to his work and how much are due to his normal aging.

Cognition and the Caped Crusader

One of the injuries we focused on in Chapter 13 was concussion. At that time we learned about not just an acute concussive incident but also about the concern with secondary impact syndrome. In this chapter on aging I want to go a bit farther and think about the repeated exposure—across a lifetime—and what that might really entail.

Since I have you on a flashback to concussion, let's begin there. The repeated effect of concussion can lead to later issues of cognitive impairment including dementia. Without a doubt many people have observed these kinds of effects since ancient times. However, this issue was brought up explicitly in the modern scientific world in 1928 by Harrison Martland (1883–1954), who described a certain neurological syndrome in a boxer that is known as being "punch drunk." The terms "dementia pugilistica" and "punch drunk" refer to appearing to be drunk when no alcohol is involved. Slurred speech, problems in maintaining balance, and generally uncoordinated arm and leg movements are common. Clearly, repeated blows to the head can lead to persistent effects on movement control and cognition. The explicit question I want to address here, though, is whether or not repeated head injury might predispose someone to degenerative diseases—such as Alzheimer's—that affect memory and cognition.

Alzheimer's disease has been described as the most prevalent of all degenerative diseases of the nervous system, affecting an estimated 25 million people worldwide in 2007. At the beginning of the twentieth century, German physician Alois Alzheimer (1864–1915) observed an interesting patient (coincidentally known by the initials "AD") who had experienced memory loss and dementia in her late forties. She became the first person diagnosed with Alzheimer's disease. Since that time we have learned that someone with Alzheimer's shows a continual deterioration in memory and functional ability such that activities of daily living eventually become impossible. When individuals with Alzheimer's disease are autopsied and their brain tissue is examined under a light microscope, hardened plaques are found that are formed from proteins called beta amyloid. The body makes amyloid and beta-amyloid proteins as a matter of course. In a healthy brain, the beta version would be broken down and gotten rid of. It is believed in people with Alzheimer's disease these proteins harden and form plaques. The plaque formation process precedes actual memory loss and dementia by many years. Similar to this, a healthy brain has a protein called tau that forms little structures called microtubules. In Alzheimer's disease, this protein has an abnormal form and results in neurofibrillary tangles. Together the plaques and neurofibrillary tangles degrade the brains neurons and are seen clearly at autopsy. The disease itself is not amenable to treatment. Genetic factors likely play a strong role in the expression of Alzheimer's. One gene in particular, called apolipoprotein E, or *APOE* for short, is a repeatedly confirmed suspect.

We don't know whether Batman is genetically predisposed to get Alzheimer's. What we want to know is whether his repeated head trauma may lead to a greater chance of his getting the disease. We discussed back in Chapter 13 that head trauma resulting in loss of consciousness and concussion was due to rotational accelerations, or rapid forward momentum of the brain. There were effects of this acceleration not only on a person's metabolism but also on his or her brain tissue. The idea has been floated that repeated concussion could help increase the likelihood of formation of amyloid plaques and neurofibrillary tangles.

Unfortunately, it is not possible to get full diagnosis and confirmation of diagnosis of Alzheimer's until autopsy, and you cannot easily follow someone who is repeatedly concussed in sports such as football or boxing until their demise and then check for the autopsy confirmation. Instead, researchers have tried to look for associations between the kinds of symptoms shown by people with Alzheimer's and those shown by people who display punch-drunk-type syndromes. Recent work, including that by Kevin Guskiewicz and colleagues from the University of North Carolina at Chapel Hill, shows a strong relation between dementia and repeated concussion in professional football players. Retired football players who developed dementia and Alzheimer's-like symptoms did so at much younger ages than did the general population.

Other researchers have also shown that the risk for Alzheimer's is higher if the concussion syndrome is worsened by repeated concussion and if there is a family risk factor for Alzheimer's. It may be that the repeated concussive incidents may increase the production of the beta amyloid protein thus leading to the plaque formation that interferes with normal brain function. This represents an unfortunate but understandable homeostatic response of the brain to the mechanical stresses of repeated injury. What we would conclude for Batman is that he is at significantly higher risk of developing Alzheimer's. Fortunately he will have at hand a suitable caregiver in the form of his brother Bob, who, because he shunned the extreme lifestyle of his driven brother Bruce, would only have a normal risk of Alzheimer's.

There is also evidence that repeated head trauma can lead to neurofibrillary tangles without the plaques seen in Alzheimer's. These can be found in areas of the brain that are key to motor co-ordination, such as the cerebellum and basal ganglia (recall those motor control advisors from Chapter 7), and memory, such as the hippocampus. This has been described as a "pugilistic Parkinson's," because it presents in a similar fashion to that seen in Parkinson's disease. Although it is yet unknown whether this is actually the case, it is possible that this kind of background could explain some of the Parkinsonian symptoms that some boxers—notably Muhammad Ali—display years after all boxing activity has stopped.

Physiology and Motor Performance

An important aspect working against our ability to perform at a high functional level as we age is sarcopenia. This term, coming from Greek for "lacking of flesh," refers to the normal lessening of strength that occurs in aging. Along with the loss of muscle mass may be increased porosity of bone (osteoporosis) and weakened bone (osteopenia). The graph shown in Figure 15.2 is meant to illustrate that from about age 30 there is a steady decline in physiological function. Shown on the figure are speed of nerve conduction in the nervous system, function of the heart and lungs, and overall ability to perform work. Kidney function and other organ systems also deteriorate. As for the loss of muscle, a lot of the normal regulation of muscle mass takes us back to Chapter 3 when we first met the insulin-like growth factors (or IGFs). Reduction in IGF levels as we age may remove a potent stimulus for maintaining muscle mass.

Let's look at what happens to our bodies as we age. More specifically let's look at what happens as we move beyond about age 30 and our physiological function begins to decline. I am going to concentrate this discussion on the motor system and our ability to activate our muscles. It is not my intention—and it would require many more pages to do so—to list all the physiological changes that occur in aging.

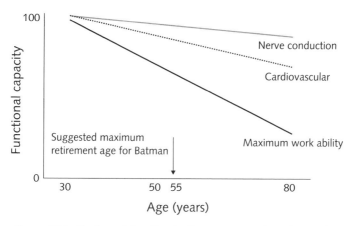

Figure 15.2. Decline of function in the nervous and cardiovascular systems linked with a decline in overall functional capacity at various ages for Batman. Data from Hertoghe (2005).

Think back to the motor unit, which we defined in Chapter 4 as a motoneuron, in the spinal cord and all the muscle fibers that it energizes. Don't be shocked, but as we age, our motoneurons die. Given our discussion above about the Hayflick limit, this shouldn't be too surprising. If the cells that relay the command for muscle to become active die, you might suppose that factors like muscle strength would decline. And clearly, that is true. As much as 50% of skeletal muscle mass may be lost between the ages of 20 and 90 years, and there is a corresponding reduction in muscle strength.

There is also death of muscle fibers, particularly those found in the fastest contracting motor units, the Type IIa group. Usually you don't really notice the extent of the decline in motoneuron number or muscle fibers that much. This is because your nervous system is exceptionally good at covering up for these changes. This is another way of saying that changes in the connections within the nervous system compensate for the age-related death of muscle fibers and motoneurons.

Imagine a muscle in your leg that may contain 250 motor units. In a large leg muscle, each motor unit might have a thousand muscle fibers in it. This relationship of motor cells to motorneurons is called the innervation ratio; in this example it would be a thousand fibers per motorneuron. Innervation (and this is scientists being really clever with naming again!) means bringing nerves to something.

Well, the number of motor units in that same muscle might drop to 125 by age 70. This means you would have lost 125 motoneurons. However, many of the muscle fibers would still be sitting in your muscle waiting to become active on command. You may have lost 50% of the motoneurons but only 10% of the muscle fibers. Shouldn't this make you half as strong? Not necessarily because the other motoneurons innervating muscle fibers in that leg muscle can send branches from their axons over to the muscle fibers that are just sitting there waiting. This is called "sprouting" and eventually leads to much larger innervation ratios—in this example, let's says it is now 1,500 fibers per neuron—that lead to a preservation of strength. By the way, this is the same process that occurs in recovery from some nerve injuries.

Batman's nervous system also would show a general slowing with aging. There is a reduced speed of conduction within the nervous system. The events involved in muscle contraction are also themselves slowed down. Despite these declines that occur in everyone's nervous system with aging, an active lifestyle—such as Batman certainly lives—can help offset the overall impact of these changes. The main reason for this goes back to the general stimulus-response model we have been using all along. If there is a maintained exercise stress across the life span, there will be a corresponding attempt to respond to minimize the effect of the stress. This means maintaining muscle mass as best as possible and maintaining needed coordination and motor skills.

Hormone levels also decline over the life span. As an adjunct to physical activity, in certain cases hormone and steroid replacement therapies can also be helpful. These are usually used only in severe cases. However, restoring hormone levels, and in particular those related to muscle mass such as the IGFs we talked about in Chapter 3, has been used extensively to help improve physical capacity with aging.

In addition to experiencing reduced muscle mass, Batman could have a problem with decreased bone-mineral density. Because of his nocturnal lifestyle he doesn't get much sun, which is a major source of vitamin D. When Batman is out and about during the day he wears the batsuit, and his skin doesn't see much light. Even as Bruce Wayne, he is mostly at business meetings inside buildings. So, his vitamin D intake from sun exposure is very low. Vitamin D, as we learned in Chapter 5, is a major regulator of bone mineralization.

So, Batman is at increased risk for osteoporosis! This risk will of course be offset by the helpful bone stimulus of being so active. Still, he ought to drink lots of vitamin D–enriched milk products and take his vitamins.

Codger or Not?

The last point to address here speaks to the chapter's subtitle—will the Caped Crusader become the caped codger? Clearly the answer is yes. However, the implied question is really when will Batman have to hang up the old cape? To consider this let's discuss some examples from sports that encompass the elements of physical power and toughness and that have physical contact as main elements: NHL ice hockey and professional boxing. We will take these real-life activities as examples that emulate the physical pounding that Batman would take in his career as a costumed crimefighter.

To give us a benchmark for how long someone could continue in a physically demanding job like being Batman, let's look specifically at the careers of NHL great Gordie Howe and former heavyweight boxing champion George Foreman. They both represent athletes who performed at a high level at a time when many other professionals would be off making commercials or providing commentary on sports broadcasts.

Gordie Howe—a.k.a. "Mr. Hockey"—was born on March 31, 1928. Howe debuted in the NHL for the Detroit Red Wings in 1946 at the age of 18. He is best known for the length of his playing career, the high level of his play, and the physical nature of his game. In fact, the term "Howe hat trick" has often been used to describe a game in which a player gets a goal, an assist, and wins a fight. During his 25-year career with Detroit, Howe won four Stanley Cup championships as well as the scoring championship and most valuable player trophy. He is third in NHL all-time scoring with 1,850 points. This includes 801 goals and 1,049 assists. Including all of his goals from his entire professional playing career (NHL and World Hockey Association [WHA]) puts Howe first in goals with an incredible 975. The point is that Gordie Howe was one of the best players in hockey history. He retired (first retirement) in 1972 at the age of 43. In his last NHL season for the Red Wings he scored 23 goals and added 29 assists for 52 points in 63 games. This would have to be considered outstanding for almost any age but is staggering for a man in his early 40s.

But there is more. He came out of retirement for the 1973–1974 season to play in the WHA with the Houston Whalers and then the New England Whalers. It is amazing that during his six seasons in the WHA, Howe had two years with more than a hundred points. Then, the most impressive feat, in my view, was in 1979–1980 when Howe played in the NHL again for the Hartford Whalers. He played in all 80 games and scored 15 goals and 26 assists at the age of 52! This is a truly amazing performance and shows that well into what many would consider the early retirement years, it is possible to produce at a high level.

The boxing career of George Foreman represents another example of performance over a long span. He was born on January 10, 1949, and won the 1968 Gold Medal for heavyweight boxing at the Mexico City Olympics. Thereafter he turned professional and won the undisputed world heavyweight championship in January 1973 by knockout over Joe Frazier. George had many memorable fights in his career, including the "Rumble in the Jungle" in which he lost to Muhammad Ali. However, of relevance to aging and performance is that Foreman had several retirements and comebacks over the years. Notably, in November of 1994 he defeated Michael Moorer by knockout to win the heavyweight title. This victory was at the age of 45, and in so doing Foreman became the oldest fighter to win the heavyweight title championship. His last fight was some years later at the "tender" age of 48. This example of George Foreman shows that even pure fighting prowess can be maintained in championship form into the fifth decade of life. Also, although he never won the heavyweight crown, the Canadian boxer George Chuvalo had a 23-year career that begin in 1956 and ended in 1979 at the age of 42. Over that time he fought 93 times, amassing 73 wins—including 64 by knockout—and 18 losses. He fought Muhammad Ali twice and went the distance but lost by decision both times. Chuvalo really does represent high-level performance for a long career.

So, how long can Batman function as Batman? Well, based on the evidence at hand I would say Batman could still operate at a high level into his early 50s. He will have lost a bit of speed, endurance, and pure physiological power as we discussed above. Despite not being able to do everything quite the way he used to, he could still achieve most of his objectives.

Also, his technical competence will help compensate for many of the gross physiological losses. I have found in my own martial arts training that when I face many "older" karate masters—those in their late 60s up to late 70s—it is not how fast you move but when you move that is important. They still seem very adept at throwing me to the ground. Let's conclude that Batman could still be Batman into his sixth decade but that he should then retire and take up his rocking chair at stately Wayne Manor. Also, in his later years he will need to rely more and more on his acolytes Robin, Batgirl, Nightwing, and whoever else he can train.

As we shall see in the next chapter, we need to make a distinction between the possibility of being able to perform at a high level as we age and the ability to remain at the peak of our performance. Don't you want to know how long Batman can really be at his peak to remain the undisputed guardian of Gotham?

CHAPTER 16

The Reign of the Bat

CAN YOU REALLY BECOME BATMAN AND REMAIN BATMAN?

> The main rule of thumb when doing Batman is, "Is it realistic or not?" That is more important than anything else.
> —From an interview with Kia Asamiya, author of *Batman: Child of Dreams* (2003)

We have explored many aspects of training and what happens to the human body as a result of training stresses. Everything we have discussed is embedded in the concepts of stress and homeostasis. We have talked about some biology, some biomechanics, and some injuries. All of this was meant to illustrate what would have happened to the fictitious Bruce Wayne or to a real person who undertook to become Batman. I have also included many quotes and comments from artists, writers, and editors for the Batman comics who all expressed the idea that an inherent part of the Batman mythology was that he wasn't a person with superhero powers. Batman is just a human being who trained himself to the ultimate extent. This general idea is shown in Figure 16.1 in a thumbnail sketch of the progression from Bruce to The Bat-Man to Batman differentiations that we have followed throughout the book.

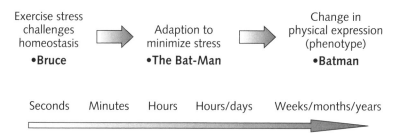

Figure 16.1. Transformation of Bruce Wayne to Batman shown in a parallel scale for physiological adaptations occurring in his body.

After having read through all this material, let's reflect briefly on whether you could become Batman if you wanted to. If so, for how long could you remain as Batman?

The short answer is that, yes, in my view and in light of everything I have outlined for you, a person could become Batman (notice I said a person, not necessarily you or I). This person would need to have the proper blend of genetic endowment, be driven at a fanatical level by some passionate goal, and have inordinate amounts of time and money to undertake all the extreme privations and training needed. Following the general stimulus-response model of maintaining homeostasis by altering biological function we have talked about all along, yes, you could bring about the necessary training adaptations to do so. If all that were in place, then, yes, you could become Batman.

However, the caveat is that it would be enormously difficult to actually be Batman. Wait a minute, Paul, I hear you say. Are you dealing from both sides of the deck here? What is the difference between becoming and being Batman? Well, I think you could prepare for and become Batman. To undertake his activities on a regular and possibly daily or nightly basis, though, would create such a large physiological stress and entail so many injuries that the possibility of remaining on top for a lifetime or even a very short career as a costumed crimefighter lacking in superpowers is very low.

You might argue this is the opposite of what I said in Chapter 15 about Batman having a crime-fighting career until age 55. However, then and there we talked about whether it was possible to perform at a high level for a long time. What we are talking about here is performing at the highest level possible—the absolute pinnacle of performance—for the longest possible time. We are really considering how long Batman could maintain his best performances. This is important because a substandard performance by Batman doesn't mean a rematch some months later. It could likely mean his death.

To continue I want to make use of the same approach as in Chapter 15. That is to take some examples from sports, namely boxing and ultimate fighting. How long can champions in these two sports remain at their peaks? We will begin with ultimate fighting and the story of Randy Couture. Couture was born in June 1963 and has won the Ultimate Fighting Championship heavyweight title seven times over an approximately ten-year span. His first championship was in 1997 (age 34) and his last in 2007 at the age of 44. So, in this grueling hard-fought contest, peak performance could be maintained over a decade. However, the longest stretch for maintaining his title did not quite total two consecutive years in that decade. Also, across his entire career, Couture has had 24 professional matches. Batman would have many more than 24 events requiring peak performance in a few weeks! Even if there were only one Batman comic title per month, and even if each story had only one encounter, he would still have at least a dozen events per year. So, when using ultimate fighting performance as the indirect gauge, the ability to be at the peak of performance is really closer to two years.

Another example I want to bring up comes from boxing and the career of the great Muhammad Ali. Born in 1942 as Cassius Clay Jr., he won the Olympic light-heavyweight gold medal at the Rome 1960 games and also had his first professional match that year. His last fight was in 1981, and over that 21-year professional career Ali had 56 wins in 61 fights. Including all titles from all sanctioning bodies, he has held eight championship belts. The longest stretch of maintaining his crown was between February 25, 1964, and February 6, 1967. So, for almost three years he was at the top and defended his title nine times.

Again, converting that timescale into Batman's yields less than a year of once-per-month challengers for Batman. Remember now, in Batman's world that is well below what could even be laughingly suggested as the minimum. Batman has many more deadly encounters than that each month. So, in events with demands such as found in ultimate fighting and boxing, it is difficult to repeat as champion or remain as champion. It can and has been done, but not for very long.

Since we equated many of Batman's activities and injury risks to professional football players in Chapter 13, I would also like to comment on the length of such a career. The average length of an NFL player's career is pretty short. There are still extremes. For example, NFL quarterback Vinny Testaverde as of 2007 had played in 21 seasons. But that is a real aberration. A few players may play for 10 or 12 years, but the ballpark average offered by the NFL Players Association is approximately three years.

So, this means that Bruce would have spent 3 to 5 years reaching his maximum physical capacity, 6 to 12 years honing his skills in martial and other arts, and then another 6 to 8 years gaining the poise and grace under pressure (the experience) needed to perform flawlessly, defend himself and Gotham, but never, ever lose. With all that 15 to 20 years of training, Bruce finally became Batman. In this world, he finally achieved his goal, but he had a very short (yet distinguished!) career.

Where does all of this leave us? Well, the conclusion I would like to leave you with is that becoming Batman would require a very unique set of circumstances including genetics, wealth, a suitable environment, and an unequaled internal drive to pursue an objective. It could be done, though. However, remaining as Batman is not realistic beyond a few years and a decade at the absolute maximum. Everything we have discussed in the last few chapters should be suggestive enough for this conclusion. You cannot have everything, I guess.

Becoming Batman the cultural icon is a dream that could be realized but not maintained for very long. However, the story of Batman is still intriguing. The sentiments raised by many people quoted in this book echo the possibility that Batman is fascinating because he *is* human. Because he is human we can see a bit of ourselves in Batman's story. It becomes exciting when we recognize the possibility that this could be realized in ourselves—even if only for a short time. I think that Batman's limitations make his story more inspiring. To me it increases his humanity. His struggles can now be seen as living life as we all live: training, getting injured, recovering, and aging. Batman becomes one who must overcome many obstacles and events, just as we all must in the real world and the superhero universe.

Appendix

BATMAN'S TRAINING MILESTONES

> "I don't believe Batman considers himself a 'super-hero.'"
> —Bruce Wayne to a dinner guest in the 2003 graphic novel *Batman: Child of Dreams*

The top training milestones from Batman's physical and martial arts training are shown in Table A.1. These are broken down to golden, silver, and modern age. For a more complete description of the relevance of the "ages," please to refer to James Kakalios's *Physics of Superheroes,* where an excellent summary of comic book history is given.

TABLE A.1. Historical milestones in the martial arts and physical training history of Batman

Comic book era	Comic, date, and reference	Event description
Golden age (1930s–mid 1950s)	Detective Comics #27, May 1939: "The Case of the Chemical Syndicate"	This is the first appearance of "the Bat-Man." No description of his training history is given, but he does appear to have significant fighting prowess dispatching several gun-wielding thugs.
	Batman #1, Spring 1940: "The Legend of the Batman—Who He Is and How He Came to Be!" (Originally found in Detective Comics #33)	This is the first attempt to describe the origin story of Batman. Bruce Wayne is shown using one hand to hold a gigantic barbell over his head. The extent of his physical training covers one panel!
	Detective Comics #38, April 1940: "Introducing Robin, the Boy Wonder"	This is the first documentation of Batman training in boxing and jujutsu, although he is shown using a "ju jitsu trick" in Detective Comics #46 from Feb. 1940 in the story "Professor Hugo Strange."
	Batman #4, Winter 1941: "Black-beard's Crew and the Yacht Society"	Batman explains to Robin that they must understand how to use all weapons but must never use deadly force.
	Batman #31, Oct/Nov 1945: "Trade Marks of Crime"	Using jujutsu, Batman disarms and throws an attacker who tries to club him with a bottle.
	Batman #113, Feb 1958: "Batman—the Superman of Planet X!"	Batman is transported to a distant planet where he has the super-powers that Superman has on Earth, including flight and invulner-ability. Not really a historical milestone for training, but there isn't much to choose from in the 1950s.
Silver age (late 1950s–early 1970s)	Giant Batman Annual #1, 1961: "How to Be the Batman"	Batman has amnesia, and Robin takes him through a training regimen of boxing and acrobatics in the hope of jogging Batman's memory and restoring all his skills.
	Batman #200, March 1968: "The Man Who Radiated Fear"	Bruce Wayne's training now shows gymnastics and acrobatics, including walking a tightrope.

	Batman #232, June 1971: "Daughter of the Demon"	Regimen now includes realistic strength, track and field, and gymnastics training.
	Batman #243, August 1972: "The Lazarus Pit"	Batman is shown using a judo arm lock on a knife-wielding attacker and saying he has "years of practice in judo."
	Batman #260, Jan/Feb 1975: "This One'll Kill You Batman"	Batman fights a huge gang of adversaries. As a "master of unarmed combat" he uses kung fu, aikido, judo, and "plain old fisticuffs."
Modern age (late 1970s–present)	Batman #404, 1986: "Chapter One: Who I Am and How I Came to Be"; reproduced in *Batman: Year One* (graphic novel, 2005)	Batman's extensive prowess in martial arts is shown. Apparently this includes smashing through bricks with his fingertips and chopping a tree down with a sidekick.
	Detective Comics #568, Nov 1986: "Eyrie"	Batman fights with martial arts weapons and improvises a stick for a "bo" staff.
	Detective Comics #598–600, 1989: "Blind Justice" story arc	Multiple flashbacks to Bruce training in Europe and Asia with ninja-like master. Introduces Henri Ducard as Bruce's major teacher who emerges again in the movie *Batman Begins*.
	Batman/Superman/Wonder Woman, Trinity (graphic novel, 2004)	Batman who "has trained a lifetime to prove them wrong" incapacitates thugs who "find courage . . . with a gun in their hands."
	Batman Begins: The Movie and Other Tales . . . : "The Man Who Falls" (graphic novel, 2005)	Bruce Wayne's odyssey around the world trying to gain fighting prowess is shown.
	Superman/Batman: Supergirl (graphic novel, 2005)	Alongside Superman, Batman uses a battle-ax to fight Darkseid's hordes in an effort to free Supergirl. Superman describes Batman as "versed in nearly every known weapon."

Bibliography

If you are interested in further reading about science and superheroes, my number one recommendation is *Physics of Superheroes* by James Kakalios (Gotham, 2005). It is a great book about science. The fact that superheroes and comic books are thrown in too only makes it better. *The Science of Superheroes* by Lois Gresh and Robert Weinberg (Wiley, 2003) is also quite good.

If you are interested in reading more on Batman, his training, and related topics check out *The Batman Handbook* by Scott Beatty (Quirk, 2005). *Becoming Batman* provides the background for Beatty's great and light look at how to actually be Batman. Also, if you want further information on Batman, anything by Scott Beatty is highly recommended. In particular, *Batman: The Ultimate Guide to the Dark Knight* (Dorling Kindersley, 2001) is fantastic, has great art, and is well-researched. A great exploration of Batman in popular culture can be found in Bradford Wright's *Comic Book Nation* (Johns Hopkins University Press, 2003).

DC Comics and Graphic Novels Cited

1939   Detective Comics #27: "The Case of the Chemical Syndicate"
        Detective Comics #29: "The Batman Meets Doctor Death"
        Detective Comics #33: "Legend of the Batman, Who He Is and How
            He Came to Be"

1940   Batman #1: "The Legend of the Batman, Who He Is and How He
            Came to Be!"
            "Professor Hugo Strange and the Monsters"
            "The Cat"
        Batman #3: "The Batman vs. the Cat-Woman!"
        Detective Comics #38: "Introducing Robin, the Boy Wonder"
        Detective Comics #46: "Professor Strange's Fear Dust"

1941   Batman #4: "Blackbeard's Crew and the Yacht Society"
        "Victory for the Dynamic Duo!"

1945   Batman #31: "Trade Marks of Crime"

1948   Batman #47: "The Origin of Batman"

1958   Batman #113: "Batman—the Superman of Planet X!"

1961   Giant Batman Annual: "How to Be the Batman"

1966   Detective Comics #349: "The Blockbuster Breaks Loose!"

1967   Detective Comics #359: "The Million Dollar Debut of Batgirl"

1968   Batman #200: "The Man Who Radiated Fear"

1969   Batman #217: "One Bullet Too Many"

1970   Detective Comics #397: "Paint a Picture of Peril"
        Detective Comics #400: "The Challenge of the Man-Bat"

1971   Batman #232: "Daughter of the Demon"
        Batman #237: "Night of the Reaper"

1972   Batman #243: "The Lazarus Pit"

1974   Detective Comics #442: "Death Flies the Haunted Sky!"

1975   Batman #260: "This One'll Kill You Batman"

1976   Richard Dragon Kung-Fu Fighter #5: "Her Name is Lady Shiva . . ."

1983   The Brave and The Bold #197: "The Autobiography of Bruce Wayne"

1984   Batman Special #1: "The Player on the Other Side"

1986   Batman #404: "Who I Am and How I Came to Be"
        Detective Comics #568: "Eyrie"
        Batman: Year One (graphic novel)
        The Dark Knight Returns (graphic novel)

1989   DC Comics #598–600: "Sleep of Reason"

1992   *Batman: Blind Justice* (graphic novel)

1993   Batman #497: "Knightfall: Part 11: The Broken Bat."
        Detective Comics #664: "Knightfall 12: Who Rules the Night"
        Batman: Venom (graphic novel)
        Batman: Vengeance of Bane #1
        Knightfall: Part 1: No Rest for the Wicked (graphic novel)

1994   Batman #509: "KnightsEnd Part One: Spirit of the Bat"
        Batman: Shadow of the Bat #29: "KnightsEnd Part Two.
        Manimal: Proving Ground"
        Batman Knightfall Part 3: Knightsend (graphic novel)

1996   Batman #529: "Tears of Blood"

1998   *Batman: Four of a Kind* (graphic novel)
        Legends of the Dark Knight Annual #5: "Wings"

1999   Batman #567: "No Man's Land: Mark of Cain: Part 1"

2002   *Bruce Wayne: Fugitive Volume 1* (graphic novel)
        Batman: The Dark Knight Returns (graphic novel)
        Batman: The Dark Knight Strikes Again (graphic novel)

2003   *Batman: Child of Dreams* (graphic novel)
        Batman / Superman / Wonder Woman: Trinity
            (graphic novel)
        Batman: No Man's Land Vol. 3 (graphic novel)
        Batman: Contagion (graphic novel)
        Batgirl: Year One (graphic novel)
        Superman/Batman #1–6: "Public Enemies"
        Batman #608–619: "Hush"

2004   Batgirl #50: "Batman versus Batgirl: Tough Love"
        Batman: Broken City (graphic novel)

2005   Batman #604: "Reasons"
        Batman Begins: The Movie and Other Tales of the Dark Knight
            (graphic novel)
        Batman: Year One (graphic novel)
        Identity Crisis (graphic novel)
        Superman/Batman: Supergirl (graphic novel)
        Superman/Batman: Public Enemies (graphic novel)

Batgirl: Kicking Assassins (graphic novel)
Batman: Dark Detective #2: "You May See a Stranger"

MOTION PICTURES AND TELEVISION PROGRAMS CITED

Batman and Robin (1949; Columbia Pictures Corporation)
Batman (1966–1968; ABC TV series)
Kung Fu (1972–1975; ABC TV series)
Batman (1989; Warner Bros.)
Batman Returns (1992; Warner Bros.)
Batman Forever (1995; Warner Bros.)
Batman & Robin (1997; Warner Bros.)
Batman Beyond (1999–2001; WB TV series)
The Last Samurai (2003; Warner Bros.)
Batman Begins (2005; Warner Bros.)
The Dark Knight (2008; Warner Bros.)
Star Wars: Episode III—The Revenge of the Sith (2005; Lucasfilm)

BOOKS AND JOURNAL ARTICLES

Preface

Beatty, S. (2001) *Batman: The ultimate guide to the Dark Knight*. Dorling Kindersley, New York.
Daniels, L. (1999) *Batman: The complete history*. Chronicle Books, San Francisco, CA.
DC Comics. (1988) *The greatest Batman stories ever told*. Warner Communications, New York.
DC Comics. (2004) *Batman*, illustrated by Neal Adams, vol. 2. Warner Communications, New York.
DC Comics. (2005) *Batman*, illustrated by Neal Adams, vol. 3. Warner Communications, New York.
Kane, B, and Andrae, T. (1989) *Batman and me: An autobiography by Bob Kane*. Eclipse Books, Forestville, CA.
Vaz, MC. (1989) *Tales of the Dark Knight: Batman's first fifty years: 1939–1989*. Random House of Canada, Toronto, ON.

Chapter 1. The "Before" Batman: How Buff Was Bruce?

Beatty, S. (2001) *Batman: The ultimate guide to the Dark Knight*. Dorling Kindersley, New York.
Sawka, MN, Cheuvront, SN, and Carter, R, III. (2005) Human water needs. *Nutrition Review* 63: S30–S39.

Sutcliffe, JF (1996) A review of *in vivo* experimental methods to determine the composition of the human body. *Physics in Medicine and Biology* 41: 791–833.

Chapter 2. Guess Who's Coming for Dinner: Bruce's Twin Brother, Bob, and the Human Genome

Allen, GE. (2003) Mendel and modern genetics: The legacy for today. *Endeavour* 27: 63–68.

Bellinge, RH, Liberles, DA, Iaschi, SP, O'Brien, PA, and Tay, GK. (2005) Myostatin and its implications on animal breeding: A review. *Animal Genetics* 36: 1–6.

Britton, SL, and Koch, LG. (2005) Animal models of complex diseases: An initial strategy. *IUBMB Life* 57: 631–638.

Brutsaert, TD, and Parra, EJ. (2006) What makes a champion? Explaining variation in human athletic performance. *Respiratory Physiology & Neurobiology* 151: 109–123.

Cummings, MR. (1988) *Human heredity: Principles and issues.* West, St. Paul, MN.

Dunn, PM. (2003) Gregor Mendel, OSA (1822–1884), founder of scientific genetics. *Archives of Disease in Childhood: Fetal and Neonatal Edition* 88: F537-F539.

Gest, H. (2004) The discovery of microorganisms by Robert Hooke and Antoni van Leeuwenhoek, Fellows of The Royal Society. *Notes and Records of the Royal Society* 58: 187–201.

Hawley, JA, and Spargo, FJ. (2006) It's all in the genes, so pick your parents wisely. *Journal of Applied Physiology* 100: 1751–1752.

Heck, AL, Barroso, CS, Callie, ME, and Bray, MS. (2004) Gene-nutrition interaction in human performance and exercise response. *Nutrition* 20: 598–602.

Judson, HF. (2003) "The greatest surprise for everyone"—Notes on the 50th anniversary of the double helix. *New England Journal of Medicine* 348: 1712–1714.

Klug, A. (2004) The discovery of the DNA double helix. *Journal of Molecular Biology* 335: 3–26.

Kostek, M, Hubal, MJ, and Petcatello, LS. (2007) Genetic roles in muscle strength. *ACSM Health & Fitness Journal* 11: 18–23.

Lopez-Munoz, F, Boya, J, and Alamo, C. (2006) Neuron theory, the cornerstone of neuroscience, on the centenary of the Nobel Prize award to Santiago Ramon y Cajal. *Brain Research Bulletin* 70: 391–405.

MacArthur, DG, and North, KN. (2005) Genes and human elite athletic performance. *Human Genetics* 116: 331–339.

McArdle, WD, Katch, FI, and Katch, VL. (2005) *Essentials of exercise physiology,* 3rd ed. Lippincott Williams & Wilkins, Baltimore, MD.

Mosher, DS, Quignon, P, Bustamante, CD, Sutter, NB, Mellersh, CS, Parker, HG, and Ostrander, EA. (2007) A mutation in the myostatin gene increases muscle mass and enhances racing performance in heterozygote dogs. *Public Library of Science: Genetics* 3: e79.

Ridley, M. (1999) *Genome.* HarperCollins, New York.

Sawka MN, Cheuvront SN, and Carter R, III. (2005) Human water needs. *Nutrition Review* 63: S30–S39.

Schuelke, M, Wagner, KR, Stolz, LE, Hubner, C, Riebel, T, Komen, W, Braun, T, Tobin, JF, and Lee, SJ. (2004) Myostatin mutation associated with gross muscle hypertrophy in a child. *New England Journal of Medicine* 350: 2682–2688.

Segal, NL. (2006) SuperQuads: A day in the life; research reviews: color-number association, finger-length ratios, twinning diets, athletic pairs. *Twin Research and Human Genetics* 9: 609–614.

Wolfarth, B, Bray, MS, Hagberg, JM, Perusse, L, Rauramaa, R, Rivera, MA, Roth, SM, Rankinen, T, and Bouchard, C. (2005) The human gene map for performance and health-related fitness phenotypes: the 2004 update. *Medicine and Science in Sports and Exercise* 37: 881–903.

Chapter 3. The Stress of Life: Holy Hormones, Batman!

Driskell, JE, Salas, E, and Johnston, JH. (2006) Decision making and performance under stress. In TW Britt, CA Castro, and AB Adler (eds.), *Military life: The psychology of serving in peace and combat* (vol. 1, pp. 128–154). Praeger Security, Westport, CT.

Goldstein, DS, and Kopin, IJ. (2007) Evolution of concepts of stress. *Stress* 10: 109–120.

Kraemer, WJ, and Ratamess, NA. (2005) Hormonal responses and adaptations to resistance exercise and training. *Sports Medicine* 35: 339–361.

Solomon, AM, and Bouloux, PMG. (2006) Modifying muscle mass—The endocrine perspective. *Journal of Endocrinology* 191: 349–360.

Viner, R. (1999) Putting stress in life: Hans Selye and the making of stress theory. *Social Studies of Science* 29: 391–410.

Chapter 4. Gaining Strength and Power: Does the Bat That Flies the Highest or the Fastest Get the Worm?

Booth, FW, Tseng, BS, Fluck, M, and Carson JA. (1998) Molecular and cellular adaptation of muscle in response to physical training. *Acta Physiologica Scandinavica* 162: 343–350.

Goldspink, G. (1999) Changes in muscle mass and phenotype and the expression of autocrine and systemic growth factors by muscle in response to stretch and overload. *Journal of Anatomy* 194 (Pt 3): 323–334.

McArdle, WD, Katch, FI, and Katch, VL. (2005) *Essentials of exercise physiology,* 3rd ed. Lippincott Williams & Wilkins, Baltimore, MD.

Parise, G, Reilly, CE, and Rudnicki, MA. (2006) Molecular regulation of myogenic progenitor populations. *Applied Physiology, Nutrition, and Metabolism* 31: 773–781.

Penfield, W, and Rasmussen, T. (1950) *The cerebral cortex of man: A clinical study of localization of function.* Macmillan, New York.

Sale, DG. (1988) Neural adaptation to resistance training. *Medicine and Science in Sports and Exercise* 20: S135-S145.

Sale, DG. (1992) Neural adaptation to strength training. In PV Komi (ed), *Strength and power in sport* (pp. 249–265). Blackwell Scientific Publications, Cambridge, MA.

Sherrington, CS. (1947) The integrative action of the nervous system. Cambridge University Press, Cambridge, UK.

Swazey, JP. (1969) *Reflexes and motor integration: Sherrington's concept of integrative action.* Harvard University Press, Cambridge, MA.

Tyc, F, and Boyadjian, A. (2006) Cortical plasticity and motor activity studied with transcranial magnetic stimulation. *Reviews in the Neurosciences* 17: 469–495.

Wernbom, M, Augustsson, J, and Thomee, R. (2007) The influence of frequency, intensity, volume and mode of strength training on whole muscle cross-sectional area in humans. *Journal of Sports Medicine.* 37: 225–264.

Chapter 5. Building the Batbones: Brittle Is Bad, But Is Bigger Better?

Andreoli, A, Monteleone, M, Van Loan, M, Promenzio, L, Tarantino, U, and De Lorenzo, A. (2001) Effects of different sports on bone density and muscle mass in highly trained athletes. *Medicine and Science of Sports and Exercise* 33: 507–511.

Carter, DR. (1984) Mechanical loading histories and cortical bone remodeling. *Calcified Tissue International* V36: S19–S24.

Enoka, RM. (2002) *Neuromechanics of human movement.* Human Kinetics, Champaign, IL.

Huiskes, R. (2000) If bone is the answer, then what is the question? *Journal of Anatomy* 197: 145–156.

Iwamoto, J, Takeda, T, and Sato, Y. (2005) Interventions to prevent bone loss in astronauts during space flight. *Keio Journal of Medicine* 54: 55–59.

Karlsson, MK, Hasserius, R, and Obrant, KJ. (1996) Bone mineral density in athletes during and after career: A comparison between loaded and unloaded skeletal regions. *Calcified Tissue International* 59: 245–248.

Sylvester, AD, Christensen, AM, and Kramer, PA. (2006) Factors influencing osteological changes in the hands and fingers of rock climbers. *Journal of Anatomy* 209: 597–609.

Chapter 6. Batmetabolism: What's For Dinner on the Dark Knight Diet

Dawkins, R. (2004) *The ancestor's tale.* Orion Books Ltd, London.

Hawley, JA, Tipton, KD, and Millard-Stafford, ML. (2006) Promoting training adaptations through nutritional interventions. *Journal of Sports Science* 24: 709–721.

Macfarlane, DJ. (2001) Automated metabolic gas analysis systems: A review. *Sports Medicine* 31: 841–861

Maughan, R. (2002) The athlete's diet: Nutritional goals and dietary strategies. *Proceedings of the Nutrition Society* 61: 87–96.

McArdle, WD, Katch, FI, and Katch, VL. (2005) *Essentials of exercise physiology,* 3rd ed. Lippincott Williams & Wilkins, Baltimore, MD.

Phillips, SM. (2006) Dietary protein for athletes: From requirements to metabolic advantage. *Applied Physiology, Nutrition, and Metabolism* 31: 647–654.

Turner, N, Hulbert, AJ, and Else, PL. (2006) Limits to physical performance and metabolism across species. *Current Opinion in Clinical Nutrition and Metabolic Care* 9: 691–696.

Westerterp, KR. (2001) Limits to sustainable human metabolic rate. *Journal of Experimental Biology* 204: 3183–3187.

Zehr, EP., and Sale, DG. (1993) Oxygen uptake, heartrate and blood lactate responses to the Chito-Ryu Seisan kata in skilled karate practitioners. *International Journal of Sports Medicine* 14: 269–274.

Chapter 7. From Bruce Wayne to Bruce Lee: Mastering Martial Moves in the Batcave

Cunnington, R, Windischberger, C, Deecke, L, and Moser E. (2003) The preparation and readiness for voluntary movement: A high-field event-related fMRI study of the Bereitschafts-BOLD response. *NeuroImage* 20: 404–412.

Driskell, JE, Willis, RP, and Cooper, C. (1992) Effect of overlearning on retention. *Journal of Applied Psychology* 77: 615–622.

Fitts, PM, and Posner, MI. (1967) *Learning and skilled performance in human performance.* Brooks/Cole, Belmont, CA.

Funakoshi, G. (2003) *The twenty guiding principles of karate: The spiritual legacy of the master.* Kodansha International, Tokyo.

Hebb, DO. (1949) *The organization of behavior.* Wiley, New York.

Krueger, WCF. (1930) Further studies in overlearning. *Journal of Experimental Psychology* 13: 152–163.

Luft, AR, and Buitrago, MM. (2005) Stages of motor skill learning. *Molecular Neurobiology* 32: 205–216.

Maguire, EA, Nannery, R, and Spiers, HJ. (2006) Navigation around London by a taxi driver with bilateral hippocampal lesions. *Brain* 129: 2894–2907.

O'Donovan, O, Cheung, J, Catley, M, McGregor, AH, and Strutton PH. (2006) An investigation of leg and trunk strength and reaction times of hard-style martial arts practitioners. *Journal of Science and Medicine in Sport* 5–12.

Schendel, JD, and Hagman, JD. (1982) On sustaining procedural skills over a prolonged retention interval. *Journal of Applied Psychology* 67: 605–610.

Schmidt, RA, and Lee, TD. (2005) *Motor control and learning: A behavioral emphasis,* 4th. ed. Human Kinetics, Champaign, IL.

Scoville, WB, and Milner, B. (1957) Loss of recent memory after bilateral hippocampal lesions. *Journal of Neurology, Neurosurgery, and Psychiatry* 20: 11–21.

Seidler, RD, and Noll, DC. (2008). Neuroanatomical correlates of motor acquisition and motor transfer. *Journal of Neurophysiology* 99: 1836–45.

Zehr, EP. (2005) Neural control of rhythmic human movement: The common core hypothesis. *Exercise and Sport Sciences Reviews* 33: 54–60.

Zehr, EP, Sale, DG, and Dowling, JJ. (1997) Ballistic movement performance in karate athletes. *Medicine and Science in Sports and Exercise* 29: 1366–1373.

Chapter 8. Everybody Was Kung Fu Fighting: But What Was Batman Doing?

Amtmann, JA. (2004) Self-reported training methods of mixed martial artists at a regional reality fighting event. *Journal of Strength Conditioning Research* 18: 194–196.

Beatty, S. (2001) *Batman: The ultimate guide to the Dark Knight*. Dorling Kindersley, New York.

Bishop, M. (1989) *Okinawan karate: Teachers, styles, and secret techniques*. A&C Black, London.

Bledsoe, GH, Hsu, EB, Grabowski, JG, Brill, JD, and Li, G. (2006) Incidence of injury in professional mixed martial arts competitions. *Journal of Sports Science and Medicine* 136–142.

Buse, GJ. (2006) No holds barred sport fighting: A 10 year review of mixed martial arts competition. *British Journal of Sports Medicine* 40: 169–172.

Discovery Channel. (2003) Unsolved history: Ninjas. [DVD.] Discovery Communications, Silver Spring, MD.

Draeger, DF. (1973a) *Classical Bujutsu*. Vol. 1 of *The martial arts and ways of Japan*. Weatherhill, New York.

Draeger, DF. (1973b) *Classical Budo*. Vol. 2 of *The martial arts and ways of Japan*. Weatherhill, New York.

Draeger, DF. (1974) *Modern Bujutsu & Budo*. Vol. 3 of *The martial arts and ways of Japan*. Weatherhill, New York.

Draeger, DF, and Smith, RW. (1997) *Comprehensive Asian fighting arts*. Kodansha International, Tokyo.

Haines, BA. (1995) *Karate's history and traditions*. Charles E. Tuttle, Tokyo.

Hatsumi, M. (1981) *Ninjutsu: History and tradition*. Unique Publications, Burbank, CA.

Inoue, M. (1987). *Bo, sai, tonfa, and nunchaku/kama* and *Tekko, tinbe, and surujin. Ancient martial arts of the Ryukyu Islands*. Volumes 1 & 2. Tokyo: Japan Publications Trading.

Lawler, J. (1996) *The martial arts encyclopedia*. Masters Press, Indianapolis, IN.

Lowry, D. (2002) *Traditions: Essays on the Japanese martial arts and ways*. Tuttle Publishing, North Clarendon, VT.

Lowry, D. (2005) *The Best of Dave Lowry: Karate Way columns 1995–2005*. Black Belt Communications, Valencia, CA.

Lowry, D. (2006) *In the dojo*. Weatherhill, Boston.

McCarthy, P. (1995) When masters meet: The 1936 meeting of Okinawan karate masters. *Furyu: The Budo Journal* 4: 1–11.

McCarthy, P. (1999a) *Koryu uchinadi*. Vol. 1 of *Ancient Okinawan martial arts*. Tuttle, Boston.

McCarthy, P. (1999b) *Koryu uchinadi*. Vol. 2 of *Ancient Okinawan martial arts*. Tuttle, Boston.

Mol, S. (2001) *Classical fighting arts of Japan: A complete guide to Koryu Jujutsu*. Kodansha International, Tokyo.

Sells, J. (1997) Chito-Ryu Karatedo: The legacy of Chitose Tsuyoshi. BuGeiSha: *Traditional Martial Artist* 1(2): 31–35.

Chapter 9. The Caped Crusader in Combat: Can You Kayo without Killing?

Draeger, DF, and Smith, RW. (1997) *Comprehensive Asian fighting arts.* Kodansha International, Tokyo.

Driskell, JE, Salas, E, and Johnston, JH. (2006) Decision making and performance under stress. In TW Britt, CA Castro, and AB Adler (eds), *Military life: The psychology of serving in peace and combat* (vol. 1, pp. 128–154). Praeger Security, Westport, CT.

Lavie, N. (2005) Distracted and confused? Selective attention under load. *Trends in Cognitive Sciences* 9: 75–82.

Lowry, D. (1995) *Sword and brush: The spirit of the martial arts.* Shambhala Publications Inc., Boston.

Lowry, D. (2002) *Traditions: Essays on the Japanese martial arts and ways.* Tuttle Publishing, North Clarendon, VT.

Lowry, D. (2005) *The Best of Dave Lowry: Karate Way Columns 1995–2005.* Black Belt Communications, Valencia, CA.

Lowry, D. (2006) *In the dojo.* Weatherhill, Boston.

Milton, J, Solodkin, A, Hlustik, P, and Small, SL. (2007) The mind of expert motor performance is cool and focused. NeuroImage 35: 804–813.

Ross, JS, Tkach, J, Ruggieri, PM, Lieber, M, and Lapresto, E. (2003) The mind's eye: Functional MR imaging evaluation of golf motor imagery. *American Journal of Neuroradiology* 24: 1036–1044.

Scaglione, R, and Cummins, W. (1994) *Karate of Okinawa: Building warrior spirit.* Person-to-Person, New York.

Takuan, S. (1986) *The unfettered mind.* Kodansha International, Tokyo.

Westbrook, A, and Ratti, O. (1970) *Aikido and the dynamic sphere: An illustrated introduction.* Charles E. Tuttle, Rutland, VT.

Chapter 10. Batman Bashes and Is Bashed by Bad Boys (and Girls): What Can He Break without Getting Broken?

Adams, B. (1985) *Deadly karate blows: The medical implications.* Unique Publications, Burbank, CA.

Adrian, MJ, and Cooper, JM. (1995) *The biomechanics of human movement.* Brown & Benchmark, Madison, WI.

Cavanagh, PR, and Landa, J. (1976) A biomechanical analysis of the karate chop. *Research Quarterly* 47: 610–618.

Chow, D, and Spangler, R. (1977) *Kung fu: History, philosophy, and technique.* Unique Publications, Burbank, CA.

Feld, MS, McNair, RE, and Wilk, SR. (1979) The physics of karate. *Scientific American* 240: 150–158.

Imamura, RT, Hreljac, A, Escamilla, RF, and Edwards, WB. (2006) A three-dimensional analysis of the center of mass for three different judo throwing techniques. *Journal of Sports Science and Medicine* 5: 122–131.

Ingber, L. (1981) *Karate: Kinematics and dynamics.* Unique Publications, Burbank, CA.

Martinez, J. (2001) *Okinawan karate: The secret art of tuite.* Javier E. Martinez, San Juan, Puerto Rico.

McCarthy, P. (1995) Bubishi: The bible of Karate. Tuttle, North Clarendon, VT.

Nagamine, S. (1994) *The essence of Okinawan Karate-do.* Charles E. Tuttle, Rutland, VT.

Viano, DC, Casson, IR, Pellman, EJ, Bir, CA, Zhang, L, Sherman, DC, and Boitano, MA. (2005) Concussion in professional football: Comparison with boxing head impacts–part 10. *Neurosurgery* 57: 1154–1172.

Walker, J. (1975) Karate strikes. *American Journal of Physics* 43: 845–849.

Walker, J. (1980) The amateur scientist. *Scientific American* 150–161.

Watanabe, J, and Avakian, L. (1984) *The secrets of judo.* Charles E. Tuttle, Rutland, VT.

Wilk, SR, McNair, RE, and Feld, MS. (1982) The physics of karate. *American Journal of Physics* 51: 783–790.

Zehr, EP, Sale, DG, and Dowling, JJ. (1997) Ballistic movement performance in karate athletes. *Medicine and Science in Sports and Exercise* 29: 1366–1373.

Chapter 11. Hardening the Batbody: Can Sticks and Stones Break His Bones?

Chow, D, and Spangler, R. (1977) *Kung fu: History, philosophy, and technique.* Unique Publications, Burbank, CA.

Kandel, ER, Schwartz, AB, and Jessel, TM. (1991) The perception of pain. In ER Kandel, JH Schwartz, and TM Jessel (eds.), *Principles of neural science* (pp. 472–491). McGraw Hill, New York.

Larose, JH, and Dae, SK. (1969) Karate hand-conditioning. *Medicine and Science in Sports and Exercise* 1: 95–98

Lowry, D. (2005) *The Best of Dave Lowry:* Karate Way *columns 1995–2005.* Black Belt Communications, Valencia, CA.

Oyama, M. (1966) *What is karate?* Japan Publications, Tokyo.

Oyama, M. (1968) *This is karate.* Japan Publications, Tokyo.

Salzman, M. (1990) *Iron & silk.* Vintage Books, New York.

Toth, R. (2007) The stories of Meibukan Gojyu Ryu karate. *Journal of Asian Martial Arts* 16: 48–61.

Webb, J. (2007) Analysis of the Wing Tsun punching methods. *Journal of Asian Martial Arts* 17: 62–81

Chapter 12. Gotham by Twilight: Working the Knight Shift

Cirelli, C. (2002) Functional genomics of sleep and circadian rhythm: Invited review: How sleep deprivation affects gene expression in the brain: A review of recent findings. *Journal of Applied Physiology* 92: 394–400

Eastman, CI, Gazda, CJ, Burgess, HJ, Crowley, SJ, and Fogg, LF. (2005) Advancing circadian rhythms before eastward flight: A strategy to prevent or reduce jet lag. *Sleep* 28: 33–44

Horne, JA. (1988) *Why we sleep: The functions of sleep in humans and other animals.* Oxford University Press, New York.

Lagerquist, O, Zehr EP, Baldwin, E, Klakowicz, P, and Collins, D. (2006) Diurnal changes in the amplitude of the Hoffmann reflex in the human soleus but not in the flexor carpi radialis muscle. *Experimental Brain Research* 170: 1–6.

Nicolau, MC, Akaarir, M, Gamundi, A, Gonzalez, J, and Rial, R V. (2000) Why we sleep: The evolutionary pathway to the mammalian sleep. *Progress in Neurobiology* 62, 379–406.

Rajaratnam, SM, and Arendt, J. (2001) Health in a 24-h society. *The Lancet* 358: 999–1005.

Reilly, T, and Edwards, B. (2007) Altered sleep-wake cycles and physical performance in athletes. *Physiology & Behavior* 90: 274–284.

Revell, VL, and Eastman, CI. (2005) How to trick mother nature into letting you fly around or stay up all night. *Journal of Biological Rhythms* 20: 353–365.

Rial et al. (2007) The trivial function of sleep. *Sleep Medicine Reviews* 11(4): 311–325.

Sharkey, KM, Fogg, LF, and Eastman, CI. (2001) Effects of melatonin administration on daytime sleep after simulated night shift work. *Journal of Sleep Research* 10: 181–192

Smith, RS, Guilleminault, C, and Efron, B. (1997) Circadian rhythms and enhanced athletic performance in the National Football League. *Sleep* 20: 362–365.

Waterhouse, J, Reilly, T, Atkinson, G, and Edwards, B. (2007) Jet lag: Trends and coping strategies. *The Lancet* 369: 1117–1129.

Chapter 13. Injury and Recovery: How Much Banging until the Batback Goes Bonk?

Beatty, S. (2001) *Batman: The ultimate guide to the Dark Knight.* Dorling Kindersley, New York.

Evans, NA. (2004) Current concepts in anabolic-androgenic steroids. *American Journal of Sports Medicine* 32: 534–542.

Greenfeld, KT. (2006, December 18) Media giant? *Sports Illustrated* 60–69.

Hall, ED, and Springer, JE. (2004) Neuroprotection and acute spinal cord injury: A reappraisal. *NeuroRx.* 1: 80–100.

Harmon, KG. (1999) Assessment and management of concussion in sport. *American Family Physician* 60: 887–92, 894.

Hartgens, F, and Kuipers, H. (2004) Effects of androgenic-anabolic steroids in athletes. *Sports Medicine* 34: 513–554.

Kuhn, CM. (2002) Anabolic steroids. *Recent Progress in Hormone Research* 57: 411–434

Levy, ML, Ozgur, BM, Berry, C, Aryan, HE, and Apuzzo, ML. (2004a) Analysis and evolution of head injury in football. *Neurosurgery* 55: 649–655.

Levy, ML, Ozgur, BM, Berry, C, Aryan, HE, and Apuzzo, ML. (2004b) Birth and evolution of the football helmet. *Neurosurgery* 55: 656–661

Lim, PA, and Tow, AM. (2007) Recovery and regeneration after spinal cord injury: A review and summary of recent literature. *Annals of the Academy of Medicine, Singapore* 36: 49–57.

Maravelias, C, Dona, A, Stefanidou, M, and Spiliopoulou, C. (2005) Adverse effects of anabolic steroids in athletes: A constant threat. *Toxicology Letters* 158: 167–175.

McCrory, P. (2002) *Cavum septi pellucidi*—A reason to ban boxers? *British Journal of Sports Medicine* 36: 157–161.

Shaw, NA. (2002) The neurophysiology of concussion. *Progress in Neurobiology* 67: 281–344

Chapter 14. Battle of the Bats: Could Batgirl Beat Batman?

Alway, SE, Grumbt, WH, Gonyea, WJ, and Stray-Gundersen, J. (1989) Contrasts in muscle and myofibers of elite male and female bodybuilders. *Journal of Applied Physiology* 67: 24–31.

Alway, SE, Grumbt, WH, Stray-Gundersen, J, and Gonyea, WJ. (1992) The effects of resistance training on elbow flexors of highly competitive bodybuilders. *Journal of Applied Physiology* 72: 1512–1521.

Cheuvront, SN, Carter, R, Deruisseau, KC, and Moffatt, RJ. (2005) Running performance differences between men and women: An update. *Sports Medicine* 35: 1017–1024.

Deschenes, MR, and Kraemer, WJ. (2002) Performance and physiologic adaptations to resistance training. *American Journal of Physical Medicine & Rehabilitation* 81: S3–16

Ford, LE, Detterline, AJ, Ho, KK, and Cao, W. (2000) Gender- and height-related limits of muscle strength in world weightlifting champions. *Journal of Applied Physiology* 89: 1061–1064.

Ivey, FM, Roth, SM, Ferrell, RE, Tracy, BL, Lemmer, JT, Hurlbut, DE, Martel, GF, Siegel, EL, Fozard, JL, Jeffrey, ME, Fleg, JL, and Hurley, BF. (2000) Effects of age, gender, and myostatin genotype on the hypertrophic response to heavy resistance strength training. *The Journals of Gerontology. Series A, Biological Sciences and Medical Sciences* 55: M641-M648.

Sale, DG, MacDougall, JD, Always, SE, and Sutton, JR. (1987) Voluntary strength and muscle characteristics in untrained men and women and male body-builders. *Journal of Applied Physiology* 62: 1786–1793

Seiler, S, De Koning, JJ, and Foster, C. (2007) The fall and rise of the gender difference in elite anaerobic performance 1952–2006. *Medicine and Science in Sports and Exercise* 39: 534–540.

Sparling, PB, O'Donnell, EM, and Snow, TK. (1998) The gender difference in distance running performance has plateaued: An analysis of world rankings from 1980 to 1996. *Medicine and Science in Sports and Exercise* 30: 1725–1729.

Chapter 15. The Aging Avenger: Could the Caped Crusader Become the Caped Codger?

Adams, JH, Graham, DI, Jennett, B. (2001) The structural basis of moderate disability after traumatic brain damage. *Journal of Neurology, Neurosurgery, and Psychiatry* 71: 521–524

Beatty, S. (2001) *Batman: The ultimate guide to the Dark Knight.* Dorling Kindersley, New York.

Castellani, RJ, Zhu, X, Lee, HG, Moreira, PI, Perry, G, and Smith, MA. (2007) Neuropathology and treatment of Alzheimer disease: Did we lose the forest for the trees? *Expert Review of Neurotherapeutics* 7: 473–485.

Corsellis, JA. (1989) Boxing and the brain. *British Medical Journal* 298: 105–109.

Greenwood, R. (2002) Head injury for neurologists. *Journal of Neurology, Neurosurgery, and Psychiatry* 73: 8i-16

Guo, Z, et al. (2000) Head injury and the risk of AD in the MIRAGE study. *Neurology* 54: 1316–1323.

Guskiewicz, KM, Marshall, SW, Bailes, J, McCrea, M, Cantu, RC, Randolph, C, and Jordan, BD. (2005) Association between recurrent concussion and late-life cognitive impairment in retired professional football players. *Neurosurgery* 57: 719–726.

Hertoghe, T. (2005) The "multiple hormone deficiency" theory of aging: Is human senescence caused mainly by multiple hormone deficiencies? *Annals of the New York Academy of Sciences* 1057: 448–465.

Kaeberlein, M, McVey, M, and Guarente, L. (2001) Using yeast to discover the fountain of youth. *Science of Aging Knowledge Environment* E1.

Kraemer, WJ, and Ratamess, NA. (2005) Hormonal responses and adaptations to resistance exercise and training. *Sports Medicine* 35: 339–361.

Martland, HS. (1928) Punch drunk. *Journal of the American Medical Association* 19: 1103–1107.

Morley, JE, Baumgartner, RN, Roubenoff, R, Mayer, J, and Nair, KS. (2001) Sarcopenia. *Journal of Laboratory and Clinical Medicine* 137: 231–243.

Solomon, AM, and Bouloux, PMG. (2006) Modifying muscle mass—The endocrine perspective. *Journal of Endocrinology* 191: 349–360.

Thomas, DR. (2007) Loss of skeletal muscle mass in aging: Examining the relationship of starvation, sarcopenia and cachexia. *Clinical Nutrition* 26: 389–399.

Troen, BR. (2003) The biology of aging. *Mt. Sinai Journal of Medicine* 70: 3–22.

index